SPENCER BAIRD OF THE SMITHSONIAN

Bairds Bunting.

John James Audubon print of Baird's bunting (*Ammodramus bairdii*), the last bird named by Audubon and the first one named for Baird.

SPENCER BAIRD

OF THE SMITHSONIAN

E. F. Rivinus and E. M. Youssef

SMITHSONIAN INSTITUTION PRESS

WASHINGTON AND LONDON

© 1992 by the Smithsonian Institution
All rights reserved
Chief Manuscript Editor: Catherine F. McKenzie
Staff Editor: Jack Kirshbaum
Designer: Alan Carter

Library of Congress Cataloging-in-Publication Data
Rivinus, E. F.
Baird of the Smithsonian / E.F. Rivinus and E.M. Youssef.
p.   cm.
Includes bibliographical references and index. ISBN 1-56098-155-5
1. Baird, Spencer Fullerton, 1823–1887. 2. Smithsonian Institution—Biography.
3. Naturalists—United States—Biography.
I. Youssef, E. M. II. Title.
QH31.B17R58   1992
508'.092—dc20
[B]   92-6897

British Library Cataloging-in-Publication data available

Manufactured in the United States of America
96 95 94 93 92   5 4 3 2 1

∞ The paper used in this publication meets the minimum requirements of the American
National Standard for Permanence of Paper for Printed Library Materials Z39.48-1984.

*The authors gratefully dedicate this book to Ahmed M. Youssef
for his patience and kind but critical analysis of many rewrites,
and mostly for his encouragement when the going got tough;
and to Marion and Flo Rivinus, for whose loving investment
in a son's education this book is a modest dividend.*

Contents

CONTENTS

Acknowledgments

WE COULD NOT HAVE FOLLOWED Baird's career nor, more important, have become acquainted with the man behind the achievements without the help of a great many people—Smithsonian staff members and important contributors outside the Institution. Our first thanks go to our friends and colleagues in the Smithsonian Archives—in particular, Libby Glenn, Bill Deiss, Bill Cox, Jim Steed, Gerald Rosenzweig, and Josephine Jamison, without whose experienced guidance and bulldog tenacity we would never have found our way through the archival labyrinth of the Baird, Henry, Rhees, and associated collections. And our second thanks go to Drs. Allen Greenlee and Tom Hartman for their generous and perceptive diagnoses of the illnesses of Mary and Spencer Baird. It is regrettable the Bairds did not have access to their help. We thank also Isabella Adona Edwards, whose research into the Baird-Rhees relationship has proven of real value to us.

We are especially grateful to Catherine McKenzie for her editorial help in smoothing our prose and gently but firmly directing us to an acceptably scholarly degree of precision in our notes and bibliography, as well as to Jack Kirshbaum, our key editor at the Smithsonian Institution Press. Others at the Press who have earned our special thanks for their experienced help in early drafts were Joe Goodwin of Smithsonian Books, managing editor Ruth Spiegel, and all the members of the design, production, and marketing staffs who have given their time and skills to turning our raw manuscript into an attractive and marketable book.

People in other areas of the Smithsonian who have been particularly helpful were Leslie Overstreet and Ellen Wells of the Rare Book Library, Carolyn Hahn of the Natural History Library, Doug Evelyn and Harry Rubenstein from the Museum of American History, David Hunt of Physical Anthropology, and Melodie Kosmacki in Spencer Baird's own Arts and Industries Building. And we are especially grateful to Richard Strauss of the Office of Printing and Photographic Services, who put so much effort into the photography of Baird artifacts for our benefit. We particularly appreciate the contribution of a good friend (nameless by request) who is a professional and respected handwriting analyst. Her voluntary characterizations of both Spencer and Mary Baird on the basis of what they revealed of themselves in their personal handwriting have constituted for us an interesting and altogether objective confirmation of much of our own analysis of their personalities at important periods of their lives.

Lastly, we thank our several contacts at Dickinson College, the Cumberland County Historical Society, the National Archives, and the United States Marine Biological Laboratory at Woods Hole for their archival and photographic assistance.

To all of you our warm thanks and a well-deserved share in any success this book may earn.

SPENCER BAIRD OF THE SMITHSONIAN

Introduction

I WELL REMEMBER when a lad of 8, uniting with two or three friends . . . in combining our joint natural history curiosities into a museum, which attracted a good deal of curiosity, and portions of which now form part of the National Museum in Washington."[1] Spencer Fullerton Baird never deviated throughout his sixty-four years from this childhood dedication. Indeed, he became the consummate collector, and when more demanding responsibilities intruded upon his direct involvement in collecting and classifying, he became a collector of collectors. Under his training and guidance virtually all the major natural scientists of the nineteenth century developed their enthusiasms and their professional competence.

Some of Baird's biographers and memoralists have attempted to trace the origin of what might be described as his obsession with collecting, classifying, and exhibiting. William H. Dall quotes Baird's daughter, Lucy, to the effect that Baird recalled walks in the country with his father, "to which he attributed the germ of that love for Nature which afterward blossomed into his passion for natural history."[2]

What seems a more persuasive, if perhaps less tangible, explanation was furnished to Baird's protégé and memorialist, George Brown Goode, by Samuel Pierpont Langley, Baird's successor as secretary of the

Smithsonian Institution, in response to Goode's query on precisely this subject. "The drawing, almost in infancy, toward what so often proves to be the work of our future lives, is one of the mysteries of our being, which I have noted in my own early childhood, and which is almost always found if sought in the biography of a worker in any special field, and always worth attention."[3]

In Baird's day, collecting specimens of natural history was mostly an avocation. He turned it into a vocation, and a highly successful one in terms of his personal goals. As a teenage amateur enthusiast, he began to collect and study seriously the characteristic fauna and flora of the Pennsylvania countryside. Upon completion of his formal education, he quickly progressed to the position of salaried professor of natural history, then to assistant secretary and curator of natural history at the newly founded Smithsonian Institution. As he advanced in the career he made for himself, he earned respect both at home and abroad as America's top native-born naturalist, to whom both scientists and politicians looked for counsel and leadership.

From the beginning of his official life, as well as before, Baird created his own work patterns to meet his goals, even while he dutifully and resourcefully performed the tasks asked of him by his superior. Throughout his twenty-eight years as assistant to Joseph Henry, secretary of the Smithsonian Institution, he satisfied all of his chief's very special demands while he built up the Institution's natural history collections to the point that they dominated the Institution itself and changed its character entirely.

In 1871 Baird wrote and persuaded Congress to legislate the criteria that resulted in the selection of himself as the first United States Commissioner of Fish and Fisheries, a duty that was added to his Smithsonian functions. Yet with the rare consistency that distinguished his entire career, he soon maneuvered this role, too, away from that which Congress had mandated and into the more congenial one of collection and study of a new and challenging taxon.

Baird took quiet but effective action to assure his own succession to the secretaryship of the Smithsonian on Joseph Henry's death, and when administrative and public duties left him little time for collecting, he dedicated comparable energy to training and directing younger collectors. Thus the flow of specimens and artifacts that arrived at the Smithsonian from exploring expeditions and from private collectors for his examination never ceased throughout his lifetime.

Although Baird's innate passion directed his goals and dominated his career, he never allowed it to obscure his very human side. He was always approachable, beloved by his students and colleagues, kindly and persuasive. He demanded much of his assistants, but never more than he demanded of himself, and throughout his life he earned the trust, respect, and affection of almost all of his colleagues and protégés.

From another standpoint, however, Baird's overweening absorption in his work, while it earned him many honors and made him generally esteemed, was not without its extracurricular cost. Although his relations with his wife and only daughter appeared intimate and affectionate, his wife, Mary, became a demanding invalid early in their married life, and a recent professional diagnosis of her condition indicates that at least some of her troubles were the result of her dutifully controlled, but sometimes passionately expressed, sense of loneliness and neglect.

In most respects Baird was a loyal and devoted family man. His numerous siblings and in-laws turned continually to him for help as the successful and influential head of both families, and he never failed to respond to their requests. Yet, while he devoted much time to family support, in his personal life, as in his profession, Baird was a completely and consistently self-contained man. He kept his work interests so separate from his personal relations as to make it challenging to a biographer to paint a single portrait of the inner man.

Baird gave every outward appearance of self-sufficiency and self-assurance. A closer look into his personal life, however, reveals him to be as consistently self-protective. He let no one penetrate his closely guarded inner space, and there are indications that he expunged selections from his journals and correspondence which he may have felt too revealing. Baird was intelligent and perceptive. He carefully, and probably accurately, assessed his limits as well as his strengths, and he took care to highlight the latter by assiduously respecting the former.

Although Baird was respected and honored among his contemporaries for his lifetime achievements, his more lasting merit rests in the heritage he bequeathed to later generations. He initiated and developed a precise method of systematic study and research in natural history; wrote many books and reports to which students still refer; discovered, educated, and supported an entire generation of natural scientists whose works have made major contributions to the field; and quietly and patiently reshaped Joseph Henry's Smithsonian Institution to embody his personal approach and goals.

Yet time has not been kind to the reputation of this nineteenth-century man of distinction. Within the Smithsonian itself, many interested visitors attend programs in the Baird Auditorium several times weekly, but few pay heed to its name or encounter there anything to arouse their curiosity in that direction.[4] In an unlighted corner near one of the two entrances stands a marble bust of a broad-faced, bearded man with a kindly expression, labeled for any who will take the trouble to read it "Spencer Fullerton Baird." However, there is no evident connection between the bust and the auditorium, and indeed, a first impression regarding the bust might be that someone had put it there to get it out of the way.

In the reading room of the Smithsonian Institution Archives, the one available copy of William Dall's 1915 biography of Baird is in such dilapidated condition that it is wrapped in paper and tied with string to keep it from falling apart, and at least one copy in the Smithsonian Institution Libraries is in comparable condition. Beside Dall's book on the archives shelf is a plain but nicely bound copy of a Ph.D dissertation by Dean Allard, "Spencer Fullerton Baird and the U.S. Fish Commission: A Study in the History of American Science"—a first-rate description and analysis of an important phase of Baird's career—but the contents are simply reproduced on xerographed microfilm pages.

Other Baird memorabilia are also exhibited in the Smithsonian Institution in ways that accord comparably little credit to the man. The Arts and Industries Building was built to house the carloads of exhibits that Baird persuaded his fellow exhibitors at Philadelphia's Centennial Exposition of 1876 to donate to the Smithsonian. He played a major role in the design of the building and supervised its construction. Nearly all the current exhibits in the building are there because of his personal efforts, yet the museum's labeling contains no mention of Baird.

A handsome and ingeniously constructed desk used by Baird as secretary of the Smithsonian appears in an exhibit of furniture craftsmanship from the Centennial Exposition of 1876, without identification or attribution. The imposing and elaborately worked silver trophy awarded to Professor Baird by the German emperor at the International Fisheries Exhibition of 1880 appears also among the 1876 exposition artifacts, but simply as an example of German craftsmanship and without any reference either to Baird or to the honor paid him.

The fadeout of Baird's image into the mists of historical oblivion may be attributed in part to the character of his work and perhaps in larger part to the self-effacing character of the man. Baird's principal achievements were in the field of systematic science, and systematic science does not loom large in public interest. Hence he occupied what is considered today a vital but fairly restricted corner even in the history of science— and one of its least spectacular ones. He was born into a family at the top of the class structure and rose early in life to the top levels of his chosen field. Baird never felt a need to seek public acclaim. His successes and the respect they generated came to him without any effort on his part to draw attention to himself.

Spencer Baird's dedication to an unspectacular field and his own lifelong lack of interest in public acclaim have combined to deprive him of the lasting recognition that is his due and for which this book has been written. Our search for Baird the man has been more penetrating and inevitably more critical than those of our predecessors—perhaps more so than his daughter would have approved. Our goal has been to illustrate the importance of the personal challenges which Baird had to overcome to make his greatness possible. The result has caused us to view both Baird and his heritage as all the more impressive and to agree wholeheartedly with the judgment of George Brown Goode that in the years since his death "his like has not been found."

Chapter One

(design ornament)

The Smithson Bequest

(design ornament)

A paradox, a paradox, a most ingenious paradox.

—From Gilbert and Sullivan,
The Pirates of Penzance

WHEN HE DIED IN 1829, James Smithson, an English scientist of aristocratic origin born under the bar sinister of illegitimacy, left his substantial estate to a nephew, but subject to the following curious entail: "In the case of the death of my said nephew without leaving a child or children he may have had under the age of twenty years, I then bequeath my whole property . . . to the United States of America to found at Washington, under the name of the Smithsonian Institution, an Establishment for the increase and diffusion of knowledge among men."[1] Even more paradoxical were the circumstances which led to the birth of James Smithson himself, from a bed of adulterous dalliance, and led ultimately to the founding of the institution which bears his name and which in turn molded the life and career of the young Pennsylvania naturalist Spencer F. Baird.

This extraordinary train of events began in the year 1764, when Elizabeth Keate Macie, a widow lady of distinguished birth and evident attractions, became pregnant in the course of an illicit relationship with Hugh Smithson, a lively baronet of her acquaintance, husband of her cousin, and a gentleman destined to rise spectacularly within the ranks of British nobility.

Hugh Smithson was a member of a genteel but not noble family. However, in 1740 he wooed and won the wealthy and titled Elizabeth Percy and began his rise to fame and fortune. He had two sons and a daughter by Elizabeth Percy and, according to one source, fathered three illegitimate offspring in addition to the son by Elizabeth Macie.[2] Smithson was reportedly a competent manager and an astute politician. Under his administration his wife's estates prospered; at the same time, he so ingratiated himself with the reigning monarch, George III, that in 1765 the crown appointed him first duke of Northumberland and authorized him to take the name of Percy.

Smithson's eldest legitimate son and heir, Earl Algernon Percy, joined the army and as a major commanded the rear guard which covered the retreat of General Thomas Gage's badly mauled redcoats from Concord and Lexington in 1775. When Smithson's legitimate daughter, Dorothy Percy, died in 1794, she bequeathed three thousand pounds to James Lewis Macie, as Elizabeth Macie's illegitimate son was still known at that time. Dorothy's generosity was the only formal evidence of any recognition of kinship to him by the Smithson-Percy-Northumberland family.

Elizabeth Keate Macie had gone discreetly to Paris for her accouchement, and on an unrecorded date in 1765 she gave birth to James Lewis Macie. Elizabeth boasted aristocratic lineage. She was a direct descendant of the Hungerfords of Studley, a family that claimed royal descent from Henry VII. The Keates had become heirs to the Studley fortune, with the result that when in 1766 her older brother died, Elizabeth inherited a substantial estate, by means of which she was evidently able to give her two sons (she had an older son by a previous marriage to a gentleman named Dickinson) a good education and ultimately to purchase a commission in the army for her oldest son, who rose to the rank of lieutenant colonel before his death.

Despite serious research efforts by a series of Smithsonian scholars, first of whom was Spencer Baird's successor, Secretary Samuel Pierpont Langley, few traces have been found of young Macie's early life. His mother evidently returned with him to England, where, when he was nine years old, a petition was submitted for his naturalization, although under terms which barred him from entering politics, the civil service, the army, or the church.[3] The next time his name surfaced was in 1782, when James Lewis Macie, age seventeen, matriculated at Pembroke College, Oxford. There he distinguished himself in the then seldom studied subjects of chemistry and mineralogy.

The scientific papers that Macie wrote in college came to the attention of some distinguished members of the prestigious Royal Society and so impressed them that he was elected to membership in the society just eleven months after his graduation in 1786—a rare distinction for one so young. During his lifetime he achieved considerable renown in scientific circles in England and on the Continent, where he spent much of his time. He wrote over two hundred papers on chemical analysis and kindred subjects. While most of his scientific conclusions have been overtaken by later and more sophisticated research, he made one lasting contribution in demonstrating that a mineral then known as "calamine" was in fact a compound composed of a native carbonate and a silicate of zinc. These elements were recognized on the strength of his analysis, and the newly discovered silicate of zinc was named smithsonite in his honor. Specimens are appropriately on exhibit in the Smithsonian's Hall of Minerals. In 1806 he had formally changed his name from Macie to Smithson, thus establishing his patrilineal connection (although his father had meanwhile changed his own name to Percy).

Despite the acclaim he achieved in his chosen scientific field, the restrictions that the rules of British nobility placed on him because of the circumstances of his birth constituted a festering sore in the psyche of this young man that continued as long as he lived. In addition, it seems evident that his ineligibility ever to accede to the title of Northumberland rankled in his soul—a trifle unrealistically, since two legitimate Percy half-brothers, both older, effectively blocked any such aspiration on his part.

Nevertheless, the intensity of Smithson's yearning for the privileged rank and recognition he felt was due him is clearly evident in the wording of the preamble to his will: "I, James Smithson, Son to Hugh, first Duke of Northumberland, and Elizabeth, Heiress of the Hungerfords of Studley and Niece to Charles, the proud Duke of Somerset, now residing in Bentinck Street, Cavendish Square, do this twenty-third day of October, one thousand eight hundred and twenty six, make this my last Will and Testament." The extent of his resentment is even more obvious in his widely quoted statement, "My name shall live in the memory of man when the titles of the Northumberlands and the Percys are extinct and forgotten."[4]

One may sympathize with, or perhaps wonder at, the degree of Smithson's concern over what he considered his deprivation of power and pelf, but the fact that the United States became the beneficiary of his desire for retaliation is a cause for national gratification for all generations of Americans. And it seems fair to predict that his name will live in the institution that he made possible at least as long as the names of Northumberland and Percy are honored in England.

James Smithson died in Genoa, Italy, in 1829 at the age of sixty-four (in Reading, Pennsylvania, Spencer Baird was just six years old), leaving a sizable estate to a rather surprising list of heirs. He provided an annuity to a former servant for his lifetime and named as his chief heir James Hungerford, the illegitimate son of his older half-brother, Lieutenant Colonel Henry Louis Dickinson. Hungerford's mother had meanwhile married a French baron, and young Hungerford had taken the surname and title of his stepfather, and called himself Baron Eunice de la Batut. Smithson willed only the income from his estate as a lifetime annuity to his nephew. In the following paragraph of his will he added, "Should the said Henry James Hungerford have a child or children, legitimate or illegitimate, I leave to such child or children, his or their heirs, executors, and assigns, after the death of his, her, or their father, the whole of my property of every kind absolutely and forever."[5] Then in an astonishing extension of his wishes, Smithson provided that should his nephew die without issue, his entire estate should go to the United States for the founding of a "Smithsonian Institution" dedicated to "the increase and diffusion of knowledge among men."

9

The wording of Smithson's will is remarkable, almost schizophrenic, in various respects. While he had what seems an outlandish dream of retribution, it was basically a dream—one that could become reality only if a twenty-three-year-old man whose immediate forebears had demonstrated noteworthy procreative capacities should die childless. One inevitably wonders whether Smithson ever really expected the reserve paragraph in his will to become effective. Many have also speculated about how he came to nominate the United States of America to fulfill his dream. Smithson had never visited the United States, he was not known to have expressed any special interest in the country or to have had any American friends or associates, and there were only one or two books about the United States in his extensive library.

Whatever the answers to these puzzling questions, the fact is that Henry James Hungerford, or de la Batut, né Henry James Dickinson, "son to my late brother, Lieutenant-Colonel Henry Louis Dickinson," did die childless in 1835, and in September of the same year the United States chargé d'affaires in London, Aaron Vail, notified Secretary of State Martin Van Buren of the Smithson bequest. (In Carlisle, Pennsylvania, young Spencer Baird was twelve years old, enrolled in his final year at the Dickinson College Preparatory School.)

With the possible exception of any residue of Dorothy Percy's 1794 bequest that might still have remained among Smithson's holdings at the time of his death, all of his estate consisted of Hungerford money. No evidence indicates that Smithson's father ever showed the slightest sense of responsibility for either Elizabeth Macie or their son, or that any Northumberland-Percy money contributed to the founding of the Smithsonian Institution.

On December 17, 1835, President Andrew Jackson advised Congress of the Smithson bequest but declared that he had no authority to accept it without approval of the Senate. Thus began ten years of often acrimonious debate in an often unappreciative Congress. It debated, first, whether even to accept the gift and after the supporters of acceptance won their case, the extent of the responsibility of the United States Treasury for the security of the fund, and finally and most significantly, the purpose to which the money should be directed.

The arguments for and against acceptance lasted two years. The former vice-president and later states' rights and proslavery senator John C. Calhoun insisted that it would be beneath our national dignity to accept a donation from a foreigner. Another articulate opponent was Senator W. C. Preston of South Carolina, who argued that Congress was not empowered to do so. Despite the eloquence of these gentlemen and their supporters, a majority of the Senate, under the leadership of future president James Buchanan (like Spencer Baird an alumnus of Dickinson College), voted in favor of authorizing the president to accept the bequest, and on July 1, 1836, the pertinent bill became law.[6]

President Jackson promptly appointed a distinguished lawyer and financier, Richard Rush of Pennsylvania, to prosecute the claim, and on May 9, 1838, he obtained a decree from the British Court of Chancery approving the claim on behalf of the United States. (The only other claimant was the senior Baron de la Batut, who had pressed a claim on behalf of his wife, the mother of Smithson's nephew. The court rejected the baron's claim on the ground that she had never been married to Hungerford's father. However, Rush, with the approval of the secretary of state, did agree to a modest annuity for the lady, the principal of which was returned to the United States on her death in 1862.)[7]

Rush promptly converted the debentures in which the estate was held into gold sovereigns, which he personally brought back to the United States by ship in ten or more boxes holding one thousand pounds each, a formidable sum for the time. (One can but wonder at the state of public safety at the time or at the courage of Rush in bringing $500,000 in gold across the Atlantic, apparently simply as baggage, although two United States Treasury agents did meet him at dockside in New York and accompany him to Washington.)

Upon receipt of the money, the secretary of the Treasury promptly had the sovereigns melted down and converted into United States coin, which he, with congressional approval, proceeded to invest in bonds of the states of Arkansas, Illinois, Michigan, and Ohio, at 6 percent interest. By 1841 these states, with the notable exception of Ohio, had defaulted on their interest payments, and the values of their bonds so depreciated that many shared the concern expressed by Richard Rush: "Fortunate it will be if the fund itself, at such an era of dishonesty and hocus-pocus, is not made away with, or dilapidated, before any public use whatever is made of the beneficent bequest."[8]

So great was the concern among responsible members of Congress that in August 1847 in the aftermath of lengthy debate between former president John Quincy Adams, in favor, and future president Andrew Johnson, against, Congress passed, and President James K. Polk signed, an enabling bill providing that the sum of $515,169, plus interest accrued up to August 1846 in the amount of $242,129, be loaned to the Treasury at 6 percent interest to be used for the "perpetual maintenance and support of the Institution." The bill further provided that "all moneys and stocks which have been or may hereafter be received into the Treasury of the United States on account of the fund bequeathed by James Smithson be and hereby are pledged to refund to the Treasury of the United States the sums hereby appropriated."[9] Thus the Smithson fund was saved, and the Treasury was properly obligated to shoulder the state bond losses.

Coincident with the debate over the responsibility of the United States for the protection of the Smithson fund, a debate over the purpose to which it should be devoted occupied the attention of nine successive congressional sessions, from the Twenty-fifth to the Twenty-ninth Congress, which finally passed the Bill of Incorporation of the Smithsonian Institution on August 10, 1846, more than ten years after President Jackson's announcement of Smithson's bequest to the United States.

Certainly the delay did not stem from lack of interest on the part of congressmen. It seemed that everyone had a favorite goal for the money. The discussions and controversies were so heated that an exasperated John Quincy Adams, chairman of the congressional committee charged with proposing a plan for the prospective institution, wrote in his diary in 1846: "In this committee no two members, excepting Mr. Marsh and myself, have agreed in opinion with regard to the future management of the fund. I doubt if there will be more harmony in the House, for never was there a benevolent and charitable purpose more unfortunately endowed than that of James Smithson, entrusted to the good faith and intelligence of the North American Congress."[10] Many members urged that it be used for the establishment of a national university; others favored an agricultural institute. The influential Senator Rufus Choate of Massachusetts, strongly abetted by his colleague in the House, the articulate George Perkins Marsh of Vermont, argued for a national library, while former president Adams initially urged that the money be devoted to a national astronomical observatory.

Among the strongest voices were the proponents of a national museum. The leader of this faction was Joel R. Poinsett, secretary of war in the Van Buren government, former United States minister to Mexico, discoverer of the plant named for him—the Poinsettia—and founder of the privately established National Institute for the Promotion of Science, the only organization of its type in the capital. Congress had already appointed the National Institute for the Promotion of Science custodian of the natural history collections sent back to Washington by the United States Exploring Expedition of 1838–1842, led by Lieutenant Charles Wilkes (and known as the Wilkes Exploring Expedition), and Poinsett had high hopes that it would be awarded the Smithson fund and become the national museum he so strongly favored. According to George Brown Goode, Poinsett nearly attained his goal. He lost out mainly because of the opposition of Adams and others to relinquishing their hard-won determination of United States government responsibility for the fund, which would have been lost had a private institution been given charge of it. They also opposed awarding the fund to the National Institute for the Promotion of Science on the ground that its membership was almost entirely made up of nonprofessionals and had never attracted respected members of the scientific community.[11] Nonetheless, the idea of establishing a museum became a major factor in the final determination of the goals of the fund.

A series of bills were considered and rejected over the years. The university and the agricultural institute ideas were abandoned, and Adams dropped his recommendation for an astronomical observatory upon the establishment of the United States Naval Observatory in 1844. Throughout the years of the debate, Adams was the most articulate and insistent protagonist of the idea that the Smithson fund should be dedicated to the highest intellectual goals, and all historians of the Smithsonian Institution credit him with having played the key role in the final outcome. The depth of his feeling for the Institution is evident in his own statement of satisfaction upon passage of the final bill of incorporation. "Of all the foundations or establishments for pious or charitable uses which ever signalized the spirit of the age or the comprehensive beneficence of the founder, none can be named more deserving of mankind than this."[12]

In the Bill of Incorporation of the Smithsonian Institution, which was finally passed by both houses and signed by President Polk on August 10, 1846, provision was made for governance of the Institution by a board of regents, headed by a chancellor and acting through their elected secretary. On the insistence of John Quincy Adams, the principle was established that only the interest of the fund should be used for operations and that the principal should be permanently invested in the Treasury of the United States.[13]

In its mandate to the board of regents, Congress noted that the Institution should include a library, a museum, and an art gallery. The influence of Senator Choate made itself felt in the provision that an amount "not to exceed" $25,000 of interest should be used for the formation of the library. (Since the annual interest on the principal barely exceeded $30,000, this provision soon became an important bone of contention between the library supporters and the new secretary of the Institution.) A further proviso called for the use of the interest, which had accrued over the ten years of debate and now amounted to $242,129, to build a suitable building to house the Institution—another source of future irritation.

The board of regents, consisting of the vice-president, the chief justice, three senators, three members of the House, and six citizens chosen at large, but no two of whom could come from the same state, met on September 6, 1846, and promptly set about the search for a secretary. Considered in the final vote were three candidates: the well-known and highly respected physicist Joseph Henry, from the faculty of Princeton University; Joel Poinsett's candidate, Francis Markoe, the executive secretary of the National Institute for the Promotion of Science and an amateur botanist and mineralogist of some standing; and Charles Pickering, a naturalist and a physician residing in Philadelphia. He was chief naturalist on the Wilkes Exploring Expedition. In the final vote of twelve regents (apparently neither the vice-president nor the chief justice participated in the voting) Henry, the professional scientist, was quite appropriately chosen over the amateur collector, Markoe, by seven votes to four, the remaining vote going to Pickering.

Thus was fulfilled the improbable dream of James Smithson, and thus the stage was set for the entrance of another dreamer, Spencer Fullerton Baird.

James Smithson was buried in the small English cemetery in Genoa, where his grave remained undistinguished for some time, even after the Smithsonian Institution was officially established seventeen years later. It is perhaps understandable, but a little sad, that the first two secretaries, Henry and Baird, found themselves too preoccupied with the actual creation and development of Smithson's institution to attend seriously to rendering homage to the man whose generous concept had done so much for them.[14]

However, in 1891, four years after Secretary Langley had succeeded Spencer Baird, the secretary himself went to Italy, where he visited Smithson's grave, collected all the information he could find about the founder's life, arranged for the perpetual care of the grave site on behalf of the Institution, and on a later visit placed at the tomb a bronze tablet that gave for the first time public recognition to James Smithson as the founder of the Smithsonian Institution.

In 1900 the Italian government announced its intention to expropriate the cemetery site in order to extend an adjacent and already encroaching quarry. At that point a motion was made by Regent Alexander Graham Bell, and approved unanimously by the board, to solicit Italian consent to the exhumation of Smithson's remains and their removal to the United States for honorable and permanent preservation in the institution that bears his name. The Italians gave their assent to the proposal, and in December 1903, Regent Bell headed a delegation to Italy to monitor the disinterment and to accompany Smithson's body to Washington.

When Smithson's body had been exhumed and placed in a suitable casket for shipment, William Henry Bishop, United States consul in Genoa, who was present with Bell and other officials at the ceremony, gave a short address in which he said:

I assure you that it is with a feeling of real emotion that I have just now cast the American flag over the body of this illustrious man, this noble but as yet little known benefactor, as it is on the verge of beginning its journey to the United States. The flag adopts him already, as it were, in the substance, for our country, to which he has so long belonged in the spirit. He is now about to receive there a portion of the outward veneration and homage he so supremely merits, and which, owing to the modest circumstances of his life, and his interment here in some sense almost forgotten, he has never had.[15]

So, in 1904, James Smithson made his first trip to America and the institution of his dreams. His sarcophagus was given an honorable place of repose in the mortuary chapel just inside the main door of the Smithsonian Castle, where he receives the respectful visits of countless beneficiaries of his brilliant gesture, and where we may hope he rests more contentedly than he could ever have if interred as a lesser figure among the mighty Percys.

Chapter Two

The World of Spencer Baird

SPENCER BAIRD WAS A LEADING ACTOR on center stage when American science came of age. George H. Daniels wrote: "Somewhere about 1815 Americans became interested in the pursuit of science to a greater extent than ever before. They founded journals, organized societies, appealed to the federal government for aid mostly without success—began sending their students to the scientific institutions of France and Germany in unprecedented numbers, and began bitterly resenting the scientific superiority of Europe."[1]

By the time of his death in 1887, Spencer Baird had experienced sixty-four of the most dramatic years of American history. It was the period of American national teenagerism, a period characterized by expansion—both territorial and cultural—conflict, brash immaturity, politico-military strife, industrial and economic achievement and ferment, and burgeoning self-awareness and self-assurance in the face of the serious challenges inevitably attending the onset of national puberty.

Particularly pertinent to an appreciation of Baird's life and work is an understanding of the state of science in America in the early nineteenth century, especially of natural science. Early explorers and colonists had noted in reports and journals the abundance and diversity of the natural resources of the New World, but the first American to demonstrate a real interest in scientific observation and explanation of the natural environment was Benjamin Franklin. Franklin launched a new movement to bring persons with a common interest in scientific matters together when in 1769 he organized the American Philosophical Society in Philadelphia. But for the most part, scientific activity was the province of wealthy amateurs, many of whom, such as John and William Bartram, Alexander Wilson, George Ord, William McClure, and foreign visitors and immigrants such as Charles Lucien Bonaparte and John James Audubon, made important contributions, though individually.

Serious obstacles to the advancement of science included the unavailability of formal training; many of the distinguished naturalists of Baird's time attended medical schools, where they at least learned anatomy. Also, there were no libraries of note; in 1816 Harvard's library contained only twenty thousand books, only a few of which were on scientific subjects. And the few museums, such as Peale's Museum in Philadelphia, were primarily concerned with providing public entertainment. Before 1840 even the relatively small collections procured by early expeditions had no repository. The items brought back by the Lewis and Clark expedition, for example, went to separate locations. The minerals were entrusted to the American Philosophical Society, the Indian relics and paleontological items to Jefferson's private collection at Monticello, and the animal skins and skeletons to Peale's Museum, where they were put on display as curiosities until ultimately they dissipated.[2]

In 1816 the Columbian Institute was organized in Washington, and in 1817 the Academy of Natural Sciences in Philadelphia was founded, followed soon after by the New York Lyceum of Natural Science and the Boston Society of Natural History. By 1821 there were a number of active natural history societies in the country, five in the state of New York alone. The year 1826 saw the first issue of Benjamin Silliman's *American Journal of Science and Arts*. Public lectures on scientific topics were often well attended in the three cities of principal scientific activity: Philadelphia, New York, and Boston. Of particular significance to Baird's future career was Joel Poinsett's organizing of the National Institute for the Promotion of Science in Washington in 1840.

The government had moved steadily into support for and reliance on science under the enlightened leadership of Presidents Thomas Jefferson, James Madison, and John Quincy Adams. Such scientifically oriented federal agencies as the United States Coast Survey, the United States Naval Observatory, the United States Patent Office, and the United States Topographical Engineers Corps were successively established.

In natural history, descriptive science, described as Baconian, was the order of the day. A historian of American science has identified the basic elements of the Baconian system: "All science must somehow rest on observation—it must begin with individual facts and pass gradually to broader and broader generalizations . . . avoiding hypotheses, and not going beyond what could be directly observed." Baird's scientific method was an enhancement of the Baconian system. And as another historian of American science has pointed out, the scientific world into which Baird entered was in the process of growth—a growth featured by steady progress toward ever greater professionalization, more corporate structure for scientific work, and a widely shared goal of making American science and scientists respected in Europe.[3]

In the socio-political arena, Americans had been pushing westward since before the Union was formed, but a major surge toward total occupation of the continent became national policy in the nineteenth century. President Jefferson sent Meriwether Lewis and William Clark to explore the western reaches of America in 1803. Major Stephen H. Long's expedition followed, with explorations of the territories between the Mississippi Valley and the Rockies in the early 1820s. Long's group was the first to include recognized scientists whose mission was to collect and describe the animals, birds, and plants that they found in these unknown territories, as well as to bring back descriptions of the Indian tribes they encountered. Other expeditions, with governmental backing or private sponsors, probed the territories acquired in the Louisiana Purchase, while "mountain men," hunters, trappers, and adventurers of all stripes accepted the risks and challenges of the frontier in search of a new life or escape from an old one.

In 1838 the United States government launched its first hydrographic and scientific survey under the auspices of the navy, which placed the colorful Lieutenant Charles Wilkes in command. Between 1838 and 1842 Wilkes's squadron sailed around the globe, surveyed and charted 280 islands in the Pacific as far west as Fiji and much of the northwest coast of North America, and confirmed the fact that Antarctica was a continent. Included on the expedition staff were several natural scientists, who collected barrels of botanical and zoological specimens and sent them back to Washington, where neither adequate buildings nor qualified curators were available for their reception and conservation. But an important principle was established: All specimens collected by official exploring parties were the property of the United States government and were to be sent to Washington.

The Mexican War (1846–1848) and the Civil War (1861–1865) diverted national attention from exploration but signally advanced the role of the army engineers in topographic research. Immediately after the Civil War the westward push recommenced in earnest, and the government's desire to extend railroad lines to the Pacific territories gave the surveying of railroad routes across the plains and through the Rockies major priority in national policy.

The surge of would-be settlers into the newly opened lands of the West was achieved, of course, at the expense of Indians and native resources such as bison. During Baird's lifetime little concern was shown to conservation, whether of peoples, wildlife, or land, despite the warnings and pleas of the farsighted and articulate seer John Wesley Powell, the indomitable explorer of the Grand Canyon.

The issue of greatest political concern to all Americans during Baird's early life was slavery. As new territories were opened to settlement, and as new states sought admission to the nation, questions of where slavery was to be accepted and where it was to be prohibited, together with such closely linked questions as the right of slave owners to recover escaped slaves who had reached free territory, dominated both political and citizen concern, and solutions were sought in such "compromises" as those of 1820–1821 and 1850.

Spencer Baird moved with his family to Washington from rural Pennsylvania in 1850, when he was twenty-seven. During the Bairds' first ten years in the Capital, the growing strain between the states over the slavery question predominated all other concerns. The several agreements that became known as the Compromise of 1850, one of which eliminated the slave trade in the District of Columbia, took effect that year. Some pens of the Washington slave dealers were located directly behind the newly erected Smithsonian Castle. They disappeared during the following months, but they must have been a disturbing feature of the area for several months after Baird's arrival.

The Union victory ended the slavery issue, and the seventies and eighties were years of relative peace, at least externally. Among the succession of presidents who took office and left it after Abraham Lincoln's death was a leader of promise, James Garfield, who became the victim of an assassin's bullet. Garfield was the only president with whom Baird maintained an active association, mostly while Garfield was serving in Congress and a member of the Board of Regents of the Smithsonian, and before his brief tenure in the White House.

Later political events of national importance with which Baird was directly associated were the purchase of Alaska, in the consideration of which his informed testimony was a crucial factor; a difficult negotiation with the British and the Canadians over fishing rights; and the great Centennial Exposition of 1876, commemorating the one hundredth anniversary of the independence of the United States.

The second half of the nineteenth century was a time of cultural expansion, too. Prominent in the literary field were Ralph Waldo Emerson and Henry Thoreau, both of whom Baird met. And the nature essayist John Burroughs was among his collectors. The French actress Sarah Bernhardt was achieving international fame for her wide range of roles (though Baird was highly critical of her role in *Camille*, which he attended while studying medicine in New York). Particularly, though, it was the era in which science came of age. Some notable scientific leaders who dominated the scene were Joseph Henry, the first secretary of the newly founded Smithsonian; Alexander Dallas Bache, grandson of Benjamin Franklin, a distinguished physicist, and the first head of the United States Coast Survey; Louis Agassiz, the famous Swiss-born geologist and naturalist; James Dwight Dana, geologist and zoologist; Benjamin Silliman, founder and coeditor with Dana of the influential *American Journal of*

Science and Arts; Asa Gray, America's most notable botanist; and Arnold Guyot, professor of physical geography at Princeton. The Smithsonian Institution, the American Association for the Advancement of Science, and the National Academy of Sciences all developed during these years; and Washington began to challenge Boston, New York, and Philadelphia as a center of major scientific importance.

Baird's reactions to the many events and activities on the national stage will tell much about his character, but crucial to the development of his personality, and indeed to an understanding of these responses, was the cultural and social milieu in which he grew up and spent his formative years. He was raised in Carlisle, a small town in rural Pennsylvania with close ties to the nearby metropolis of Philadelphia. In the early nineteenth century the rules of social and community behavior in cities and towns along the eastern seaboard generally followed patterns imported from Victorian England. In Carlisle, as in similar towns, "patterns of daily work and community life before 1860 had," in an apt description by Curtis Hinsley, "been predominantly local and personal." Baird's accounts of his youthful life, as recorded in his daily journals, reflect Hinsley's observation that "if small communities restricted acceptable behavior, within those horizons they also provided a sense of comfort, coherence, and control."[4] Small-town society was rigidly stratified. Spencer Baird's grandmother was Lydia Spencer Biddle. The Biddles, and consequently the Bairds, were an accepted part of the upper-crust elite, accentuated in Carlisle by the close relationships that existed between members of its upper class and their social counterparts in Philadelphia. As a Biddle, Spencer Baird acquired top social status at birth. For that he never needed to strive.

The social life of "nice" young people in communities such as Carlisle was dictated by local standards of behavior and closely monitored by their elders. Baird tells in his journal of ice cream socials, evenings of charades, musical presentations, sleigh rides, walks in the country, and comparably innocent diversions.[5] Sex was unmentionable, and alcohol was used socially but with discretion. Young males who contemplated contrary behavior in either category sought the anonymity of the big city, and young ladies were expected to approach the altar on their wedding day in a "state of innocence." Country towns were too small and social pressures too strong to admit of exceptions to the rules.

In terms of everyday life, it was the era of the extended family. Uncles, aunts, cousins, nephews, and nieces all communicated frequently— particularly when one or another needed help, and it seemed that some- one always did—and the acknowledged family head (in the Baird- Churchill family complex it was Spencer) shouldered the principal burden of family support. Marital bonds were also established and maintained on a very different basis than that we know today. Allegiance, as in the polit- ical issues of the time, was to "the Union," and certainly in the Baird fam- ily it called for a degree of selfless devotion on Spencer's part.

However, on his appointment as assistant secretary of the Smithsonian Institution in 1850, Baird moved to Washington, the capital of the nation, and for the rest of his life and career he was immersed in and influenced by urban life and culture. The Washington to which the Baird family moved in 1850 bore little resemblance to the one we know today, or even to the older, more developed American cities of his time. According to one historian,

> Householders still dumped garbage and slops into the alleys and roadways. The result, unpleasant when the city had contained only a few hundred families, was a menace to health when that number tripled. Pigs scavenged freely, dug hog wallows in the roads, and besmirched buildings and fences. Slaughter houses heightened the nauseous orders. Rats and cockroaches in- fested most dwellings, including the White House. In summer, flies swarmed from stables and the dung on the streets, and mosquitoes bred by millions in the stagnant ponds scattered through the city. Faulty drainage about some of the public pumps exposed whole neighborhoods to dysen- tery and typhoid fever. Fear of a cholera epidemic like that of 1832 inspired Mayor Seaton in 1849 to appoint ward "sanitary committees" to assist the board of health in seeing that lime was spread over the worst danger spots, but the mortality rate that year ran close to 35 per 1,000, nearly half among children under one year of age. Infant mortality was appalling.[6]

Apparently, lectures and sermons on serious subjects gave some relief from the abysmal conditions, for they drew good crowds, particularly in Washington, where entertainments were few. Making calls occupied much of the time and energy of upper-class ladies, and everyone who "was somebody" was invited to presidential levees at the White House. Even for grand social occasions, though, the comforts of modern life were not always in evidence. Baird described the excruciating celebration at the Grant inauguration in 1873. "There was a ball in the evening in a new building erected for the purpose, 350 feet by 150; & it was so cold that the guests wore all the wrappings they could gather together, & they had to chop up the chicken salad with hatchets to get a chance to eat it. It was so cold that it is said the breath as it rose into the air gave the appearance of a company engaged in Smoking."[7] Baird offers an example of some of the exigencies of household administration in a letter to the Washington Department of Health, dated November 10, 1866. "You will confer a favor by having my privies cleaned tonight or as soon thereafter as possible."[8]

For the lower classes, however, life was even harder. There were no governmental support programs for the sick, the aged, or the unemployed; widows often found themselves in desperate straits; and free Negroes had to put up bonds, or be sponsored, to get permits to settle in the District. A major civic concern among whites was that Negroes who purchased their freedom, or who were freed by Maryland or Virginia masters, would settle in the District of Columbia, where life for free blacks, while rough by modern standards, was still better than in slave states.

Pertinent, too, are a few notes about the logistics of daily life in Baird's time. Transportation was by foot, horsepower (literally), train, and steamboat. There were few enough senders and receivers to make it possible to send a letter from Washington to Philadelphia or New York advising the receiver of plans to arrive the next day. Express services were reliable enough and fast enough for the Bairds, in Washington, to order weekly supplies of meat, tubs of butter, and similar staples from Carlisle farmers and fresh fish from the Fulton Fish Market in New York. Whiskey could be bought by the barrel so cheaply that it was the principal preservative used by Baird and his collectors for the shipment and storage of zoological specimens.

Chapter Three

The Early Baird

1823–1846

Heroes must rise by small degrees to glory
'Tis *stairs* that lead them to the atick story.

—From a letter to Baird from
his grandmother, 1845.

ON OCTOBER 17, 1815, nine years after James Macie had become James Smithson, the distinguished citizens of far-off Reading, Pennsylvania, joined in celebration of the marriage of one of their leading lawyers, Samuel Baird, to the socially well connected Lydia MacFunn Biddle, of nearby Carlisle. The marriage united the members of two of eastern Pennsylvania's elite families. Samuel Baird was a direct descendant of the Potts family, in whose honor the surrounding towns of Pottstown, Potts Grove, and Pottsville had been named. Lydia was closely related to the socially and civically prominent Biddle and Penrose families of Philadelphia. American tradition provided for no social status comparable to that of the Northumberland Percys in England, but nonetheless the Baird children were assured by their birth of top social recognition in the eastern United States.

Before Samuel's untimely death in the cholera epidemic of 1833, Lydia bore him four sons and three daughters. Their third child and third son was born on February 3, 1823, and christened Spencer in honor of his maternal grandmother, Lydia Spencer Biddle. After Samuel's death, Lydia moved with her large family to Carlisle, where she had been brought up and where her mother and a number of close relatives lived. Spencer throughout his life identified himself with Carlisle. But it is clear from his daughter Lucy's accounts of his walks with his father, and from his own recollection of the little museum of natural history curiosities, described in his letter to Levi Mingle (see p. 199n.1), that his lifelong passion for natural history had taken solid root well before he left Reading.

While their mother was getting settled in Carlisle with the rest of the family, Spencer and his next older brother, Sam, went to a boarding school at Port Deposit, Maryland. He obviously remembered it with some affection, since he revisited the site many years later and wrote to Sam urging him to do the same. In the autumn of 1835 both boys transferred to the grammar school which had just been established in Carlisle under the auspices of Dickinson College.

Spencer graduated from the grammar school in 1836 at the age of thirteen. That fall, as Congress began its debates on the propriety of accepting the Smithson bequest, he entered the freshman class at Dickinson College, from which he graduated four years later in a class of nineteen. While he achieved no notable distinction as a student, two extracurricular activities were of special importance. First, he began the serious collection and study of specimens of local natural history, particularly birds, in partnership with his oldest brother, William; and second, he began to keep a daily journal, from which an intimate portrait of his activities, though not of his philosophy of life or his place in it, may be drawn. Throughout his life he never confided his deeper feelings in writing.

The congressional debate years from 1836 to 1846 were active and important ones in Baird's life. Many of his waking hours he spent afield with dog, gun, or fishing gear, usually in company with brothers, cousins, or local friends. His companions' participation was for sport, Spencer's for collecting. He recorded in his journal how he spent many an evening skinning and preparing the kill or catch of the day. Virtually every entry includes a meticulous record (always noting the weather conditions of the day) of where and with whom he had hunted or fished that day, and the species they had shot or caught. Each December 31 he summarized his totals for the year. "During the past year," he noted on December 31, 1842, "I walked about 2100 miles in one pair of laced boots, half-soled three times. Shot about 650 birds, of which 75 wild ducks, 5 crows, 6 hawks, 3 owls."[1]

During these years the Baird brothers William and Spencer moved into the public eye with the publication in respected journals of several of their articles. In 1843 their descriptions of two new species of flycatchers appeared in the *Proceedings* of the Academy of Natural Sciences in Philadelphia. The following year "The Birds of Cumberland County" was published in Benjamin Silliman's *American Journal of Science and Arts*, and "The Trees and Shrubs of Cumberland County" appeared in 1845 in the *Gettysburg Linnaean Journal*.

The seriousness and the energy with which young Baird pursued his collecting activity during these years are apparent from the list of natural history specimens in the collections he contributed to the Smithsonian Institution at the time of his appointment—collections that filled two freight cars. Listed in the Institution's annual report of 1850, Baird's donation was impressive:

> About 500 species of North American Birds, in skins, consisting of about twenty-five hundred specimens in the various stages of age, sex, and season.
> About two hundred and fifty specimens of European Birds, in one thousand specimens.
> Eggs of about one hundred and fifty species of North American Birds .... The nests accompany the eggs of many of these species.
> Nests and eggs of about seventy-five species of European Birds.
> A collection of the Reptiles and Fishes of the United States, at present contained in more than five hundred glass jars, and numerous barrels, kegs, and tin vessels. Most of the species are represented by numerous specimens, amounting in certain cases to hundreds and even thousands of a single species . . . in addition to these a good collection of the fresh water Fishes and Reptiles of Central and Eastern Europe.
> . . . Embryos of many Birds, Mammals, and Batrachian Reptiles.

Skulls and Skeletons of many North America vertebrata, amounting to about six hundred specimens.

. . . A large collection of fossil bones from various caves in Pennsylvania and Virginia.[2]

Spencer's brother Will was one of the two family members who had the greatest early influence on Spencer's life and character, and perhaps the most lasting influence, the other being his grandmother Lydia Spencer Biddle. The relationship between Spencer and Will during these years was warmer and closer than any between other members of the Baird family. Both were keenly interested in the outdoors, and especially in birds. They collected together, prepared their specimens together, co-wrote their several ornithological publications, and corresponded frequently and intimately after Will left Carlisle for a job in Washington. Will sent Spencer money when he could, urged him to pursue medical studies "because no means of livelihood . . . is to be obtained in America from Ornithology," and in general filled the role of fatherly older brother. There was feeling and sensitivity for each other not seen in any of Spencer's other relationships. Each seemed to know what would interest the other and when he would need help.

Lydia Spencer Biddle was Carlisle's social leader and a dominant personality around whom the Biddle, Baird, and Penrose families revolved. Spencer told in his journal that on Christmas Day, 1843, the company who dined at his grandmother's house included her five children, three children-in-law, and twenty-three grandchildren. In a description of her great-grandmother, Spencer's daughter, Lucy, wrote, "Her granddaughters would sometimes object to wearing some garment which she considered suitable, on the ground that it was not the fashion, and would be met with the crushing reply, 'When I was young, anything that Miss Spencer wore *was* the fashion.'"[3]

The Biddle name was safe in the custody of Lydia Spencer. Although she had acquired the Biddle name only through her marriage, she bore it proudly, and in her the Biddle connection was acknowledged without question by the Biddle families of both Carlisle and Philadelphia. Indeed, had Lydia Spencer not upheld her Biddle-ism so strongly, the Baird family would have had at best a distant and indirect claim to it. For them the

Biddle name had been superseded in 1752 when Spencer's great-grandmother, an earlier Lydia Biddle, married a British naval officer, Captain William MacFunn. Captain MacFunn died when his son, William Biddle MacFunn, was only three years old, apparently without leaving his widow well provided for. Her brother, Edward Biddle, reportedly agreed to assume the expense of young William's education on condition that the boy's name be changed to William MacFunn Biddle. This was done, thus preserving the Biddle name and associated social status for William's descendants, including Spencer Fullerton Baird.[4]

Bearing his grandmother's name, Spencer was evidently one of her favorites. He spent a good deal of time at her house, and they corresponded regularly when he was away from Carlisle. In an early letter she gave him advice in two areas, which he followed throughout his life. "Indeed my dear Spence a kind polite act never is unrewarded. Therefore, independently of the pleasure all good minds feel in giving pleasure, you are certain of your reward by having it returned. I hope you will always remember this and never let an opportunity pass of doing kind, good, and civil acts. . . . Laziness, dear Spencer, is a horrid misfortune. Never indulge it, but employ every moment in gaining something worth having or knowing." Characteristic also was her response to a request from Spencer a few years later for four dollars to buy a French dictionary. "When the gratification is to feed the mind and clothe the intelect [*sic*], helping you through the journey of life, I am not the one to refuse. Hoping, Dear Spencer you may realise the value of this book is the constant desire of your affectionate Grandmother, Lydia Biddle."[5]

Grandmother Biddle need not have felt any concern that Spencer might give in to laziness during his years in Carlisle. Although he showed no interest in athletics per se, he was a passionate walker, often covering twenty-five to forty miles in a single day.[6] His self-imposed discipline, even at an early age, was extraordinary. In addition to his collecting and walking, he immersed himself in a formidable program of study. He taught himself a reading knowledge of French, German, Spanish, Italian, and Danish; studied algebra, geometry, calculus, chemistry, and physics; set himself upon a reading program that included works by Shakespeare, Carlyle, Emerson, Goethe, Hegel, Schiller (the latter three in German), and Racine and Terence (in original French and a French translation, respectively), plus every book he could obtain on natural history subjects. Years later he wrote to a relative, "My own preferences in early childhood were in the line of mathematics and languages, and I used to get up at 4 o'clock in the morning, make my own fire in mid-winter, and devote myself to abstruse studies that I now can scarcely understand."[7]

Baird also began at this time the extensive and widespread correspondence with fellow naturalists that he continued throughout life. Just before his graduation from Dickinson in 1840, he wrote the following, oft-quoted letter to John James Audubon:

> Dear Sir,
> I herewith send you the description of a species of *Tyrannula* an account of which I have been able to find, neither in your Ornithological Biography and Synopsis, nor in Nuttall's Ornithology. I have obtained three specimens, all in low, swampy thickets. Two of them I have stuffed, the third (obtained last Saturday) [May 30, 1840] I have in spirits and would gladly send it to you, had I the opportunity. Their habits were very similar to those of the Little Tyrant Flycatcher. (*Musicapa Pusilla*). Male.

There follow three lengthy paragraphs of description of this and a rather similar bird that Baird had also collected. Both proved to be flycatcher species new to science at that time, the yellow bellied (*Empidonax flaviventris*) and the least (*E. minimus*). He continued:

> You see, Sir, that I have taken (after much hesitation) the liberty of writing to you. I am but a boy [he was seventeen], and very inexperienced, as you no doubt will observe from my description of the Flycatcher. My brother last year commenced a study of our Birds, and after some months I joined him. He has gone elsewhere to settle and I am left alone. . . . I have already trespassed too much on your patience, and will conclude by saying, that if I can be of the slightest assistance to you in any way, be assured that although others may tender it more ably, yet none can more cheerfully. I am, Sir, etc.[8]

Audubon replied:

> On my return from Charleston, S.C. yesterday, I found your kind favor of the 4th inst. in which you have the goodness to inform me that you have discovered a new species of flycatcher, and which, if the bird corresponds to

your description, is, indeed, likely to prove itself hitherto undescribed, for although you speak of yourself as being a youth, your style and the descriptions you have sent me prove to me that an old head may from time to time be found on young shoulders.[9]

Thus began a friendship and collaboration, which was unique for Audubon and which continued up until shortly before Audubon's death in 1851.

In 1840, after his graduation, Baird made excursions to Philadelphia, New York, and Boston, the major centers of natural science study in the first half of the nineteenth century. During these trips he met and established close relationships with nearly all the leading naturalists of the day—in particular, John Cassin of the Academy of Natural Sciences in Philadelphia; George N. Lawrence, a prominent New York ornithologist; Dr. Thomas M. Brewer, a Boston oologist of note; Asa Gray, a Boston botanist; and Joseph Leidy, a paleontologist in Philadelphia—all of whom became Baird's close friends, partners, and supporters throughout his later life.

In the course of a visit to Boston in 1847 he also met the already famous Louis Agassiz and began an association and collaboration with him that continued up until Agassiz' death, despite a succession of prickly ups and downs. During that same visit to Boston, Baird met Ralph Waldo Emerson, whose writings he had often praised enthusiastically, and traveled with him to Concord for an introduction to Henry Thoreau. A cryptic entry in his journal regarding this meeting speaks for itself. "Saw R. W. Emerson and with him to Henry Thoreau's. Visited battle ground at Concord. Then to Lexington where dined. Home by Waltham, Weston, and Wayland."[10] Baird never again made any reference either to Emerson or to Thoreau.

Two events of importance in Spencer Baird's life took place in 1840. His brother Will, who had been his mentor and collaborator in his ornithological pursuits, went to Washington, where their uncle, Charles Penrose, who had been appointed assistant solicitor general of the Treasury, offered him a clerkship. Then, in the fall of that year, Spencer enrolled as a medical student at the College of Physicians and Surgeons in New York, under the patronage of Dr. Middleton Goldsmith. Will Baird urged him to continue these studies, but Spencer actually had no intention of becoming a physician. As William Deiss has noted in his paper on Baird's early life, there was no training available for students of natural history at that time, and the only place an aspiring naturalist could learn anatomy and related subjects was in medical school.[11]

Baird described in his daily journal entries the lectures he attended and the dissections he performed, many on animal specimens. "[Jan] 23, Thursday. Dissecting opossum all day."[12] But much of his time and attention was given to extracurricular pursuits. He met Audubon, with whom he immediately hit it off famously. Audubon gave him many valuable specimens for his collections and coached him in drawing. He visited other collectors in New York and spent happy hours at the laboratory of John J. Bell, the leading taxidermist of the day. But by February 1842 Spencer had had enough of medical school, and he took advantage of an attack of flu to return to Carlisle for convalescence. He never resumed medical studies.

The following summer Will Baird wrote his brother that there was an opening in Washington for a curator for the collections of the Wilkes Exploring Expedition. These collections had been stored in the Patent Office building under the nominal supervision of Joel Poinsett's National Institute for the Promotion of Science. No serious effort had ever been made to identify or classify the myriad specimens of natural history in the collections, but the expedition's scientists were now clamoring that this be done. Will urged Spencer to come to Washington and apply for the job.

Spencer responded at once, walking from Carlisle to Baltimore to save money, and taking "the cars" (as he described the train) from there. He visited the executive secretary of the National Institute, Francis Markoe, whose collections of minerals and fossils greatly impressed the young Baird. Noted ornithologist John Townsend of Philadelphia was ultimately appointed curator, but Markoe was impressed enough by Baird to appoint him a corresponding member of the National Institute, supplementing a similar honor accorded Baird at about the same time by the Academy of Natural Sciences in Philadelphia.

Shortly after Baird returned from Washington, he received an alluring invitation from Audubon to join an expedition "towards the Rocky Mountains at least to the Yellowstone River, and up the latter stream four hundreds of miles, and *perhaps* go across the Rocky Mountains."[13] Baird's reaction was interesting, and significant. Initially he protested that "while nothing would delight me more," he would not be able to afford the expenses of the trip. Audubon promptly offered to pay Baird's way himself. Meanwhile, Baird had passed Audubon's letter on to his mother and Will, and had discussed the project with other friends. Ultimately he turned the invitation down on the ground that his mother was concerned about his health; he experienced occasional palpitations, which, however, had never interfered with his strenuous walks. In a later letter to Audubon, he wrote, "A thousand times I wished that the fears of my friends had not prevented me from accompanying you to the scenes of action." But he had noted no such regrets in correspondence to others or in his journal, and there is no evidence to suggest that he had pleaded with his mother for permission to go; thus it is hard to escape the conclusion that he himself had little desire to go on the expedition.

In November 1843 Baird made a second trip to Washington, again at Will's invitation—a trip that was to lead to a major turning in his life. He met Lieutenant Wilkes of the famous exploring expedition, and more significantly, he met James Dwight Dana, who had been a member of the expedition. Dana had written the expedition reports on geology, mineralogy, and crustacea, and was engaged in sorting, describing, and trying to rearrange the expedition's crustacea specimens, which had been thoroughly mixed up and had their labels removed by an incompetent "curator." Baird spent two months as a volunteer assistant to Dana and so impressed him that three years later Dana urged him to apply for the position of assistant secretary of the newborn Smithsonian Institution.

Baird's continued association with his alma mater, Dickinson College, bore first fruit in July 1845 when he was appointed honorary professor of natural science and curator of the natural history cabinet at the college. He noted in his journal that the appointment involved "no salary and nothing to do," but his grandmother saw the value of the honor more clearly. In a letter of congratulations she wrote:

Although at present there is no Salary attached to the situation, yet as the institution rises in fame and importance . . . there will be ample compensation made for the support of its professor. Besides, dear Spencer, the appointment is so honorable to a young man of your age, that the fame and credit is almost worth a principality to a young man who wishes to establish himself scientifically in the world. . . .

. . . indeed I think this beginning of your career most excellent and promising, especially if you have the patience to wait until your turn comes . . . therefore, dear Spencer, as you have mounted the first step, I most sincerely pray and hope your progress may be steadily onward and sure. And should you, before you reach the Topmost Towering hight [*sic*] of this arduous ascent require a little proping [*sic*] or helping up, your grandmother's hand shall be extended to you as long as she has the power.[14]

A further benefit was that Baird could then order at college expense scientific books which he would not have been able to afford with his own limited resources, as well as cabinets, jars, and laboratory equipment, and even the indispensable cheap whiskey for storage of specimens.

Grandmother Biddle's prediction came true a year later when, at commencement, July 6, 1846, Baird was appointed full professor of natural history at an annual salary of four hundred dollars, his teaching duties to commence in September. His letter to his grandmother is indicative of his appreciation of the support he had always received from her. "To you, dear grandmother, I owe a great many thanks for encouraging me when no one else did in devoting myself to my favorite pursuits so eagerly, and for prophesying the event which has taken place." In her letter of affectionate congratulations, his grandmother wrote: "I greatly rejoice Dear Spencer in your rising fame, a few more years I trust will find you at the top of the *Ladder*. It is stairs that lead one to the attic story."[15]

Lydia Biddle lived long enough to see her grandson well launched on his career in Washington, in fulfillment of her predictions and of her abiding faith in him. She died in Carlisle in 1858, aged 92. When Will Baird's tour in Washington ended, he settled in his birthplace, Reading, Pennsylvania, where he established a law practice and over the years served in a number of state and local offices, including that of mayor of Reading. He married but lost his only son when the child was at an early age. He and Spencer remained on close terms, although in the absence of their former joint interests and projects, their letters became fewer. Will suffered increasingly bad health and died on October 19, 1872.

In the year 1846, as Spencer Baird first attained professional status as a professor of natural history, two crucial and basically fortuitous developments took place, changing the pattern of his life radically and forever. Congress passed, and President Polk signed into law, the act incorporating the Smithsonian Institution, and Baird took Mary Helen Churchill as his wife.

Chapter Four

Years of Change

1846–1850

Chiefly the mold of a man's fortune is in his own hands.

—Francis Bacon, "On Fortune"

MARY HELEN CHURCHILL was the only daughter and eldest child of Brigadier General Sylvester Churchill and Lucy Hunter, his wife. Mary was born on August 30, 1821, in Windsor, Vermont, where General Churchill, a native Vermonter and then a captain, was in residence. Few details of Mary's early life are available. She evidently spent much of her childhood in Vermont, where she apparently received an excellent education and where she developed an affectionate relationship with an old family friend, the Honorable George Perkins Marsh, who was to play an important role, both in furtherance of her husband's career and as family counselor. Mary and her three younger brothers followed their father to the various army posts to which he was assigned in a steadily advancing professional military career.

While stationed at Fort Johnson, near Smithville, North Carolina, in the early 1840s, the Churchills became close friends with the family of a military colleague, George Blaney, whose wife, Mary, was the younger sister of Spencer's mother, Lydia Biddle Baird. George Blaney died at Fort Johnson in 1842, and his widow returned to Carlisle to be near her mother and sisters.

As tension grew between the United States and Mexico in the latter part of 1844, Colonel Churchill was ordered to a more active post. Mrs. Churchill looked for a place where she could settle with her daughter, Mary Helen, and her youngest son, Charles. She welcomed an invitation from her friend Mary Blaney to come to Carlisle, where she would find friends at the army post as well as in civilian circles. The Churchills arrived in Carlisle on November 5, 1844, and took lodgings in a house adjacent to that of Grandmother Biddle.

Spencer and Mary promptly met, and as promptly fell in love. Spencer had led an active social life up until that time, and the early pages of his journal are full of the names of young ladies whom he had squired to parties or on excursions. But after Mary's arrival he clearly had eyes only for her, and she for him.

They were a serious young couple, as is evident in the letters they wrote each other during Mary's absences on visits to her father. They discussed Spencer's explanations of the magnetic telegraph, Emerson's essays, "dreamy transcendentalism," and "car music" from trains. Spencer told of going to a Thursday evening social at his grandmother's, but added that he hated to "waste" an evening a week on frivolity—a sentiment with which Mary expressed herself in complete accord: "I do think it is really wicked to lead such a life, and after this winter I intend to be very sedate and quiet, and do much more as I please, provided you will help me decide what I do please, and teach me how to do it."[1]

Aside from these few letters, there is little information about Mary and Spencer's courtship years, since Baird made no reference in his journal to his relationship with Mary or his feelings about her, and Mary kept no diary. Spencer and Mary's daughter, Lucy, told some years later her mother's recollections of how Spencer would bring his books when he came to spend the evening in her company, and would fall asleep in his chair. Mary also recalled an occasion when they were taking a walk along a stream where Spencer spotted some fish new to him, and having no net with which to catch them, he borrowed Mary's bonnet for the purpose.[2]

Throughout their years of courtship they remained devoted, although clearly not passionate; but after Spencer's appointment to a salaried position at Dickinson, they decided to get married. They made no formal announcement of their engagement, but that it was family knowledge is evident from a letter Spencer wrote to his brother Will on August 4, 1846.

> I do not suppose that you will be much surprised at my telling you that I am engaged to be married, since you knew that already; but that it is to come off next Saturday will probably make you open your eyes. As Mary and Myself possess enough between us to make a start, (she having upwards of $200 per ann.) there is no especial reason why we should wait. Before Mr. Emory [president of Dickinson College] went away I asked him whether he thought my prospects of an increase of salary were sufficiently good to warrant my taking such a step, and that immediately. He answered most emphatically that he thought they were, and advised me to do so by all means. . . . So having obtained the consent of the Col. which arrived last Sunday, we concluded to have it all over so that I may be settled before College commences. We will be married in the Morning, and go down to Philadelphia. . . . In all probability Mother will go with us, as you know it would be highly improper for a young gentleman & lady to go off all alone. . . . everything is to be in the quietest manner, no bridesmaids, white bonnets, or such stuff. Nobody to be invited but the family, & [the Reverend] M'Clintock [professor of mathematics at Dickinson] to perform the ceremony.[3]

Will was ill and could not be present, but his reply is characteristic. "If I could be there would be willing to comply with the old custom which would compel me to dance in my stocking feet, that is provided I could do it in a dark place." Baird's journal notes on his honeymoon are comparably cryptic.

> August 8, 1846, Saturday. Clear in morn, gusty in even. Married at 9 A.M. by Prof. McClintock to Mary Helen Churchill, daughter of Colonel C. . . . None present but family. Left in cars for Phila. accompanied by mother. Got in at 9. Went to U.S. Hotel.
>
> 12, Wednesday, Went to Pottstown with wife, reached at 11 1/2. Went to hill with Lizzie Hawley. Found mother there.
>
> 13, 14, 15, 16, Did nothing much but loaf and eat peaches.[4]

William H. Dall provides a description of the youthful Mary in his biography of Baird.

Mary Helen Churchill, Prof. Baird's bride, was a well educated, highly intelligent, and tactful young woman. For the period she was exceedingly well read, and she had an unusual appreciation of good English. Without being strictly a blonde, she had light brown hair and a fair complexion, was of medium height and as a young woman slender. Probably she never laid claim to beauty other than that given by Nature in the spring of one's years, but a charming smile, a face lighted up by intelligence and cordiality, aided by a delicate sense of humor and a wit which enlivened conversation without stinging, made her a delightful hostess and companion.[5]

Mary was a year older than Spencer. Having traveled with her family, she actually had more "worldly" experience than her husband at the time they were married. She was an intelligent woman and had an excellent writing style. Her letters are interesting, informative, and clear in even the most complex descriptions. Yet when she married, she followed the standard of the time—her husband came first. As Baird noted in his letters to friends, she helped him a great deal with his correspondence, and she was of particular value to him in transcribing large portions of a German encyclopedia of natural history which he was translating and editing for a New York publisher and which provided them with a welcome source of extra income during the early days of their marriage. They economized on living expenses by residing with Mrs. Churchill.

It is characteristic of Baird that he made no mention of his married life in either his journal or his letters for nearly two years, until the following entry appears, dated February 7, 1848: "Studied Salmonidae Agassiz. Mary taken sick in night. At 16+/– minutes of 3 next morning, 8th, a daughter born," and in Mary's handwriting at the end of the entry, "Lucy Hunter Baird."[6]

During the years prior to Lucy's birth, Baird made trips to Philadelphia and Boston, during which he and Mary communicated almost daily in long, affectionate letters filled with family and local news. Then on January 3, 1850, in answer to a demand for information about his marriage from his friend James Dwight Dana, he wrote:

You ask me about my family. I wonder I have not spoken or written of them before now, as I am rather given to loquacity on this subject. My wife is a daughter of Gen. Churchill, Inspector-General of the Army, and a first-rate one she is too. Not the least fear of snakes, salamanders, and such

other Zoological interestings; cats only are to her an aversion. Well educated and acquainted with several tongues, she usually reads over all my letters, crossing i's and dotting t's, sticking in here a period, and there a
comma, and converting my figure 7's into 7's. In my absence she answers
letters of correspondents, and in my presence reads them. She transcribes
my illegible Mss., correcting it withal, and does not grudge the money I
spend on books. In addition to all her literary accomplishments, she regu-
lates her family well (myself included) and her daughter is the cleanest and
most neatly dressed child in town. So much for the Frau.

My daughter and only child Lucy is about 23 months old, talks like a
young steamboat, is passionately fond of Natural History, admiring snakes
above all things. Of these she usually has one or more as playthings, which
range from six inches to six feet in length (living). She will stand for hours
at a time diving after the fish or salamanders which I keep in tubs in my
room. A friend gave her a sugar fish some time ago, which she immediately
insisted should be put in a bottle. Her chief admiration is of ducks, one of
which, mounted on wheels (wooden) and the size of life, is her plaything
from morning till night. She spends her time chiefly in dragging about this
duck, and "writing" ducks and the like with her pencil.

Now beat the above if you can.[7]

During these years Baird was fully involved with his teaching responsibilities at Dickinson College. He took his tasks seriously, but he also enjoyed them,—particularly his association with his students. In a letter to
his brother Will, he wrote:

I have been kept working like a horse, at the rate of from three to five
recitations every day until now. Old Caldwell and Prof. Emory returned a
few days ago however, and this will lighten my load, as we all had to divide
the recitations of the absentees till their return. . . . The Sophs recite in
Geometry, the Freshmen in Animal Physiology, the preparatory classes in
Arithmetic & Algebra. Next Session (after Christmas) I take the Seniors in
Nat. Theology. I like the business of teaching very much, & believe I am a
favorite with the Students.[8]

An important part of Baird's popularity and of his enjoyment of teaching came from the practice (which he was perhaps the first to introduce in
American education) of taking his students on field excursions to observe
at first hand the natural phenomena they had studied in books. Some
years later, after he had moved on to another way of life, he wrote to one
of his former students: "Spring is upon us again, and you can imagine
how much I think of the times when I led my boys to the mts. after sala-

manders and other [illegible]. I doubt whether I shall ever enjoy such fun again."[9]

In January 1847, six months after the establishment of the Smithsonian Institution, Baird received the following letter from James Dwight Dana, whom he had assisted in 1843, classifying the crustacea specimens in the Wilkes expedition collection:

> I have just written Dr. Pickering [a member of the Board of Regents of the Smithsonian] that you would make a good curator for the Smithsonian Institution. What do you say to it? Salary $1500.00 with house rent, as I understand. If you wish such a situation you should write at once and send your credentials to Professor Henry, and enclose a copy also to the Hon. R. D. Owen, who is one of the Regents. I would give you all of my influence and the best recommendation.

Dana wrote again in early February, urging Baird to get all the recommendations he could, particularly one from "a Political man . . . since much depends on favor in all Washington appointments."[10]

Baird wrote at once to Joseph Henry and also to an old friend of his father's and a fellow Dickinson alumnus, James Buchanan, then secretary of state, requesting him to "say a word to any member of the board of regents which would be of influence in their decision." In a second letter to Henry he enclosed letters of recommendation from S. G. Morton, head of the Academy of Natural Sciences in Philadelphia, from John Cassin, curator at the academy, from Audubon, and from Dana, and he added that Asa Gray, the well-known botanist, had also offered to write separately in his support.

Henry's reply was cordial but brief, and hardly encouraging. "Your letters and testimonials in relation to the office of Curator of the Smithsonian Institution have been received and put on file to be considered when the time arrives for the appointment to be made." But he added, "The Board of Regents I think will not appoint a Curator until the building is in a proper condition to receive the specimens of Natural History and this will probably not be the case under five years."[11]

Baird had zeroed in on the target of his dreams, however, and Henry and several of the regents were soon deluged with supportive letters from scientific and political persons of note. Mary Baird, too, wrote to her old friend, George Perkins Marsh, then a member of Congress and a regent of the Smithsonian. Marsh replied: "You know me well enough to believe me without an oath, when I assure you that it will give me great pleasure to serve Mr. Baird to the utmost of my power . . . I will endeavor to assure him the good will of Messrs Evarts, Choate, and Hilliard [regents], as well as the Assistant Secretary, Mr. Jewett of Providence, and if I can advance his interests in any other way, I shall certainly not forget to do so."[12]

While he waited for a call from the Smithsonian, Baird was offered two other opportunities through the good offices of George P. Marsh. In January 1847 the president of the University of Vermont invited Baird to fill the chair of chemistry and natural history at the university at the inviting annual salary of one thousand dollars, and Marsh warmly endorsed the offer. Baird obviously turned the proposal down (although no correspondence is available on the subject), but Marsh's next assist proved more to his liking, and ultimately more profitable. On Marsh's recommendation, Charles Rudolph Garrigue, a New York publisher, offered Baird a contract to translate, and revise for an American readership, a German encyclopedia of science, F. A. Brockhaus's *Bilder Atlas zum Conversations Lexicon*, which had been published in Leipzig and had attracted very favorable attention in Europe. Baird took on this task, which occupied all of his spare time over the next two years. When published, as the *Iconographic Encyclopedia of Science, Literature, and Art* in 1852, this work spread Baird's reputation throughout the American scientific community. Of more immediate benefit to the young marrieds, it added substantially to their very limited income, since Garrigue paid one dollar per page for accepted copy.[13]

Marsh then invited Baird to come to Washington to meet both himself and Secretary Henry, writing with characteristic humor, "Let me introduce you to Mr. H. *provided* that you will for the time lay aside a little of your modesty, and swagger enough to make a proper impression."[14] On July 11, 1848, Baird met and spent three hours with Henry, and with him visited the Smithsonian Castle, then under construction. He apparently "swaggered" sufficiently, as their relationship prospered from that day forth.

During this period one of Baird's closest relationships came to an end, rather sadly. On the 16th of July 1847 he visited his friend and sponsor John James Audubon for the last time. Audubon lived until 1851, but there appears to have been no further communication between them. Baird entered a cryptic note in his journal, "Found Mr. A. much changed."[15]

Over the next two years Baird continued to teach his classes at Dickinson. The college catalogue for 1847–1848 lists him as professor of natural history (teaching the juniors "Mechanics, Hydrostatics, Pneumatics, Acoustics, Electricity, and Electro-Magnetism, and Chemistry" and conducting classes for seniors in "Mineralogy, Animal and Vegetable Physiology, . . . Optics, and Astronomy") and names him, as well, "Curator of the Museum." In addition, he continued to lead his students on his ever-popular field excursions. Away from the college he continued to add to his own growing collections and to extend his contacts with the prominent natural scientists of the day, most notably, Louis Agassiz. Early in 1848 Baird and Agassiz agreed to collaborate on a book describing the freshwater fishes of North America, in which both shared strong interest.[16]

At about the same time, Baird received an honorary degree from the Philadelphia College of Medicine. And while working on his translation and revision of the *Bilder Atlas*, he continued his language studies on his own. Also in 1849 he said good-bye to his sponsor and now close friend George P. Marsh, who departed for Constantinople as United States minister to the Ottoman Empire.

Baird made another trip to Washington in April 1849, and wrote to Mary that he was developing a close and warm relationship with Joseph Henry that augured well for his prospects.[17] He continued to solicit recommendations from potential supporters, and on December 11, 1849, Secretary Henry wrote him:

> I have told you that you are my choice and if nothing occurs to change my opinion of your character, of which I see not the slightest prospect, I shall nominate you to the Board in due time. You must recollect, however, (and I know you do) that in all the appointments I must be governed by what I consider to be the best for the Institution. I shall know no friendship in the choice, and if you are elected it will be because all things considered, you are the best man; you will therefore owe your election to your own reputation.[18]

On July 5, 1850, Spencer Baird's lifelong dream of becoming curator at a major museum came true. The Board of Regents of the Smithsonian Institution approved the secretary's proposal to appoint an assistant secretary "to take charge of the cabinet and to act as naturalist of the Institution." Henry promptly nominated Professor Spencer Fullerton Baird to the post, and he was promptly confirmed. Baird received the news by telegram from the senior assistant secretary, Charles Coffin Jewett, with whom he had come to be on excellent terms, and the following letter from Secretary Henry came three days later:

> I presume that you have received the official announcement of your appointment and that you will not hesitate to accept the office. I can assure you that nothing on my part shall be wanting to render your position as agreeable and as profitable to you as the character of the position will permit. I think that the office will afford you an opportunity of prosecuting your favorite study to the best advantage, while it will enable you to render important service to the cause of knowledge in our country by the assistance and cooperation you will render me in the line of your publications. . . . I presume that . . . you will be able to settle all your business at Carlisle and to commence operations in Washington about the 1st of Oct. I shall return myself at or before that time.
>
> I remain very truly your friend,
Joseph Henry[19]

Chapter Five

𑀰

Spencer and Mary and Lucy

𑀰

THE BAIRD'S COURTSHIP and marriage could hardly have been described in terms of a passionate romance, but it was a relationship that was warm and loving, often in the face of obstacles that only sincere mutual love could have overcome. It was a true and heartfelt partnership which kept Spencer and Mary together without rancor or notable strain for over forty years and terminated only with Spencer's death.

In later years their daughter, Lucy, recalled that her mother had never had any particular taste for natural history but that she was always interested in any activity in which her husband was involved. In his letter to Dana describing his family situation, Baird had noted that he relied on Mary's editorial help with his correspondence, and he mentioned on several occasions the extent to which she cooperated with him in transcribing large portions of his revisions of the *Bilder Atlas*.

For the first few years of their marriage, especially when they moved to a new life of their own in Washington, Mary's concerns were predominantly domestic and maternal. However, after the Bairds moved from the first home in Washington, a boardinghouse, into their own house at 322 New York Avenue, Mary began to play an actively supporting role to her husband in the social life of the city. She proved an excellent housekeeper and an agreeable hostess and was especially loved by the young collectors and scientists who worked with Baird at the Smithsonian. Every Sunday evening for years, the Bairds had open house for these young men, and when they were in the field, they relied on the letters that Mary wrote regularly to each of them for the personal and social news that Baird never included in his.

The Bairds entertained frequently, and they put up a steady succession of visiting scientists, friends, and members of both their families. Despite their frequently expressed concern over money, they always had one or more servants, and the length of time that some of these continued in the Bairds' service speaks well of Mary's management. A free black man, Solomon Brown, was a staff assistant employed by the Smithsonian. He worked closely with Baird in both his natural history and his foreign exchange functions and consequently became well acquainted with the Baird family. Later, one of Baird's memorialists quoted Brown: "Baird was as near a perfect man as ever I met with, and I do not see how such a man could get a wife equal to himself; but that is what he did, for she was as sweet as he was. I never saw either one angry."[1]

Mary had long suffered from headaches and from periods of depression, but in the early 1850s, not long after the family had settled in Washington, she began to be troubled seriously by periodic spasms of abdominal pain with accompanying gastrointestinal disturbances that obliged her to spend many days in bed. She was often subject to nervous crises during these attacks, and only Spencer's presence at her bedside seemed to soothe her. Over the years there were many days when he was unable to go to the Smithsonian because Mary needed him near her. Baird's close associate in later years, George Brown Goode, recalled, "I have known him to sit for many hours at her bedside, holding her hand in one of his while with the other he went on with his writing."[2]

Baird spent hours consulting with or writing to physicians far and near, describing and discussing her symptoms. He followed up on every new suggestion for a chemical or medical preparation or mechanical device that might help her. He took her to the best doctors in Washington, Philadelphia, New York, and Boston. In his journal he noted in detail all her periods of illness—how many days she was confined to bed, when she felt able to get up though remaining upstairs, and when she was finally able to dress and come downstairs. Characteristically, he delegated her care to no one else. He alone administered her hypodermics and other treatments, often commenting in his journal that he had had little sleep, having been up with Mary much of the night. In later years he had an elevator installed in their Massachusetts Avenue house, and much of his correspondence was with railroad officials, arranging for private cars and special routings to insure the greatest comfort for her on their summer trips to Woods Hole, Massachusetts.

None of the many distinguished doctors who treated Mary's problems in the context of nineteenth-century medical knowledge was able to find their cause or relieve her symptoms for long. However, Dr. Allen T. Greenlee, presently of the George Washington University Hospital, generously accepted the challenge of studying Baird's extensive file of journal entries and letters to and from medical correspondents regarding Mary's case and of researching nineteenth-century medical and pharmaceutical literature in order to identify the terms then in use.

Mary's mysterious condition has been passed over by Baird's biographers and memorialists, yet her invalidism constituted such an elemental burden on Spencer Baird's life and activities that it seems pertinent to quote Dr. Greenlee's perceptive diagnosis.

We can divide Mary's health chronologically into four general periods. I am missing data concerning her health as a child and adolescent. Our first period for which we do have data consists of her early married life primarily in the 1840s. During this period we have no mention of any abdominal or pelvic problems. We do find mention of frequent headaches, backaches as well as frank commentary about her loneliness, missing Spencer, etc. There are also entries which link her physical concerns with the psychological. For example, "Lucy fretful/Mary's back hurts, therefore." Also "misses him. Back headache." Indeed Mary's own lamentation about passing on her mental and physical constitutions to Lucy seems to place the two factors at parity in Mary's own mind.

In moving into the 1850s and 1860s Mary's health takes a marked turn for the worse. Two new major problems arise. First, there are bowel problems. From Spencer's journal and also from his letter to Dr. William Hammond, we are given a long history of "colic" which consists of abdominal pain. Some are in the lower abdomen, but some decidedly upper abdominal and, therefore, I think less likely to be of pelvic origin. Further we have mention of bloating, excessive flatulence and some tendency toward diarrhea. Her psychological health during this period is less often mentioned although there is mention of extreme nervousness. These are not the comments that link her emotional state with her physical state. Perhaps Spencer found it easier to deal with Mary as a sick person rather than as an emotionally needy and unfulfilled person I suspect she was. In an interesting letter from Baird to Marsh in October of 1856 Spencer describes a miraculous recovery within three days of changing physicians. To quote, "troubles of years, weariness, weak back, headache, and all of that were dissipated like a charm and to it succeeded moderate enjoyment of life, large appetite, ability to walk four or five miles in the course of a day, etc." He goes on to discuss [Dr.] Hodge's assessment that Mary's problems were uterine and . . . this may have meaning beyond the obvious.

I find it odd that there is no mention of what, if any, treatment was given. Spencer's journal is certainly not lacking in detail in this regard and yet here when his wife goes from being bedridden to walking five miles there is no mention of treatment. I suspect the reason for this is that Dr. Hodge applied not the science of medicine but the art. He probably talked to her.

The second major health problem to arise during this period is gynecologic—repeated bouts of "neuralgia in the pubic region." I was not able to discern a cyclical pattern to this symptom, but in her letters from the hospital in New York, she mentions "monthly suffering" and states that she went there to be cured of what caused painful menstruation. Indeed she seems in fine health as her hospitalization is prolonged as they await her period. The contemplated surgery—probably was hysterectomy—they ultimately decide to put off as she was near menopause and Dr. Emmet felt her health would improve post menopause. Indeed, during the 1870s at which time I suspect she had become post-menopausal, there does seem to have been a relative improvement in her health. It is interesting that she also appeared to take a more active role in Spencer's work during this decade. Was this secondary to her improved health? I suspect a little of both scenarios apply.

At this point I feel I have enough data to speculate about probable underlying disease. The disease, endometriosis, can explain the majority of her symptoms. Endometriosis is a disease wherein islets of functioning endometrial (uterine) tissue reside outside the uterine cavity. The disease is often quiet until the 20s and generally resolves, or at least improves, following menopause. Depending on the location of the endometriosis, a wide variety of symptoms may occur. Quite commonly the bowel is affected. This could present with a tendency toward diarrhea, particularly before menstrual periods, painful bowel movements, constipation, bloating, etc.

One of the major complications of endometriosis involves a tendency to lead to internal scarring or adhesions. Frequently the uterus becomes fixed to the sacral area and can certainly account for Mary's pubic neuralgias and back pain. One entry describes her back pain as sacral, which would certainly fit with a diagnosis of endometriosis. There are two common problems associated with endometriosis which I did not have sufficient data to comment on—commonly endometriosis leads to painful intercourse (dyspareunia) and infertility. I do not know if there were attempts to parent children after Lucy, and Spencer is discrete [*sic*] in never discussing his sex life.

While improvement after menopause would be expected, complete recovery is by no means assured. The extensive scarring caused by endometriosis could certainly lead to permanent chronic pain. It is here that Mary runs into another major medical problem—too much medicine. Beginning in about 1866 she begins fairly continuous treatment with Morphine. There is little doubt that by the 1880s she is addicted with increasing dosage requirements, prompt occurrence of abdominal cramping as the effects of the Morphine wear off. In addition to Morphine she was treated with many other medications/poisons. Many of her symptoms were undoubtedly drug toxicities. . . .

To summarize my findings, I do feel that her early years with Spencer were hard for her. Many of the symptoms she described—headache in particular—seem to have been caused, in great part, by her loneliness. During the 1850s new symptoms seemed to evolve including gastro-intestinal and menstrual-related pains. It is at this point that I believe she had begun to have symptomatic endometriosis. . . . The lack of periodicity in her symptoms and the often prolonged periods of being bedridden was probably the result of the psychological social components of her illness. Mary lived as a sick dependent person probably far beyond the true disability caused by her physical illness. . . .

Her final decade seems to have been dominated by her chronic pains. Unfortunately her problems were compounded by iatrogenesis notably morphine addiction.[3]

Certainly Mary had occasion to suffer emotionally during their early years from loneliness and a sense of neglect, in part from her husband's frequent absences and in part from his compulsion to work. There were only nine years in their forty-one years of marriage in which he was not away on one or more trips, sometimes for a month at a time; and he was off to Philadelphia and New York only two months after Mary and Lucy joined him in Washington. Baird tells in both journal and letters that when in Washington he regularly worked fifteen hours a day. Their summer interludes at the seashore simply provided him with a new and different focus for his professional activity.

Whenever Spencer and Mary were apart, they wrote to each other at least every other day, and if one did not hear from the other, the first part of the next letter would be filled with expressions of concern. Was something wrong? illness? accident? All their letters contained expressions of the deepest affection and love.[4] Mary clearly adored her husband and was extremely proud of him. "It must be delightful to you who can both see, and know when you do see, to be among so many new things of interest," she wrote on one occasion. "I am glad and proud that my husband is neither blind nor ignorant." And then, with a characteristic bit of self-denigration, she added, "It is enough for me to be so, Dear, dear husband."

Baird's letters were filled with endearments: "dear wifey," "my precious Polly," "dear Pollywog," "my darling wife." He tried to ease her loneliness, sometimes a little clumsily: "I cannot stop now to explain fully"; or, "Unless matters require my presence imperatively at home, I shall stay here. . . . Tell me whether I must come home right off"; or, "My dearest little Polly, Please don't get blue if you can help it. If you don't see me before very long, it will be my misfortune, not my fault."

Mary tried to keep a stiff upper lip most of the time and would reply, "Don't interrupt your work" or "I feel better today." But there were times when she could not resist telling of her loneliness: "for I am here all alone," "lonesome and passed evening alone with a violent headache," "miss you; went upstairs and cried in loneliness." Mary was, of course, quite alone in a strange city where she had no friends of her own, and as the political winds shifted, frequent turnovers even among casual acquaintances probably made the development of new friendships difficult at best. Furthermore, the cultural environment in which she lived provided few outlets for female activity beyond domestic chores and formal social calls.

Mary was clearly not an outgoing type and was thus all the more dependent on Spencer and sensitive to his absences and preoccupations. Furthermore, she shows in her letters evidence of a strong sense of inferiority, which doubtless underlay her periods of depression. In one letter she refers to her happy relations with the Marsh family. "I know they do what I think precious few can be accused of, *really like me*." And with regard to her association with her mother, she wrote, "I mean to be a good daughter, but often feel I fail in many things."

Still, throughout most of their long married life their letters were filled with expressions of deep affection for each other and for Lucy. They had many pet names for each other. Spencer was "Pincher," "Whacks," "Whacky"; Mary was "Polly," "Pollywog," and in one instance "My own dearest Salamanerine Pollywog." Mary often used baby talk in her letters, particularly if she pretended to be speaking for both herself and Lucy: "luv him dee," and "I am real dood," and "We are dood little drils." Both made frequent humorous plays on words, introduced little family jokes, and in general gave every indication of close and loving family intimacy.

The Bairds remained lovingly faithful to each other, and in the final analysis Mary's influence was a great asset to Spencer throughout his years as assistant secretary. In her own subtle way she kept him from being carried away with the importance of his roles by obliging him to be concerned with a demanding home and family life. She helped him with his work whenever and wherever possible, cared for and raised his child, ran his household so that it could accommodate a continuous succession of guests, and was a cordial and agreeable hostess and companion in Washington's social life. In countless small ways she looked after his personal needs and let him know how deeply she cared for him. Her management of their domestic life provided him with the stable base that enabled him to focus his principal energies on the work to which he was dedicated, in the assurance that he was loved and needed.

However, as Mary grew older, the stresses of her illness, her underlying sense of neglect, and her lack of self-esteem resulted in both physical and personality changes. She put on a great deal of weight, and the "slender young woman" described by Dall came to weigh upwards of two hundred pounds. Although the immediate pains of her endometriosis abated after her menopause, she became, if anything, an even more dependent invalid. In February 1887, when his own health had gravely deteriorated, Spencer wrote to her cousin Safford Hale, "Mary is almost as much of an invalid as I am, although she has recovered entirely from those distressing spasms and neuralgic pains that have troubled her so much in the last 20 or 30 years."[5] He added that she continued to be bedridden much of the time and to demand his constant care and attention and—though he did not mention it to Hale—her daily morphine injections.

Spencer's own health failed progressively during the 1880s, but there is little evidence that Mary relaxed her hold over him or made any effort to divert her attention from her own complaints to care for him. Even when his brother Sam died in 1884, Spencer was obliged to explain to his sister Rebecca his inability to attend the funeral. "Mary requires such constant vigilance that I do not dare to leave her. Her paroxysms of neuralgic pain come on at any time; they sometimes strike like a blow and require my most prompt attention."[6] This, despite the fact that Lucy was by then thirty-six years old, lived with the family, and was assuredly familiar with her mother's condition. Only Spencer would do. It seems reasonable to assume, extrapolating from Dr. Greenlee's analysis, that Mary's later illnesses were perhaps in part an expression of her inner anger, supported by her need for morphine and causing a vengeful, if subliminal, determination to hold her husband ever closer.

Spencer and Mary's only child was born on February 8, 1848. In good spirits Spencer wrote his grandmother two days later. "I would have written to you before now telling you of your promotion to the rank of Great Grandmother, but thought the telegraphic notice sent would answer until I could have more time. . . . The Grandmothers (Baird especially) say it is a fine child, and quite good looking, but I must confess I do not see in what it consists. It is a larger likeness of those two specimens I have in my jar in the closet."[7] Baird proposed to name the child Lydia Spencer in her honor, but his grandmother turned down the offer with thanks, insisting that the honor should go to Mary's mother, Lucy Hunter.

Lucy was the first grandchild in both the Baird and Churchill families. She was the apple of her father's eye throughout his life and was her mother's only companion during her father's absences. Although doted upon by both parents, she was not spoiled. She was expected to behave properly in public and to obey her parents' instructions promptly and without question. Her Churchill grandparents were particularly devoted to her, and she spent much time in their charge, often for long periods during her mother's sessions of illness. When a Confederate attack on Washington threatened in 1861, the Churchills (the general was by this time retired) took Lucy with them to Carlisle while Mary stayed in Washington with her husband.

In her childhood Lucy developed a lisp, which seems to have been infinitely charming to her parents and her Churchill grandparents. Letters to and from all of them were filled with affectionate baby talk, such as "we 'ove oo so," or "dood bye dee Mumma from oo ittle baby." Both parents addressed Lucy as "Tot" or "Baby" until late in life, and in 1879 the secretary of the Smithsonian Institution was still signing letters to his thirty-one-year-old daughter "Daddy Whacks" or "Your Whacky."

A letter that Baird wrote to five-year-old Lucy in 1855 offers an appealing example of his affectionate early relationship with his daughter.

> To Miss Lucy Hunter
> Daughter of the Assistant Secretary of the Smithsonian Institution
> Mademoiselle
> I love you dearly and want to have you for my daughter if you are not otherwise engaged. I live in a very good house at 332 New York Avenue between ninth and tenth on the south side, and if you will come and live with me, you shall have a book case half filled with books and toys. I have a prairie dog that don't bite and [you] may have it to play with. There are some nice little girls in the neighborhood with whom you may play.
> If you conclude to accept my proposition, you may come on to Washington any time you please, and I will meet you at the cars and bring you to my house. You must write to me and say if you will come and when.
>
> Very respectfully
Your obedient Serv't
Spencer F. Baird
>
> P.S. I forgot to say that I have oysters and ice cream sometimes at my house, and not unfrequently turkey with plenty of skin and stuffing.[8]

This letter reveals the typical tenor of communications between Baird and his daughter—lightly teasing, warm and loving, filled with fun, and on his part almost always including mention of some animal. He never forgot to bring her presents on his return from trips, usually books, and it often fell to his lot to see to her physical and health needs. A number of notes in his journal concern time taken off work to take Lucy to the dentist.

Baird was very proud of Lucy, and they developed a close relationship early and continued it as long as he lived. In the latter years of his life Lucy took over the companionship role that invalid Mary no longer provided him. They took walks together, she accompanied him on social calls, and she acted as his hostess in Mary's absence. Baird supplied her with intellectual information of all kinds, and he devoted much time and correspondence to searches on behalf of her latest whims, which were many and varied.

Lucy had her foibles, some of which also added to her father's problems. She was terrified of thunderstorms, and the family always had to travel to New England by train because Lucy was frightened of sea travel. What Baird described to Dana as her early enthusiasm for natural history wore off pretty fast, as did a succession of other "passionate" interests, from stamp collecting to ceramics. Baird even had to try to persuade his sister Molly to change the plan of the house she was building on the lot adjacent to the Bairds' because her existing plan threatened to intrude into Lucy's garden. "Gardening is really the only thing in the world she cares about, and it is a source of as much gratification to Mary and me as it is to her to do it to see her pottering about her plants a dozen times a day, intensely interested in the development of a rose, or the probability of a big crop of aphids." [9]

Lucy had an active social life with her parents. She was never pushed into the background, and accompanied them to presidential levees, openings, exhibits, lectures, and similar social gatherings. She received callers with her mother and presumably accompanied her on the usual round of calls on which the ladies of Washington spent many of their leisure hours. Lucy also did her part in entertaining the continual parade of visitors in the Baird home, and she never lacked for contact with eligible bachelors among the young scientists and collectors who worked with her father and to whom the Baird home was open every Sunday evening. However, there never appears to have been any romantic interest on either side, and Lucy never married. Her life was greatly affected by her mother's chronic ill health. She must have, to some extent, helped her father care for her mother, particularly during his frequent absences, and this duty fell entirely on her shoulders after his death.

Lucy and her mother moved to Philadelphia after Baird's death. Mary lived another four years in Lucy's care, after which time Lucy continued a quiet but active social life up until her own death in 1913. She spent a good deal of time typing portions of her father's journals (erasing in many cases his notations of the size of the morphine doses he had administered to her mother), and writing her own memories of him, which she turned over to his official biographer, William Healy Dall, and which constitute a large portion of Dall's biography.

A contemporary portrait of James Smithson in the dress of an Oxford student.

The grave in Genoa, Italy, in which James Smithson was initially buried. Exhumed in 1904, under the supervision of Regent Alexander Graham Bell, Smithson's remains now rest in the crypt in the Smithsonian Castle.

Lydia MacFunn Biddle Baird, Spencer's mother.

Spencer F. Baird, 1840, on graduation from Dickinson College.

James Dwight Dana (1813–1895), geologist and zoologist, at whose urging Baird applied for the job of assistant secretary of the Smithsonian Institution.

Dickinson College, Carlisle, Pennsylvania. From an illustration in the *Collegian* 1, no. 1 (March 1849).

William MacFunn Baird, Spencer's oldest brother and close companion.

Lydia Spencer Biddle, Baird's grandmother and affectionate supporter
in his early years.

Carlisle market, where young Baird purchased many specimens of local birds and fish for his collections. Photo courtesy Cumberland County Historical Society.

ICONOGRAPHIC ENCYCLOPÆDIA

OF

SCIENCE, LITERATURE, AND ART;

SYSTEMATICALLY ARRANGED BY

G. HECK.

WITH FIVE HUNDRED STEEL ENGRAVINGS,

BY THE MOST DISTINGUISHED ARTISTS OF GERMANY.

THE TEXT TRANSLATED AND EDITED BY

SPENCER F. BAIRD, A.M., M.D.,

PROFESSOR OF NATURAL SCIENCES IN DICKINSON COLLEGE, CARLISLE, PA.

PROSPECTUS.

THE ICONOGRAPHIC ENCYCLOPÆDIA will embrace (in a series of 500 Quarto Steel Engravings, and upwards of 2000 pages of letter-press in large 8vo.) all the branches of human knowledge which can be illustrated by pictorial representations, viz :—

I.—Mathematics,	VI.—Naval Sciences,
II.—Natural and Medical Sciences,	VII.—Architecture,
III.—Geography,	VIII.—Mythology, &c.,
IV.—Ethnology,	IX.—The Fine Arts,
V.—Military Sciences,	X.—Technology,

with all their respective subdivisions.

The work will be published in 25 monthly portfolios, each containing 20 Engravings and eighty pages of Letter-press.

PRICE ONE DOLLAR EACH PART.

Subscriptions taken for the whole work only.

Title page and an illustration from the *Iconographic Encyclopedia*, Baird's translation and revision of the German *Bilder Atlas zum Conversations Lexicon*, the publication of which contributed greatly to Baird's reputation as well as to his income.

Baird at the time of his appointment as assistant secretary of the Smithsonian, 1850.

Mary Helen Churchill Baird as a young matron.

Chapter Six

Assistant Secretary

1850–1865

I have enough to do, but you know I never feared work.

—Spencer Fullerton Baird, from a
letter to George P. Marsh, 1851

THE PROPER MISSION of the Smithsonian Institution was far from agreed upon by 1850 when Baird received his appointment as junior assistant secretary. Although never imagined at that time by either Joseph Henry or any member of the Board of Regents, the appointment of Spencer Baird and the acceptance of his collections were to change completely the concept of the Institution as envisioned by Henry. In comparison with current totals his was a modest collection, but it became the cornerstone on which was built the National Museum of Natural History. And so persevering was Baird in pursuit of his aims that over the next three decades he steadily reshaped and reorganized the Smithsonian Institution to embody his scientific concepts.

Professor Joseph Henry accepted the invitation of the Board of Regents to become the first secretary of the Smithsonian Institution only after long and careful thought, and his final decision was made on predominantly ideological grounds. He had developed his own interpretation of Smithson's vaguely worded wishes, which, in his estimation, called for the development of entirely new knowledge and its diffusion to all of mankind. He had no sympathy with the congressional mandate for the creation of a library and a museum, since he viewed institutions of that kind as repositories of knowledge already acquired, not as contributors to its increase. This interpretation soon brought him into conflict with at least two of the most influential members of the board.

Secretary Henry was willing to accept Baird's collection on the ground that it included newly discovered American fauna and that Baird's studies of the development of American vertebrates and their relationships provided new insights into the science of natural history. To that end he encouraged Baird to continue his collecting. Also, Henry probably saw some political merit in his support of Baird. It was clear that the strongest opponent with whom he would have to deal was the library faction. By encouraging Baird, he could hope to keep the museum sponsors in his camp.

Even more important factors in Henry's choice of Baird for the assistant secretaryship were Baird's writing and publishing experience, together with his knowledge of languages.[1] Henry counted on Baird to handle the publishing and the wide distribution of the original research papers, which he considered the key function of the Institution, and to organize within the Smithsonian an international exchange of scientific and other learned publications from any source, American or foreign, desirous of utilizing this free channel.

Thus when Baird arrived at the Smithsonian, he found that a very full plate had been arranged for his consumption as assistant secretary. He was expected to attend personally to all the chores involved in the printing of Smithsonian publications. Most important in Henry's view were the Institution's annual reports, in each of which were published the year's collection of scholarly papers accepted by the secretary from scientific contributors. Henry felt that these papers would reflect the importance of the scientific scholarship being developed in the United States. Baird noted in his daily journal entries the hours he spent in visits to and negotiations with printers, binders, paper suppliers, lithographers, and engravers.

Even more exacting was his work in connection with the international exchange service. This involved the receiving, packing, and arranging for shipment abroad of books, journals, reports, and other scholarly materials that originated in American universities, colleges, and other institutions and that the authors wished to have distributed to their counterparts overseas. Baird also received, sorted, and distributed to American addressees comparable materials from foreign sources. In Secretary Henry's opinion this was an important facet of the Smithsonian's mandate for the diffusion of knowledge, through which Europeans would receive a full exposure to the progress of scholarship in America, and American scholars could be kept up to date on the latest developments in science abroad.

Baird was responsible for organizing and implementing a system for this exchange service. Few employees were available to help in the Smithsonian of the 1850s, with the result that Baird was obliged to do much of the physical labor as well as the planning. Entries in his diary for a three-day period provide an excellent description of this task and show the attention to detail that characterized all of his work.

Monday, June 21, 1852
Furnished packages for Dr. Flügel [the Smithsonian's forwarding agent in Leipzig]. Fill 25 boxes of about 4 2/3 capacity each. Wt. about 170 lbs. & less /ft.125. wt. 4280 lbs. Package amount to

	Institution	Packages
Norway	4	7
Sweden	6	14
Denmark	5	9
Holland	11	19
Russia	11	16
Germany	67	133
Belgium	8	15
Switzerland	10	19
Batavia	1	2
Individuals	24	37
	147	271

Tuesday, June 22, 1852

	Institution	Packages
France	54	70
Italy	25	29
Individuals	10	10
	89	109

Contained in 9 boxes, 45 feet, 1530 lbs.

Wednesday, June 23, 1852
Finished rest of packages including England and Africa, & S. America

	Institution	Packages
Portugal	1	2
Spain	4	5
England	60	113
Individuals	28	34
	93	154

	Institution	Packages
Greece, Turkey		
Asia, Africa	17	19
America	16	19
	33	38

Summary

Insts.	*Parcels*	*Capacity*	*Wt*	*Boxes*
362	572	263	9885	46

Baird went into comparable detail on each shipment, and noted in a special aside on June 24, 1852: "Time spent in making up packages 4 1/2 days. Boxing, etc. 1 day. Assisted throughout by Ch. Girard, at various times by Mess'rs Taylor, Burr, Alfred Ames, Dr. Woodhouse, and Dr. Foreman. Average of three persons per day of 5 hours each."[2]

Besides meeting these demanding requirements to the secretary's satisfaction, Baird was also continuing the translation and editing of the *Bilder Atlas*, which he had started in Carlisle and which was finally published in 1852. At the same time, he was developing his network of collectors, personally receiving, sorting, identifying, and classifying the continuous flow of specimens beginning to arrive from exploring parties and other contacts. He distributed duplicates unneeded by the Smithsonian to other museums and institutions in sufficient numbers to satisfy Joseph Henry, who felt that the Smithsonian should hold only holotypes of each newly discovered species or taxon. The remainder Baird either prepared for storage or exhibited in the limited space allowed him in the not-yet-completed Smithsonian building. He also assembled and shipped collecting tools, guns, ammunition, preserving whiskey, and other supplies requested by his field workers, and he corresponded with all.

The extent of his correspondence, personally handwritten during those early years, beggars the imagination. On January 1, 1861, Baird noted in his journal:

> During the past year my own individual correspondence was as follows:
> Letters written, registered, and copied, 3050
> Pages filled of quarto letterbook copied by self, 2100
> Of these about 60 letters and 20 pp. copies were on private business. All the rest strictly Smithsonian.
> Of the 3050 letters 190 and upwards were drafts of letters for Prof. Henry.[3]

Baird described, besides the aforementioned duties, several associated duties in a letter to Minister Marsh in February 1851.

> I have already mentioned my having enough to do. You will believe me when I mention some more items of business. The American Association [for the Advancement of Science] at the New Haven meeting made me Permanent, quasi-perpetual, Secretary; the duties to consist mainly in making up and publishing the semi-annual transactions. This has taken much of my time. The forthcoming volume, now in press, will occupy some 600 8vo. pp. I am also obliged to attend the meetings which take place, the Spring one in Cincinnati (May), and the Summer, Albany (Aug.). The Association perpetrated an excellent joke in voting me $300 per annum for my services. The reality of the thing is that there are not enough funds to pay for half the volume, much less 300 dollars additional. [Baird did have to wait a few years for his money, but he was ultimately paid in full by the Association.]
> Item—I have undertaken the reptiles of the [Wilkes] Exploring Expedition, to be completed in 2 years at 500 dollars per annum. The work and pay I shall however turn over to my assistant, Charles Girard, formerly with Agassiz, who is more competent for the labor than I am. It will however require a good deal of my time, at the most favorable view.

Item—The Iconographic [*Bilder Atlas*]. You would not expect me to do much translating, nor do I. I put out the different articles all around, revising some, and correcting the proof of others. Garrigue expects to have all out by September next. . . .

I say nothing of such trifles as making out Zoological reports for Army officers, writing 8 or 10 letters every day, attending to dozens of diurnal and nocturnal visitors, etc. These are thrown into the bargain.[4]

There are frustrating gaps in Baird's journal entries during these early years, partly owing to the substantial increase in his work load and partly to the pressures of getting settled with his family in a new urban environment. These gaps may also be related to Baird's reluctance to record his part in an important controversy over the role of the Smithsonian. He gives few details of his continuing collecting activities, which were considerable. The 1850s constituted the first great period of government-sponsored exploration of the West and of the associated collection and shipment of all specimens of natural history characteristic of these unknown and unexploited territories. Secretary Henry fully supported all efforts to "increase and diffuse" this new knowledge of the land, and he counted on his assistant secretary to fulfill the natural history mandate of the Institution.

Henry could hardly have found a more ideal assistant for this goal. Baird had the passionate interest, the knowledge and experience, and the broad range of scientific contacts for the job; and in addition, he had married the daughter of the inspector general of the United States Army, and the army was in charge of staffing and conducting all terrestrial exploration. On August 6, 1850, before Baird had even reported for duty at the Smithsonian, General Churchill issued the following instruction, addressed to "any officer of the Army":

Sir: The bearer of this is my Son-in-law, Prof. S. F. Baird, connected by appointment with the Smithsonian Institution at Washington, for which he is engaged in collecting Specimens in Natural History. He will be much obliged, in behalf thereof, and it will be very gratifying to me, if you and those under your command can afford him any aid in his pursuits, for the benefit of science, and you may be assured that the collections will be safely deposited and preserved.

Very respectfully,
S. Churchill[5]

Baird took advantage of the same source of influence to assure that all collections would be shipped back to Washington through army channels and at army expense.

Not the least of his preoccupations in his first days in Washington was the domestic problem of getting settled in an altogether new environment and of satisfying his wife in the important choice of living arrangements. When Baird arrived in Washington, he brought with him his carefully packed and labeled collections, and he left his wife and child to follow a month or so later. The firmness of Mary's control over domestic arrangements and her husband's reliance on her judgement in such matters is evident in their correspondence during this time. He and Mary exchanged letters daily, and his are full of descriptions of the available boardinghouse accommodations. In letter after letter he included plans of rooms, space, prices. Mary answered each in turn, and their exchange gives an interesting picture of their respective approaches to domestic concerns.

Baird's attitude was let's-get-it-done, whereas Mary wanted things just right and was unwilling to accept a spur-of-the-moment decision. To each of his descriptions she replied with more questions, restating what she felt was important and what not. She assured him that she would live anywhere as long as it was not too expensive; but at the same time she must have a parlor in which to receive people and accommodations for Lucy and her nurse. Mary finally resolved the matter in November by going to Washington herself. They settled in a boardinghouse run by a Mrs. Wise and resided there for four years.

Despite the gaps in Baird's journal keeping in these early years, he did record a few points of special interest. In 1852 the regents voted him an increase in annual salary to two thousand dollars. Of longer term significance, in 1853 Mary Baird began to suffer the physical problems that made her a semi-invalid for most of her life. So that she might escape the heat of Washington, the Bairds started a regular practice of spending the summer months at various seashore points, in itself a serendipitous development that had major consequences in Baird's future.

In 1854 the Baird family moved into a house of their own, located at 332 New York Avenue, "a part of the city then considered good, and where many distinguished people resided." The Bairds had another active exchange of letters at this time on the subject of his efforts to purchase, during visits to New York and Philadelphia, a bed and a sofa. He sent descriptions, drawings, and prices, but Mary found his descriptions inadequate and costs too high. She finally acceded to his almost desperate pleas and took the train to Philadelphia, where they could make the decisions together.

That same year appeared the first of a continual series of publications written by Baird individually and with colleagues. "A Catalogue of North American Serpents," co-written by Baird and Charles Girard, was published in volume 2 of the *Smithsonian Miscellaneous Collections* and was based on the authors' work with the Wilkes Exploring Expedition collections, as noted by Baird in his February 1851 letter to George Marsh. In 1857 the first volume of the monumental *Pacific Railroad Survey Report* was published. It contained descriptions of the natural history specimens collected by teams of explorers reconnoitering possible routes for a railroad connection with the Pacific coast. This volume, over one thousand pages, was written by Baird and published under the title *General Report on North American Mammals*.

During the years 1857 through 1860, in addition to his many active responsibilities, Baird wrote and published a succession of important works in his field, including several volumes of the *Pacific Railroad Survey Report*: a revised edition of volume one entitled *The Mammals of North America* (volume 8), *Catalogue of North American Birds* (volume 9), and *The Reptiles and Amphibians of North America* (volume 10). Baird appears to have been the sole author of the mammals catalogue, but he had some assistance with the others. His colleagues and friends John Cassin and George N. Lawrence were coauthors of volume 9, and Charles Girard participated in the writing of volume 10. Nevertheless, it is clear from Baird's journal entries and correspondence with Brewer and Lawrence, and his many letters to artists, engravers, and printers, that he personally reviewed all texts prepared by his coauthors and revised many of them, and that the tedious labor of reading and checking proof, judging and correcting the quality of coloring and engraving of all the illustrations, verifying bills and invoices, and seeing the volumes through all the phases of publication fell on his shoulders alone.

But in 1854 Baird may have come close to losing his job at the Smithsonian in the culmination of a crisis that had been brewing before his arrival in the form of a dispute between Secretary Henry and the senior assistant secretary, Charles Coffin Jewett, with whom Baird had established very friendly relations. Fortunately, Baird managed to distance himself from the issue before it reached its crisis in 1855, when Henry, with the support of a majority of the regents, fired Jewett, and Baird became from that time on the Smithsonian's only assistant secretary.

An entirely different event of major importance in terms of Baird's aspirations, as well as his responsibilities, took place in 1857 when Congress formally transferred to the Smithsonian Institution custody of all of the government's natural history collections from the Wilkes Exploring Expedition and from early survey parties and military expeditions. All of these collections had up to then been stored in the Patent Office building under the nominal care of Joel Poinsett's National Institute. Congress's action was significant for two reasons. It vastly increased the museum role of the Smithsonian, and even more important, it introduced the concept of a federal share in the funding of the Institution.

Joseph Henry had successfully resisted previous pressures to transfer these collections to the Smithsonian on the ground that the creation of a national museum, however desirable from other points of view, was not an appropriate use of Smithson's funds, which were specifically directed to be used for the increase and diffusion of knowledge *among men*, without any national identification. He adamantly insisted that if Congress wished to create a national museum, he would be willing to accept suzerainty over it only if federal money were provided for its support and if it were to have a separate, national identity. He won his case. In the act transferring the Patent Office collections to the Smithsonian, the sum of four thousand dollars of federal money was provided for its upkeep, and thus was created, in 1858, the United States National Museum, under Smithsonian management but separately funded and for years separately identified. Spencer Baird was promptly made curator of the museum collections and operations.

In 1861 Fort Sumter fell, and the nation began the agony of four long years of civil war. In the threatening days following the first battle of Bull Run and Maryland's refusal to let Union troops pass through Baltimore to reinforce the defenses of Washington, General and Mrs. Churchill took little Lucy with them to the apparent safety of Carlisle. However, Spencer and Mary remained in Washington until summer, when Mary joined her parents and daughter in the relative cool of Carlisle and Spencer undertook a collecting trip to New Jersey, New York, and New England, followed by a conference in Montreal.

Baird deplored the division of the nation and particularly feared the potential threat to his beloved collections should Washington become a combat area. He promptly took pains to pack up his egg collections and put them in a safe area for storage. For his own part, he felt no obligation to participate. Even though he had reached an age that should have freed him from any call to military service, he played it safe by hiring a substitute to meet any draft call directed his way after the draft law was passed in 1863. In the absence of opportunities for further accumulations of collections from explorers in the West, he turned to a new collecting source in the far North; he continued to write volumes of letters; he made business trips to Philadelphia and Boston; and he wrote and published in 1864 *A Review of North American Birds.*

Mary's periods of painful illness increased in number and duration during these years, placing a severe additional burden on Baird. In 1862 Mary's mother died, and General Churchill lived only a few months longer. To Baird fell the tasks of arranging the funerals, obtaining a vault for the family in Washington's Oak Hill Cemetery, and seeing to the moving of the bodies to their final resting place.

Notable among Baird's writings during the war was his first and only effort in relatively theoretical analysis. In 1864, perhaps in response to criticisms of his work as "purely descriptive" which had been made by Agassiz and others, Baird submitted for publication in the *Proceedings* of the newly founded National Academy of Sciences an important monograph entitled "The Distribution and Migrations of North American Birds." In it he offered a theory of the continental boundaries that governed the divisions between eastern and western North American bird species, and he explained consequent migration routes, geographic variations in size and coloration of species, and changes through hybridization of related species where their ranges overlapped. He drew his conclusions and illustrated them from his taxonomic studies, but his thesis was both experimental and innovative, and fully consonant with Darwin's theory of natural selection.

Even before the war ended, an important new exploration began under the auspices of the Western Union Telegraph Company. The series of frustrating failures that had plagued efforts to lay cable lines under the Atlantic to Europe led the company's planners to consider seriously an alternate route through western Canada and Russian America (Alaska), across the narrow Bering Strait, and from there over the landmass of Siberia to a linkup with European facilities. The United States government supported Western Union in this endeavor, and Baird promptly seized the opportunity to attach naturalists to the survey team and to establish the Smithsonian's claim to their collections. The leader of the naturalists was an enterprising young man whom Baird had "discovered" and trained, named Robert Kennicott. Baird's knowledge of the natural resources of Alaska, gathered from the reports of Kennicott and his companions, proved to be of major importance in the decision by Congress to purchase Alaska from the Russians.

In 1865 a serious fire occurred in the recently completed Smithsonian building. According to accounts written at the time, workmen engaged in hanging pictures in the second floor gallery brought a stove into the room, since it was very cold, and they inserted the stovepipe into a ventilating flue in the wall next to but not connected to the chimney flue. A fire that resulted burnt out the entire upper story of the main building plus the towers on both the north and south sides.

In the final reckoning, the damage to the building was not severe and was promptly repaired with due attention to additional fireproofing. Of far greater significance was the loss of early records, publications, and manuscripts, including the early official correspondence of both the secretary and the assistant secretary. A collection of 150 Indian paintings by John Mix Stanley, on loan to the Institution, was almost entirely destroyed. But perhaps most serious was the loss of all of the personal effects of James Smithson, including many of his original manuscripts.

That year, too, the war ended, and shortly afterward the nation faced the tragedy of the assassination of Abraham Lincoln, whom Baird had always revered. Altogether, the first half of Spencer Baird's assistant secretaryship was an eventful period—for the nation and for himself. And of perhaps greatest importance to his career, both current and future, was the development of his relationship with his chief, Joseph Henry.

Chapter Seven

The Baird–Henry Relationship

A WISE OLDER FRIEND, Professor John Torrey, wrote the following to Spencer Baird in 1854, as the most serious dispute over the mission of the Smithsonian Institution peaked—a dispute that involved both assistant secretaries of the Institution in varying degrees of opposition to Secretary Henry.

> I received your previous letter and am gratified with its tone, and with your declarations, which I fully believe. Prof. Henry feels friendship for you, and I have no doubt his former confidence in you will return when he gets through the present difficulty. . . . I see no reason why you should not get along pleasantly with the Secretary for he certainly does *as much* for your favorite science as for any other department of human knowledge. As to the museum he means, as you know, to establish one, but it is evident that it cannot exceed rather narrow limits without absorbing too large a share of the income.[1]

Baird eventually weathered this crisis and stayed on as Henry's only assistant and deputy for twenty-four years. However, his relationship with the secretary, which had begun on the level of a warm and intimate friendship, was conducted on a cooperative but formal basis in the aftermath of this blowup.

Although Baird's enthusiasms and ultimate goals differed from those of Joseph Henry, their substantive differences were not at issue in 1854 and, indeed, never brought them into conflict. Within limits that Baird appreciated, Henry supported his assistant secretary's work throughout their many years of professional association. Baird, for his part, never attempted to challenge his chief on substantive grounds and never permitted his collecting to intrude on the work the secretary demanded of him, and despite claims to the contrary by some later writers, no evidence indicates that he ever tried to pursue his personal aims in any way unknown to the secretary. Spencer Baird was too honest, consistent, and dutiful a person to have been underhanded vis-à-vis his chief, while Joseph Henry was too perceptive and watchful a manager to have overlooked or tolerated any effort on the part of a deputy to undermine him. Baird's part in the conflict of 1854 at the Smithsonian related to his irritation at the secretary's stringent and, to him at the time, oppressive managerial style, but not to any opposition to Henry's concept of the purpose of the Institution.

The first direct contact between Baird and Henry occurred in February, 1847, when, at James Dwight Dana's suggestion, Baird applied to Henry for the position of curator of natural history at the Smithsonian. In a letter to Henry that same month Baird stated, "Should I go to Washington, my collections would of course accompany me," and he described succinctly what these consisted of.[2] Over the following three years they corresponded frequently and on very friendly terms. Henry twice during that period approved expenditures of Smithsonian funds for Baird projects, both times in 1848. The first expenditure was to cover the cost of making engravings of illustrations for two proposed volumes on fish that Baird planned to co-write with Louis Agassiz; the second, six months later, was made in response to a letter that Baird wrote to "ask if it will be in accordance with your views for me to make an expedition, partly at the expense of the Smithsonian Institution, for the purpose of collecting specimens for its future museum."

In the same letter Baird described fully his goals and methods.

I have been making vast collections of specimens here this summer, especially illustrating the transformations of reptiles and fishes. I count my specimens of the larvae of the salamanders, frogs, toads, &c., in their different stages, by the quart, and gallon in many cases. I have succeeded in disentangling most of the knots in the natural history of these animals, and can do what I am sure no one else can—exhibit full series, and render a complete account of them, as far as they occur in this neighborhood.

Henry wrote Baird that he had promptly approved the amount of seventy-five dollars to help with Baird's expenses and added, "I am much pleased to learn that you are still so much engaged in your researches and collections."[3]

Baird accounted for his expenditures a few months later in a long letter to Henry in which he noted: "I am overloaded with treasures, duplicates of great value and uniques. In fact I am greatly at a loss to know where to stow all my goods, I wish they were all transferred to the cellars of the Smithsonian Institution."[4]

Baird met the secretary when he went to Washington at George Perkins Marsh's invitation in April 1849. He wrote of his visit to Mary. "Prof. Henry and I are very intimate. Took tea with him Friday and Saturday evenings, and shall visit him again soon today by special request. I staid till 12 o'clock last night, and we laid vast plans for the future. I am just the man for the place et cetera. I forgot to say that Prof. H. wanted me to bring bag and baggage and stay with him." In July 1849 he wrote to Mary, "We get on amazingly, are thick as pickpockets. Begs me to see him very often"; and in December, "After breakfast I went to Prof. Henry's who immediately took me to task for not complying with his invitation to come to his house, and insisted on sending his servant round to the Irving for my baggage, which accordingly he did."[5]

On April 23, 1850, Henry sent Baird "a certificate of appointment as the agent for the Smithsonian Institution" in connection with the distribution of a circular of instructions to collectors of natural history items. But in this letter he added pointed notes about the loyalty he would expect from his assistants, and concluded:

> I shall therefore expect of you not only assistance in the way of taking charge of the collections in Natural History, but also in the publications—the correspondence and other business. On the other hand, I will furnish you with every facility in my power, compatible with the interests of the Institution, for the promotion of your own studies, and shall in all cases consider your reputation as identified with that of the Institution.

And the very next day Henry wrote again.

> In behalf of the Smithsonian Institution I authorize you to take charge of making collections in Natural History, intended for the Smithsonian Museum, and to request of officers of the Army and Navy of the U. States and of other persons such assistance as you may think necessary for the accomplishment of the intended object.[6]

Thus it is clear that while the courtship was warm, neither party to it could have claimed either ignorance or nonacceptance of the aims or interests of the other by the time they pledged their contractual vows on July 5, 1850, when Spencer Baird became assistant secretary of the Institution.

For the first few years everything seems to have gone smoothly. Baird reported to work at the Smithsonian on October 1, 1850. He wrote to Mary on October 6, "Went to church . . . with Prof. Henry, and afterwards accompanied him home to dinner. . . . Prof. Henry is disposed to do everything necessary towards making me comfortable, and I yet see no reason to repent my acceptance of that appointment." On June 5, 1851, by which time he had been with the Smithsonian very nearly a year, Baird wrote to Minister Marsh in Constantinople, "No one could be kinder or more considerate than he [Henry], and I flatter myself he considers his Asst Secretary a prize in a small way."[7]

Unfortunately, however, Baird had, probably unwittingly, stepped into a dispute of very serious proportions between Henry and the senior assistant secretary, Charles Coffin Jewett. The latter was a distinguished librarian. He had been hired by the regents rather than by the secretary with the understanding that he was to carry out that part of the Smithsonian's mandate from Congress which called for "the gradual formation of a library composed of valuable works pertaining to all departments of human knowledge."[8]

Jewett had many friends in Congress and on the Board of Regents who strongly supported his clear design to make the library the principal element of the Institution—a proposition which Joseph Henry vehemently opposed. However, the support for a library was so strong in Congress that in section 8 of the act establishing the Smithsonian, the regents were instructed to make available from the interest from the Smithson fund an amount "not exceeding twenty-five thousand dollars annually" for library acquisitions. Since the entire income from the Smithson fund amounted to no more than thirty thousand dollars, Henry reluctantly agreed to a compromise with the regents whereby 50 percent of the income of the Institution would be devoted to library acquisitions.

Henry and Jewett were continually at odds. Their quarrel reached a crescendo in 1855, and the secretary obtained the approval of a majority of the regents to fire Jewett. This move so infuriated Jewett's principal sponsor on the board, the influential senator Rufus Choate, that Choate submitted his resignation in letters to the president of the Senate and the Speaker of the House. The resulting imbroglio ended in an investigation by a select committee of the House, which covered not only this issue but Henry's overall administration of the Smithsonian. Henry came off with a clean slate, and Jewett returned to Boston and other librarianship; but the record of the investigation shows that Baird, too, was sharply questioned, and that his own tenure at the Institution may even have been at risk during these events.[9]

Baird had been an altogether free spirit before he became associated with the Smithsonian. Even as a professor at Dickinson he enjoyed academic freedom, since he was the only professor of natural history and there was no one looking over his shoulder to approve or question either his choice of subject matter or his teaching methods. Under Joseph Henry he encountered an entirely different atmosphere. Henry was a kind and thoughtful person but a stern administrator who was not disposed to share authority in the area of his responsibility. A major focus of the hearing before the select committee dealt with the secretary's claim that he had the right to open and read any letters addressed to staff members which were "on public business," and there were references to other evidence of the tight rein with which Henry exerted control over his staff.

Jewett had been very friendly toward Baird and had made some effort to promote his cause with Henry while his application was pending. Indeed it was Jewett who first telegraphed Baird the news of his appointment. In Baird's letters to Mary from Washington he frequently mentioned meetings and talks with Jewett. It seems likely that the two assistant secretaries had exchanged mutual confidences about restrictive elements in Henry's administration which they found irritating. And this in turn brought them into ever closer association.

In his testimony before the select committee, Jewett described a discussion with Henry in which he reported that the secretary had made the following statement in a conversation with him: "I perceive that I have traitors in my camp," and "applied the remark to Professor Baird . . . that he had ascertained . . . that an article abusing him was to appear in Putnam's Magazine . . . written by an intimate friend of Professor Baird's; and that he (Professor Baird) had given the writer the facts." Baird's own testimony is instructive.

QUESTION: Have you ever put in a written form your complaints in regard to the Institution, that you recollect?
ANSWER: That is a question that I prefer not answering. I may state that I have made a memorandum of such things, but as a purely private matter.

It developed that Baird had given his memorandum to Senator Choate, "not as preferring a public complaint before a Regent, but as a confidential communication to a friend whom I had known years before." When the members of the committee requested a copy of the memorandum, Baird made various excuses and finally claimed that he could not locate it. The committee eventually moved on to other matters.

Another passage from the committee's questioning of Baird dealt with the Putnam article that Henry had mentioned to Jewett.

QUESTION: Has the secretary ever used towards you ungentlemanly and abusive language; and if so, in what respect?
ANSWER: I have had one (at least) interview with the secretary, in which there was a somewhat warm discussion in regard to certain supposed facts. This was in reference to an article for appearance in Putnam's Magazine, by a friend of mine, and supposed to have been prepared at my suggestion or instigation. The data of which were supposed to have been derived from myself. Professor Henry charged me with having been concerned, in that way, with the article, which I denied. The circumstances of the interview I cannot recall, my memory of facts not being very good. I have no recollection of the interview beyond the facts stated, and that it was a warm one and lasted some time. It concluded, however, I think, with a considerable weakening, as far as I could judge, of the impressions of the secretary in regard to the circumstances. I denied entirely the allegations.

It is curious that Baird's memorandum to Choate has never appeared, that the gaps in his otherwise faithful journal keeping occur just in the years of the controversy, and that Baird's letters during the period make no mention of it.[10] It seems clear from the above, however, that Baird had been frustrated by Henry's tight controls and that he had developed a closer association with Jewett, who was obviously looking for allies, than was either wise or safe under the circumstances.

The eminent botanist John Torrey, who had known Joseph Henry well when they were both at Princeton, wrote a cautionary letter to Baird on May 13, 1854, at the height of the battle.

> I wish that I was in Washington, and that we could have had a quiet talk for an hour on matters relating to the Smithsonian. (I write now in entire confidence and without the knowledge of Prof. Henry . . . who would probably object to my course). It is evident that a very considerable combination exists, to revolutionize the Institution, and to induce Prof. H. to resign. It is equally evident that Prof. Jewett is the leader of the combination, and that he has staked all on the result. He will most *certainly be foiled*, for the Regents *must* make common cause with Prof. H. as he is their agent, and they have endorsed his doings. His acts are their acts. Prof. H. has often expressed the kindest feelings toward you, but has felt grieved that you have been so much in the councils of those who have so earnestly opposed him. He does not think that you have intended to injure him, but that in your earnestness to advance your favorite sciences, you have inadvertently been drawn in to the views of those who have been secretly and openly attacking him. It is very clear that matters cannot go on so. The Institution is a house divided against itself. From what I know of the Regents, I am *certain* they will sustain Prof. H. and will carry out his plans—while those who cannot work with him will be the losers. . . . I don't make these remarks in the way of threat. You know me too well for that . . . but I am desirous that you should keep entirely aloof from the controversy now going on. Let Mr. Jewett fight his own battle.[11]

Henry confirmed Torrey's assessment of his feelings toward Baird during this difficult period in a letter he wrote to his friend Alexander Bache (himself no partisan of Baird) in July 1853.

> I had a serious talk with Baird a few days ago, just before he left for the north. He was as pliant and affectionate as a young dog, but I fear he will sin again, and nothing but a strong arm and a few hard knocks will keep

him in the right course. I informed him that I intended to submit a set of rules to the Board for the regulation of the duty of the assistants, among which would be one forbidding anything being sent from the Institution to the press without a thorough examination and approval.[12]

On the basis of Torrey's advice, or perhaps even before receiving it, Baird did manage to put sufficient distance between himself and the Jewett camp to satisfy Professor Henry that he was not an active mutineer. He stayed with the Smithsonian, and there is no available indication that he ever again had any contact with his former friend and associate Jewett. This was the one serious crisis in Baird's thirty-year relationship with Henry. But the entire sequence of events is of particular interest, both for itself and because it reveals a side of Baird that he or someone with access to his private papers obviously preferred to keep out of the record.

Following the Jewett affair, no relaxation was evident in Henry's administrative strictness toward Baird or anyone else under his authority. On August 5, 1856, in a letter to Baird, who was summering at Beasley's Point, New Jersey, Henry stated firmly, "Girard informed me that he could not find the key to your desk. . . . though I may not have an occasion in your absence to look into anything in your possession, I must have the means of doing so at any time." In another letter the secretary asserted "that more attention [needs to] be given to the affairs of the Institution than they have received during the past year," and he frequently chided Baird either directly or indirectly with reference to "things which have to be put in order."[13]

In August 1868 Henry wrote the following letter to Baird:

My dear Sir
Accompanying this we send you letters and other documents . . . in reference to a business concerning which our records exhibit but a partial exposition. This matter certainly illustrates the impropriety of mixing up the affairs of the Institution with those of other parties, and of attempting to conduct our business under two hands. This system must eventually lead to trouble, and I protest against its continuation.

Prof. S. F. Baird

Truly yours,
Joseph Henry
Sec'y Sm Inst[14]

Baird probably continued on occasion to chafe inwardly at the secretary's firm control. However, he was basically respectful and dutiful towards his seniors, and through his appointment to the Smithsonian Institution he realized the dream he had nurtured from the time he was a teenager to become curator of a major natural collection. Thus there was little likelihood that he would allow occasional irritation at Henry's strict but essentially cooperative managerial style to jeopardize that association. Letter after letter from Baird to numerous correspondents during 1868 and 1869 included impassioned pleas to address their letters on topics not directly related to the Smithsonian to his home, and letters calling for action by the Smithsonian to Henry, not to him.

However, it was some time after the Jewett affair before Baird felt altogether secure in his relationship with his chief. Even as late as 1866 A. A. Gould, president of the Boston Society of Natural History, wrote to ask Baird whether he would be interested in the directorship of the society. In his response, Baird stated:

> I hardly know what to say in reply to your question whether I am a fixture here or not. I have no immediate reason to anticipate any [illegible] disruption from the S.I. under present circumstances, although what further changes may follow the separation of the Library [Joseph Henry had the entire Smithsonian library transferred to the Library of Congress in 1866.] I cannot tell. . . . At present my relations with Prof. Henry are satisfactory, and my position generally very agreeable. I try to do my duty to both him and the S.I. [illegible] carrying out his policy, even where I myself might prefer a different course. As his assistant, appointed by Prof. Henry to assist him in his [illegible], I do not allow any personal views to interfere with my official conduct. How soon all this may change from one cause or another, however, no one can tell. . . . Under present circumstances I would then say that I may be considered a fixture here and not available for another position. . . . I shall at any rate consider it a high compliment to have been thought of in this connection, and it would strengthen my hands here very much in any event to have the position offered to my acceptance, even though I might not be able to take it.[15]

In 1873, although Henry had fifteen years earlier given Baird full responsibility for the direction of the United States National Museum, Baird had occasion to chafe at Henry's retention of financial control. On February 13, 1873, Baird wrote in reply to an inquiry from Peter Parker, a regent:

I am charged with the determination as to the expenditure of the Congressional appropriation for the National Museum, & expected to meet all the requirements out of that fund. . . . Prof Henry feels responsible to the Board of Regents for the disbursement of the Congressional appropriation, & is therefore unwilling to permit any Bill to go to the Disbursing Clerk of the Interior Department without receiving his endorsement. This is in some respects an inconvenience, and I would be glad if he could see his way clear towards allowing my own endorsement of correctness to suffice. . . . I do not wish to act independently of Prof. Henry in matters of general policy; but I would greatly prefer to be permitted to send the Bills, directly, for payment, instead of having to wait for Prof. Henry's convenience for their examination; especially, as, in the pressure of his other occupations, days sometimes elapse without the opportunity of that quiet conference necessary to explain to him the details of the Bills.

He hoped the regents might be able to persuade Henry to let go, as he was obviously unable to himself.[16]

Thus it is evident that in business matters Henry retained a firm upper hand and that Baird was respectfully dutiful. Social relations between the Henrys and the Bairds appear to have been cordial, but there were no more effusive comments like those of the early years. In a letter to Minister Marsh in 1870 Baird wrote, "Mr. and Mrs. Edmunds [influential senator from Vermont] are our most 'rite'-mate friends in Washington . . . in fact form the only household in which we feel at all at home," to which was added, but in Mary's handwriting, "always excepting the Henrys."[17]

The differing views of Henry and Baird regarding a natural history museum as a function of the Smithsonian were of much longer term significance, and they might well have resulted in a Jewett-type confrontation had they not been softened both by personality factors and by a degree of sympathetic understanding on both sides which did not exist in the case of the library. Henry's feelings about a museum were somewhat complex and centered on his sense of responsibility as custodian of the Smithson fund. He expressed them most clearly in his final annual report, after he had turned over the charge of the United States National Museum to Baird and after he had been obliged to take under the Smithsonian's wing not only Baird's collections but the extensive collections sent back to the Institution by the many exploring expeditions, including the Wilkes exploration collection, and the carloads of materials donated to the Smithsonian by the exhibitors at the Centennial Exposition of 1876.

The functions of the Institution and the Museum are entirely different; those of the Institution being first, to enlarge the bounds of human thought by assisting men of science to make original investigations in all branches of knowledge, to publish these at the expense of the Smithson fund, and to present copies of them to all the principal libraries of the world; second, to institute investigations in various branches of science and explorations for the collection of specimens in natural history and ethnology *to be distributed to museums and other establishments* [italics ours]; third, to diffuse knowledge by carrying on an extended series of exchanges by which the accounts of all the original researches in science, the educational progress, and the general advance of civilization in the New World are exchanged for similar works of the Old World. To carry out this plan the Institution requires no costly building, but merely accommodations for receiving and distributing its collections.

The Museum, on the other hand, is intended to embrace a collection of specimens of nature and art which shall exhibit the natural resources and industries of the country, or to present at one view the materials essential to the condition of high civilization which exists in the different States of the American Union; to show the various processes of manufacture which have been adopted by us, as well as those used in foreign countries; in short, to form a great educational establishment by means of which the inhabitants of our own country, as well as those of foreign lands who visit our shores, may be informed as to the means which exist in the United States for the enjoyment of human life in the present, and the improvement of these means in the future.

The support of such an establishment must, of necessity, be derived from Congress and no part of the Smithson fund should be devoted to this purpose, since it is evident from the will of Smithson that he intended his benefaction for the good of mankind, and therefore all expenditures on local objects, or even on those limited to the United States, are not in conformity with the intentions of the donor.[18]

Henry expressed his principal concern in a letter to a friend, J. P. Lesley, in 1876. "But now comes the danger. The appropriations of Congress for the Museum are fitful and can only be obtained in the name of the Smithsonian Institution by a process to which I am not fitted, that of lobbying. If the appropriation fail in any year, the expense of maintaining the Museum must fall upon the Institution."[19]

Joseph Henry had maintained this reasoning and this concern from the very start of his administration of the Smithsonian. His statement makes clear, however, how he could accept Baird and his collections, and his willingness to provide Smithsonian funds in support of explorers and their accumulations of natural history specimens. It even indicated how he could rationalize his (reluctant) acceptance of the Wilkes and Centennial materials—many of which were indeed distributed to other museums by Baird—since both were accompanied by supporting funds from Congress and assigned to a national museum under the aegis of, but separate from, the Smithsonian Institution.

Baird's position was simpler and more direct. From the start, his unwavering goal was to be the curator in charge of a major natural history collection. While he, too, never deviated from pursuit of his objective, his approach was quite different from that of Jewett. He had been hired by Henry "to render such assistance to the secretary as he may require," and his sense of responsibility was therefore to Henry, whereas Jewett had been appointed by the regents for a function which Choate, Marsh, and others backed him for, despite the expressed opposition of the secretary. Baird never sought confrontation; indeed, he avoided it unless it was thrust upon him. His methods were more subtle.

Hence Baird continued actively to add to the Smithsonian's collections of natural history and North American native archaeology and to distribute duplicates to other museums or collectors. He continued to urge nearly all his correspondents (and there were hundreds) to send in specimens of reptiles, bird nests and eggs, local fish, and anything they or their friends might find in nearby Indian burial mounds or middens; he saw to it that qualified naturalists were assigned to the staffs of all government exploring expeditions, and he supplied them with all the tools of the collector's trade, often at Smithsonian expense; he successfully persuaded most of the exhibitors at the Centennial Exposition to donate the contents of their exhibits to the Smithsonian Institution; and he lobbied actively with his many friends and contacts in Congress to establish a national museum and to provide funds and authorization for a building to house what the Smithsonian building could no longer contain.

But there is no way to imagine that he did all this behind Joseph Henry's back, especially in light of the strict and detailed monitoring to which Henry subjected all Institution correspondence and the care with which he controlled all expenditures of Smithsonian funds. In every annual report to the regents, the secretary spoke with pride of the growth of the Institution's collections and provided space for a special report by Baird on the museum. In short, Baird was successful because, unlike Jewett, he never attempted to intrude into Joseph Henry's managerial domain, never tried to siphon off Smithson fund money for his ends, and kept Henry fully informed by seeking his approval for what he was doing. While there are letters to Baird from staff members reporting that Henry was on the warpath about the odor emanating from the basement where Baird stored skins, which Henry also considered to be the source of fleas, we have found no written evidence that the secretary ever called a halt to Baird's collecting activities or that he ever reprimanded Baird on any matter of substance.

Chapter Eight

A Collector of Collectors

IN THE SMITHSONIAN'S ANNUAL REPORT for the year 1855, Joseph Henry reported: "Though the statement may excite surprise, yet I may assert, on the authority of Professor Baird, corroborated by the opinion of others well qualified to judge, that no collection of animals in the United States, nor indeed in the world, can even now pretend to rival the richness of the museum of the Smithsonian Institution in specimens which tend to illustrate the natural history of the continent of North America."[1]

When Spencer Baird accepted the appointment of assistant secretary in 1850, the Smithsonian Institution collection totaled 6,000 natural history specimens. By 1861, when government exploration ceased for the duration of the Civil War, the collection had grown to over 150,000 catalogued items. And there could be no disputing the fact that the man responsible for this spectacular development was Assistant Secretary Baird.

Soon after he went on duty, Baird became too busy with publishing, overseas distribution, and other tasks assigned him by Joseph Henry—as well as with the sorting, classification, and storage of all the incoming collections—to continue collecting more than sporadically himself. He became instead a collector of collectors.

Early in his Carlisle years Baird had learned to supplement his own collection through trades with fellow enthusiasts. It was a time when, in the absence of either museums or game laws, most amateur naturalists amassed private collections of the taxa which interested them. Like most collectors, they actively traded specimens among themselves. The young Baird had corresponded with most of the ornithologists of the time. He recorded in his journal for 1841 his visits to Audubon in New York and the specimens of birds Audubon had given him from his own collection. He also noted trades he had made with New York's foremost taxidermist, John J. Bell, and particularly with a prominent amateur collector, J. P. Giraud, "with whom I went to see his [Giraud's] collection of birds, which is the finest I have seen. Gave him a Cape May warbler. He gave me a Red Phalarope . . . obtained a number of rare American bird skins from Peale [Titian Peale, a naturalist on the Wilkes Exploring Expedition and interested in all collections for the Peale family museum in Philadelphia], for which I am to send Helices, fossils, coins, etc."[2]

By the time he received his appointment to the Smithsonian, Baird was well known among the members of the American natural history community, and he had formed productive contacts with prominent naturalists overseas. When he was given charge of the museum of the already important Smithsonian Institution, he became one of the most widely known and respected naturalists in America. Enjoying the backing of the many congressional supporters of a museum and the recognition of American and European scientists, he held a position that was both politically and scientifically important.

Baird did not wait for his formal appointment to exploit his new leverage. In early 1850 he drafted a letter for Henry's approval which, when formalized, was widely distributed with its printed enclosure during the next several years.

> The Smithsonian Institution, being anxious to lay the foundations of a collection of American Natural History, would respectfully ask assistance in furtherance of this object from the friends of science generally, and espe-

cially from officers of the Army and Navy. Any specimens of animals, plants, minerals, and fossil remains will be acceptable; especially of such as may be enumerated in the following brief directions for their preservation. These objects may be forwarded, either directly to the Smithsonian Institution at Washington, or to the undersigned at Carlisle, Pa., who has been requested by Prof. Henry to act temporarily as agent for such collections. All contributions will, of course, be duly credited to their respective donors in the Museum and in the reports of the Institution.[3]

Baird's widely distributed circular, together with General Churchill's memorandum to all army officers, introducing his son-in-law and urging them to collect for him, were both issued just as the government launched its prewar series of exploring and surveying expeditions under army auspices. In combination they provided Baird with a whole new force of enthusiastic and energetic collectors both military and civilian. In addition, his status as an official of the Smithsonian enabled him to place civilian naturalists chosen by him on expedition staffs. Soon every government-sponsored expedition included one or more of Baird's "missionaries," as he called them, or else a military man who had been detailed to the Smithsonian for a period of training by Baird and equipped with apparatus for collecting and preserving specimens.

Baird personally found time to plan and assemble the apparatus for each expedition, which usually included alcohol, normally cheap whiskey. The whiskey was often doctored to lessen its attraction to nonscientific personnel of the expeditions. One of Baird's collectors wrote that he had nearly made teetotalers of thirsty members of his expedition by letting them see what else was in the cask besides whiskey. Also included in the apparatus was arsenic, powder and shot, often a gun, dissecting tools, egg blowers, containers of various sizes, and beads, mirrors, knives, and comparable items for trading with Indians. In her reminiscences of her father, Lucy Baird wrote, "No bride ever devoted more thought and attention to her trousseau than did my father to the fitting out of each of these explorers, and he watched the progress of each missionary with anxious personal interest."[4]

The list of distinguished army and navy officers whom Baird counted among his collectors reads like a historical Who's Who. The army officers included Captain (later General) George B. McClellan, Major (later General) William B. Emory, Colonel George Hammond (later surgeon general of the army), Lieutenant John Irwin (awarded the Congressional Medal of Honor and subsequently promoted to brigadier general), Captain Richard H. Pratt (founder of the Carlisle Indian School), Lieutenant Darius N. Couch (who resigned from the army for a time and worked for the Smithsonian, rejoined the army in the Civil War, and attained the rank of brigadier general), and Captain R. B. Marcy (subsequently a major general and father-in-law of General McClellan). On the navy side were Captain David G. Farragut, Commander John Rogers, in command of the United States North Pacific Exploring Expedition (also known as the Ringgold Expedition after its first commander, Captain Cadwallader Ringgold), Commodore Matthew C. Perry of the Japan Expedition, Arctic explorer Dr. E. K. Kane, and Captain J. M. Gillis (whose recommendations led to the founding of the United States Naval Observatory and who later commanded several important astronomical expeditions to Chile).

The most important of the one hundred or more western expeditions in which Baird had a significant interest included the Exploration and Survey of the Valley of the Great Salt Lake of Utah in 1849, under Captain Howard Stansbury; the Expedition down the Zuni and Colorado Rivers in 1851, under Captain Lorenzo Sitgreaves; the Exploring of the Red River of Louisiana in 1852, conducted by Captains Marcy and Mc-Clellan; and the United States and Mexican Boundary Survey from 1855 through 1857, which was under the command of one of Baird's most active correspondents, Major Emory. The most important of the expeditions in terms of their collections and the reports that resulted from them were the four separate explorations conducting surveys for a railroad route across the continent to the Pacific coast. During the three-year period from 1852 through 1854 alone, Baird was receiving materials and information from twenty-six separate expeditions.

He was also successful in enlisting the cooperation of a number of other government departments and offices that were conducting their own surveys and researches. These included the United States Department of State, the United States Navy Department, the United States

Signal Service, the Department of Treasury Lifesaving Service, the Lighthouse Board, the General Land Office, the Office of Indian Affairs, and the Office of Education.

With the outbreak of war in 1861, Baird's army sources dried up for a time, but even before the attack on Fort Sumter he had turned his attention to a rich natural history treasure trove north of the border. Indeed, before he joined the Smithsonian, he had become interested in the fauna of the Arctic, and on February 19, 1850, he wrote to Assistant Secretary Jewett: "I have . . . a plan for getting specimens of arctic animals from the posts of the Hudson's Bay company; as also for enlisting the different missionary associations in our behalf. A correspondence with Methodist and Baptist Union has already been started, with this end."[5]

There is no evidence that his appeals to Methodist and Baptist missionaries proved productive, but the Hudson's Bay Company became a major source of Smithsonian collections during the war and for several years thereafter. The man who became most instrumental in exploiting this treasure for Baird was Robert Kennicott, a young naturalist from Chicago who had studied natural history with a good friend of Baird's, Jared Kirtland, and had himself subsequently become one of Baird's special protégés. In 1857 Kennicott became curator of natural history at Northwestern University. That summer he embarked on a four-month collecting expedition into western Canada, during the course of which he became acquainted with and won the esteem and cooperation of many of the officers of the Hudson's Bay Company, whose help was to prove invaluable to him—and ultimately to Baird.

Shortly after his return from this venture, Kennicott made his first visit to the Smithsonian, arriving in December of 1857 and remaining under Baird's tutelage through the following April. During this time he and Baird laid plans for a scientific expedition to be undertaken by Kennicott throughout what was then referred to as central British America and into a portion of Russian America (Alaska). Chief sponsor was to be the Smithsonian Institution, but the University of Michigan, the Audubon Club of Chicago, and the Chicago Academy of Science also provided support.

Since it was obvious that Kennicott would require major assistance from many of the far-flung posts of the Hudson's Bay Company, a letter signed by Joseph Henry (but almost certainly drafted by Spencer Baird) went to the governor, Sir George Simpson, head of the company in Canada, requesting his advice and assistance in carrying out the enterprise. The Hudson's Bay Company's resident representatives had, almost since its founding in 1670, collected specimens of the natural history resources in their principal territory, known as Rupert's Land. For a time they had sent their findings to London and Montreal, but they had received from their British and Canadian recipients few indications of appreciation or encouragement for their efforts, with the result that much of their activity had become dormant. This new contact with the Smithsonian and its personable agent, Kennicott, had the immediate effect of reawakening local enthusiasm.

On receipt of Secretary Henry's letter, Governor Simpson issued to company officers a circular letter to which he attached a copy of the Henry request, giving his approval to all efforts they might make to cooperate with Kennicott and, most important, authorizing free transportation via company facilities for any collections he might make. A historian of this era of the company's activities notes, "There is no doubt that this was one circular they took seriously."[6]

Kennicott set out on his adventurous expedition on April 20, 1859. Over the next three years he was effectively the guest of the company. He traveled on company steamboats and in company canoes, and he spent the winters in company forts and stations. He also hired Indians and Eskimos who trapped and hunted for the company to collect for him, "for you know that there is very little chance of my ever killing such things as musk oxen, barren ground bear and reindeer. . . . I can only hope to get them by hiring the Indians to bring them in from a great distance."[7] And Kennicott relied on the company to arrange the transport of his collections to points from which they could be shipped to Washington.

Baird provided much appreciated reciprocal support to the company officers and factors. He corresponded regularly with Kennicott's company friends and helpers; he sent them a continual flow of books, both scientific and literary, newspapers, and journals—all greatly cherished where contact with the outside world was rare and infrequent; and he provided

Kennicott with an ingredient of special value, whiskey. Alcohol was expressly forbidden by company regulations, but "Kennicott realized that a little alcohol for his Mackenzie mates would go a long way toward securing their support, so when he received liquor from home . . . ostensibly to preserve specimens, he assiduously divided a good portion of it among 'the gentlemen.'" Baird's shipments were not limited to books, alcohol, and collecting apparatus. One list of items requested by Kennicott, and furnished by Baird, presumably with the help of Mary and Lucy, included:

5000 common sewing needles
200 darning needles
3 lbs. good white and black linen thread
Cheap colored silk ribbons
6 dozen common colored cotton handkerchiefs
5 dozen common pipe beads
Cheap pocket knives
Gold and silver tinsel hatcords
Gold and silver sham "jewelry"
Calico shirts.[8]

Baird's support was important to Kennicott, but it is clear that Kennicott's personality was his greatest asset. One can detect in his many letters to Baird during his two-year sojourn in the Mackenzie District that he was liked and respected by all with whom he came in contact, and that Simpson's instruction to provide him with transportation and assistance was carried out as much from motives of affection as from orders.

Kennicott was obliged to return to the States in 1862 because of his father's illness. But this by no means ended the relationship of the Smithsonian Institution with the Hudson's Bay Company. Although Governor Simpson had died in 1860, Baird, through Kennicott, developed warm and cooperative working relationships with three of the company's most important officials: the chief trader, Bernard Ross; Roderick Ross Mac-Farlane, "the company's most prolific collector in the Mackenzie region"; and Alexander Grant Dallas, who had succeeded George Simpson as the new governor of Rupert's Land. Baird so successfully sustained these contacts that between 1863 and 1868, when company personnel changes and other factors gradually brought the exchanges to a halt, the Institution received thousands of bird and mammal skins and skeletons, the eggs of virtually all bird species that nested in the North, fish, insects, plants, and fossils, and examples of the clothing, weapons, and utensils of the various tribes of Indians and Eskimos of Western Canada.

The Arctic was not Baird's only productive source of natural history specimens during the war years. In his contribution to the Smithsonian annual report for 1863, he noted:

> In addition to the collections obtained from the British possessions in North America, by Mr. Kennicott, specimens have been received from other points and other parties. Among these are a series of birds and eggs from Labrador, gathered by Mr. Henry Connolly; as well as a large amount of new material from Mexico, collected by John Xantus under the auspices and at the expense of the Institution, consisting of birds, fishes, reptiles, shells, &c. Another series from the same country has been presented by Dr. Sartorius, who has for a number of years, been one of the meteorological observers of the Institution. Interesting collections have been received, also, from Dr. A. Van Frantzius of Costa Rica; from Mr. Osbert Salvin of Guatemala; from Captain J. M. Dow, of Panama; specimens from Cuba have been presented by Mr. C. Wright and Prof. Poey; from Trinidad by Mr. Galody, United States consul; from Jamaica by Mr. W. T. March; from Salvador by the Hon. C. T. Buckalew [U.S. minister], now of the United States Senate. A valuable contribution of birds and mammals has also been received from Prof. Sumichrast of Orizaba. These collections are all intended to illustrate the natural history of the American continents, to the investigation of whose extended regions the Institution has especially directed its labors.

In the same report Secretary Henry noted that collections entered in the record book, each of which he pointed out incorporated a number of specimens, amounted to 66,075 in 1861, 74,764 in 1862, and 86,847 in 1863. He also noted with satisfaction that by the end of 1863, 94,713 specimens had been distributed to other museums or institutions.[9]

Soon after the war ended in 1865, government exploring and topographic surveying expeditions were renewed in support of the postwar surge of westward settlement. Four separate, and in some cases competitive, expeditions were being funded by Congress. One, headed by Clarence King, later the first chief of the United States Geological Survey, was conducting a survey of the fortieth parallel; a second, under

Lieutenant George M. Wheeler, was surveying the territory west of the one hundredth meridian; Ferdinand V. Hayden headed a survey of the United States territories; and Major John Wesley Powell led a party surveying the Rocky Mountain region. All were under instructions to collect, preserve, and send back to the Smithsonian Institution specimens of natural history. And at least one member of each expedition had been selected for the task or given collecting instruction and necessary equipment by Baird.

In 1865 Kennicott was chosen to lead the Western Union Telegraph Expedition northward in search of a western cable route. Before his untimely death in 1866, the cable project had been abandoned, but the members of the expedition continued to explore the upper Yukon and on up the coast of Alaska. William H. Dall assumed Kennicott's mantle, and explored and collected all the way to the Bering Strait.

A few years later, when President Ulysses S. Grant appointed Baird United States Commissioner of Fish and Fisheries (a post he held concurrently with his position as assistant secretary of the Smithsonian), he made collecting and the study of marine biology the primary function of the scientists with him at his summer station at Woods Hole, Massachusetts. In consequence, during the first summer alone, 106 species of marine fish were collected for the Smithsonian. Under Professor Addison E. Verrill of Yale University, Baird's most important collaborator at the station, a collection of marine invertebrates totaling hundreds of thousands of specimens of over 2,000 species was accumulated during five or six years, and all originals were deposited in the United States National Museum.

Although from the very beginning of Baird's career at the Smithsonian he was steadily receiving casks and carloads of natural history specimens from official expeditions in the field and from institutional sources nearer at hand, he always kept an eye out for other collections of interest, and he consistently demonstrated ingenuity in procuring them and in assisting those who brought them to his attention. Both these talents became evident soon after his appointment to the Smithsonian.

In 1851 Jean Louis Berlandier, a French scientist and collector who had been recruited by the Mexican government to be its naturalist on the

United States and Mexican Boundary Survey Commission, drowned during a commission operation, leaving in the hands of his common-law
Mexican widow and their children an extensive and valuable collection of
archaeological and natural history specimens, many paintings and
sketches done with great skill by Berlandier, and a large file of meteoro-
logical reports and scientific papers that he had prepared. Lieutenant
Darius N. Couch was Baird's man on the commission, and he wrote to
Baird urging that the Smithsonian purchase the collection from
Berlandier's widow. Although he tried, Baird could not raise enough
funds from either the Smithsonian or the government for the purpose,
but Lieutenant Couch was so impressed with the collection that he
bought it with his own money. By agreement with Baird, he sent the collection to the Smithsonian for safekeeping, noting that it consisted of

> a labor of 24 years. Ranges from the Sabine to California. There is about
> 150 bottles of diff. [illegible], species of vertebrata, mostly snakes, lizards,
> etc.—a few birds, several cubic feet of minerals, lare [sic] box of plants,
> some twelve sq. ft. of insects nicely preserved in glass cases, paintings of all
> the Indian tribes in Old Mexico, sketches of Mex. scenery, meteorological
> reports, observations, with files of manuscripts relating to the labors. It's
> very valuable. Probably been abused somewhat.[10]

The Smithsonian did purchase some items from the Berlandier collection,
but not enough to reimburse Lieutenant Couch for his investment. So
Baird played another role in support of his collector: he helped Couch to
find purchasers among other museums and private collectors.

In later years it was often Baird himself who put up money for the purchase of collections. In a letter to a wealthy benefactor, Mrs. Robert L.
Stuart, dated May 7, 1873, he wrote:

> I may confess to you what I have not dared to say even to Mrs. B., that I
> have spent a great deal more myself than I could well afford in buying from
> my own means certain specimens and collections which I knew the Institu-
> tion needed, and which could not be obtained in any other way. The temp-
> tation to come myself to the rescue was in such cases irresistible, and I do
> not suppose that $2000 would cover the amount of my substance laid out in
> this way.

And in a letter of January 13, 1876, to another correspondent, whose request for a personal loan he had tactfully turned down, he wrote: "One

additional cause of being cramped was my contribution in a moment of enthusiasm a week or two ago of $150 towards an exploration of the antiquities of Nicaragua for the benefit of the National Museum. I have very foolishly spent several hundred dollars a year as an average for ten or fifteen years to do such work. . . . I continually vow I won't do it again, but I do."[11]

Baird cemented the loyalty of his collectors by the extent to which he found time to give personal attention to each of them. Smithsonian archivist William Deiss has written:

> No question was too unimportant, no letter too trivial for Baird's personal attention. An amateur naturalist writing to Baird for the first time always received a detailed and courteous response . . . collectors were repaid with Baird's gratitude and help, with their own sense of accomplishment, and perhaps more importantly, with fame. When Baird listed accessions and praised his collectors in the pages of the Smithsonian Annual Report . . . when he named new species after their collectors, he was conferring on them an enduring fame, the acquisition of which had been a motivation for naturalists for centuries.[12]

His enthusiastic praise was often a reward in itself. A letter he wrote on September 28, 1851, to Captain Stewart van Vliet in St. Louis is typical.

> I returned from the North East Saturday night, and lost no time yesterday (Monday) in unpacking your box which had been here some time. Everything was in perfect order and I was delighted to find my anticipations more than realized by the examination. The fossils are *magnificent*, far superior to anything I ever saw before. A little careful [illegible] will exhibit some nearly perfect skulls. Several are quite different from any received before, and will undoubtedly prove new to science. From your modest way of speaking about them I had not anticipated quite such a treat. . . . The Mountain sheep is capital. The best plumaged specimen I ever saw. . . . Indeed the entire collection is charming—that is the very word.[13]

Baird served his collectors in many more tangible ways, too. Captain George B. McClellan wrote a manuscript for a book on bayonet exercises, and Baird spent many hours in visits and correspondence arranging with the J. B. Lippincott Company for its publication. He helped many of his collectors to sell specimens from their personal collections, managed and invested their money for them while they were in the field, and often forwarded their mail and kept in touch with their families on their behalf.

He not infrequently intervened with the secretaries of war and of the navy to assist the military collectors. He arranged a transfer for John Xantus when the latter had problems with an unsympathetic commander, and he later arranged for him to be released from the army and assigned as observer for the Coast Survey in Baja Mexico. Ultimately he persuaded the secretary of state to appoint Xantus United States consul in Colima, Mexico. For another particularly competent collector, Sergeant John Feilner, Baird successfully pulled strings to secure an officer's commission.

It would be impossible to name all of Baird's nonmilitary collectors, but a few were distinguished or famous enough to merit notice. Baird had considerable correspondence with the widely known popular naturalist John Burroughs, beginning in 1871 when Burroughs sent him the nest and eggs of a black-throated blue warbler. It continued when Burroughs asked for the use of some of the plates in Baird's *History of North American Birds: Land Birds* to illustrate his *Wake Robin*. (Baird supplied the prints but noted that the ones requested were actually look-alikes, for example, a western hermit thrush for an eastern, a house finch for a purple finch, and urged that the substitutions be duly footnoted.) The following year Burroughs asked Baird if he would help him to join Hayden's expedition, but "in some capacity that would leave me free to indulge my tastes and pursuits," as well as to draw a salary, "as I could not afford to loose [*sic*] it."[14]

Susan Fenimore Cooper, daughter of the well-known author James Fenimore Cooper, collected fish from northern New York lakes and streams for Baird, and Baird supplied John Howard Payne, the author of "Home Sweet Home," with copper tanks, alcohol, and dip nets when Payne took up his duties as United States consul in Tunis.[15] One of Baird's most faithful collectors was his sponsor, counselor, and close friend George P. Marsh, who devoted a good deal of time away from his diplomatic duties in the Ottoman Empire to acquiring specimens of Near Eastern fauna and shipping them to his younger friend. Marsh wrote Baird a typically delightful letter from Constantinople on August 23, 1850.

> I was fully resolved not to write to you until I could say, "herewith I send a cask of fish," but yours of July 7th which I have just received is irresistible. However, I don't anticipate much, for I have been collecting the small fish of the Bosphorus for several weeks and have now about 20 species, with ten

or twelve individuals of a kind, in spirits. They will be sent to Smyrna next week and be shipped from there about the middle of September. The larger fish are interesting, but I don't know what to do with them. There are many lizards and salamanders, but the lizards are almost impossible to catch, and besides the people are afraid of them. Scorpions are not yet in season. They will be plenty in October. I have a good many snails and some bulimi I suppose that *hibernate* in summer. What ignorant wretches! It's a real Hibernicism, isn't it. I shall pick you up all the rubbish I can, but I think I shall only send the fishes next week and keep the rest to fill a box. The other day, I found my fisherman had caught a dozen fish whose sting is poisonous, and lest I should be hurt, he had carefully cut off the dangerous part! Well I told him that was just what I wanted. So he has gone in search of more. I could do a great deal better for you, but the expense of every material and of every sort of work is so enormous, that the revenue of the Smithsonian would not suffice for one naturalist at Constantinople. . . . We mean to go to Egypt this winter and back by way of Syria, if my poor wife is well enough. What particular thing do you want me to look for in those countries? . . . The natural history of the Bosphorus, though you would find it interesting and full of life, is not striking to an ignoramus. There being no forests, and scarcely any trees, there are few birds. Hawks of various kinds abound. There are a few storks, two kinds of gulls very abundant and very tame, and the "ame damnee" by thousands. [Note: Flocks of Manx shearwaters (*Procellaria puffinus*) fly continuously throughout the day up and down the Bosphorus from their nesting grounds on the Black Sea coast to feeding grounds in the Sea of Marmara. Because of their restless, unceasing flight they are known locally as the "lost souls," *âmes damnées*, and legends abound as to whose souls.] There are many fish principally small, and quite a variety of shellfish, but in Coleoptera, as I learned from Mr. Souza the Spanish minister, who is a good entomologist, and others, it is the richest place in the world. I have saved a few remarkable ones and shall catch more. . . . Take care of yourself, my dear boy. You are destined to great things, if you do not exhaust yourself too early by overwork.[16]

Baird sent Marsh on May 2, 1852, possibly the most unusual instruction ever levied on a minister plenipotential of the United States.

By all means send me lots of Salamandrosus. I want him exceedingly. You must have several species of salamanders, some in water, some on land, under rocks, etc. (N.B. See printed directions enclosed.) I won't give much for a live ostrich, but will give a bottle of first rate Scuppernong wine from North Carolina, when you come back, for his skeleton. It would be a prize indeed. But I *must* have a camel's head at least, if not his whole skeleton. And what of Hyaenas, Jackals, & the like of which travellers speak. Are such fabulous? I fear me so. I want some dog skulls too; these I know abound. The fresh water fish you sent me from old Nilus were nice—and still nicer I have a book which tells me about them. . . . Send me different species of unios or fresh water mussels in alcohol. Shall I send more, or has the Sultan yet introduced the Maine liquor law?[17]

Another important source of collectors for Baird was a lively and progressively varying group of young naturalists whom Baird had in most cases recruited and brought to Washington when they wrote to him with some inquiry that signaled to him their serious interest. Lucy Baird noted in her reminiscences that

> many young naturalists who were studying in the Museum as well as assisting in its work lodged in the Smithsonian towers. By the kindness of Professor Henry many of the unused rooms, too high up for business purposes, and situated conveniently for access to their work were assigned to such young students as lodgings. They supplied their own furniture and linen and were looked after for a small fee by some of the colored employees of the Institution.[18]

The group ultimately rented a house nearby and nominated themselves the Megatherium Club. Robert Kennicott, who was one of the members, wrote his father in 1863, expressing a bit of the flavor of the Megatherium. "It is five o'clock, when the Megatherium takes its prey, that the most interesting characters of the animal are seen. Then it roars with delight and makes up for the hard work of the day by much fun and conduction. . . . We den in various rat holes about the building, in the high towers and other queer places where the air is plentiful and fresh." He added that their "keeper" was Professor Baird, "just about the best and most wonderful man I ever did see. Their motto? 'Never let your evening's amusement be the subject of your morning's reflections.'"[19]

Future American scientists of note, many of whom were members of the Megatherium and all of whom worked under Baird and were trained by him, included William Stimpson, Robert Kennicott, Edward D. Cope, Addison E. Verrill, Fielding Meek, Ferdinand V. Hayden, Theodore N. Gill, James G. Cooper, and Elliott Coues. To this list should be added John H. Clark and Caleb Kennerly, both former students of Baird at Dickinson and both of whom participated as naturalists in major western expeditions; William H. Dall, prominent zoologist and explorer, who became Baird's first biographer; and Robert Ridgway, coauthor with Baird and Thomas M. Brewer of *A History of North American Birds: Land Birds* and ultimately curator of birds at the Smithsonian. As one of Baird's distinguished memorialists noted, "There was scarcely a young naturalist of serious purpose . . . who had not in some way received help and encouragement from Professor Baird."[20]

Baird kept up an active correspondence with all of these men when they were in the field. When they were in Washington, helping to sort and classify specimens and assisting Baird in his other Smithsonian tasks, the Bairds welcomed them on Sunday evenings and often on holidays for a meal and the chance to meet important and established scientists such as Louis Agassiz and Thomas Brewer. Baird wrote his sister Molly on Christmas Day, 1875, "Mary insisted on having the usual Christmas gathering of Smithsonian homeless boys, and the table is now set for fourteen persons."[21]

In later years an important contributor of exotic animal specimens to the United States National Museum was the showman P. T. Barnum. Barnum had known Secretary Henry and as early as 1873 had sent the Smithsonian the carcass of a Bactrian camel. By 1878 Baird and Barnum were in regular contact, and the carcasses, or at least the skins and skeletons, of all animals which died in the circus menagerie were shipped to the Smithsonian. Barnum requested one *quid pro quo* in a letter to Baird dated October 25, 1882. After noting his intention to bring to the United States for exhibit a group of "semi-civilized or rather *uncivilized*" natives, he added:

> Now when our agents strike *Holland* or Dutch *colonies*, we have before found that the authorities are *reluctant* about letting their people leave the country unless they are first satisfied that the party taking them is responsible and will return them according to agreement. . . . One agent writes me that he needs an endorsement of the U.S. Secretary of State, but I think from former experience this is impracticable. It struck me, however, that the Smithsonian Institution, with its big seal, &c, might be about as effective as any document from *other* branches of the U.S. Government, & therefore I hasten to trespass most unwarrantably upon your time by laying these facts before you, in the hope that you will kindly think of some manner in which you & your institution will be willing to supply some document which, when shown to these foreign governments, will convince them

that our firm are *responsible* for the return of any people or animals (including *sub rosa* a white elephant from Siam) which we may agree to return. . . . Of course I don't want the Smithsonian or any institution or person to guarantee us in the remotest manner, but we need . . . *Something* that will *show* to these governments that we are solid, honorable, and reliable.[22]

Baird complied.

In letters dated June 21, 1884, and September 27, 1885, Barnum promised Baird that the Smithsonian would receive either the skeleton or the skin of the famous elephant Jumbo whenever the animal died, adding in the second letter, "for which *you now have the means of reciprocating generously* by contributing such duplicate birds, animals, casts, &c as you can spare to my pet 'Barnum Museum of Natural History' at Tufts College." Jumbo did die unexpectedly early in an accident, but the Smithsonian never profited from Barnum's promises. The curator of the Barnum Museum of Natural History, Professor John P. Marshall, and the president of the college, the Reverend E. H. Capen, both persuaded the aging Barnum that the Smithsonian was not fulfilling its side of the bargain in either the quantity or quality of its contributions, with the result that Barnum wrote to Capen on November 20, 1885: "Yours and Prof. Marshall's letters indicate that Prof. Baird cannot or *will not* carry out his promises—so hereafter I will (unless my partners object) have all our dead animals sent to Prof. Ward to use for museum in exchange or otherwise. . . . I am disappointed in Smithsonian's meanness & now I want this matter simplified so that *I* need not be often bothered with details of skins and bones."[23]

Baird was well into his final illness by the time of this contretemps. W. T. Hornaday, then taxidermist at the United States National Museum, tried manfully to persuade Barnum to keep his promises, but in vain. Jumbo's bones ended up at the American Museum of Natural History in New York, and his skin at the Tufts College museum, where it was subsequently destroyed in a fire.

It is tempting to go on describing Baird's contacts, correspondence, and sometimes conflicts with his multitudes of other collectors—with Lieutenant John Irwin, who obtained for the Smithsonian the great Tucson meteorite but wrote Baird in high Irish dudgeon when his find was exhibited under the name of another; with the eccentric Hungarian John Xantus, whom Baird had helped despite Joseph Henry's concern about Xantus's sometimes erratic behavior ("From all the impressions I have received relative to the moral character of this man," Henry wrote, "I think he is not to be trusted, and that it will be safest in the future for the Inst. to let him slide.");[24] with Ferdinand V. Hayden, who through the survey that bears his name deserves much of the credit for establishing Yellowstone National Park; with Sgt. John Feilner, whom Baird helped to receive an officer's commission and who was ambushed and killed by a Sioux war party when collecting for the Smithsonian; and with José Zeledon, perhaps Costa Rica's first natural scientist. However, other authors have done ample justice to all of these, with the possible exception of Zeledon, and in the final analysis, all simply merit mention here as prominent members of Spencer Baird's collection of collectors.

Chapter Nine

Spencer Baird and Louis Agassiz

A PRICKLY ASSOCIATION

NOT LONG AFTER WEATHERING THE HAZARDS of his involvement in the Jewett affair, Baird ran into a troublesome and potentially serious controversy with the most notable and popular natural scientist of the day, the eminent Professor Louis Agassiz. More important for Baird, he was a member of the Smithsonian's Board of Regents and a close associate of Joseph Henry.

Some professional jealousy and conflict between the two may have been inevitable, but it was made doubly so by the elemental differences in their respective attitudes and styles of work. Agassiz had arrived in the United States with an already established reputation, fortified by a personal charm that made him one of the most sought-after public speakers of the day as well as a formidable fund-raiser. He was an eminently capable taxonomist, but he believed that the discovery and morphological classification of a new species was at best a beginning, and worthwhile only to the extent that it might lead the researcher to the discovery of broad scientific generalizations through inductive reasoning. He wrote:

> When less was known of plants and animals the discovery of new species was the great object. This has been carried too far, and is now almost the lowest kind of scientific work. The discovery of a new species as such does

not change a feature in the science of natural history. . . . It is merely adding to the enumeration of objects. We should look rather for the fundamental relations among animals. . . . The origin of life is the great question of the day.[1]

Baird, who was sixteen years younger than Agassiz, had acquired only a limited reputation by the time they first met, and indeed Agassiz played a not inconsiderable role in the younger man's advancement. However, it soon became evident that Baird's scientific method was precisely the one that Agassiz condemned. Baird's approach was pure Baconian and rested on the conviction that general truths in science would surface of themselves from the comparative study of many specimens.

Initially, Baird's relations with Agassiz were warm and based on mutual esteem. They corresponded at first and then met during a visit that Baird made to Boston in July 1847. Baird had turned his research attention from birds to fish by that time, and he and Agassiz hit it off at once, since the subject was of mutual interest. Early in 1848 Baird and Agassiz made an agreement to co-write a book on the freshwater fishes of North America. In his letter to Joseph Henry of June 9, 1849, Baird requested money for an expedition to collect specimens and explained:

> Professor Agassiz and I, when in Washington together, arranged a system of explorations, for the sake of more speedily and systematically getting a complete view of the ichthyology of our country. I undertook the streams of Western and Middle Virginia, as also of southern Pennsylvania, but shall be unable to carry out the plan on my own resources. I have done this in obedience to my own tendencies, strengthened by the earnest advice of Professor Agassiz, who said that such collections as these would be of unique and inestimable value.[2]

Henry approved a grant of seventy-five dollars for the purpose, the first such grant extended with Smithsonian funds.

Agassiz had been impressed by Baird's work on the *Iconographic Encyclopedia* and agreed to review revised portions of the text, as is evident in a letter from Baird to his brother Will in December 1849. "I do not wish to hurry you about the geology, but would like it as soon as convenient. It will come on in a few months and Professor Agassiz can attend to the revision immediately." When Baird attended the 1849 meeting of the American Association for the Advancement of Science in Boston, he stayed with the Agassiz family, and in October of that year Agassiz wrote to Baird, "I have written to-day to Prof. Henry about the Conservatorship of the Museum in such terms as to let him feel how important your connection with that Institution might be for its advance in the Nat. Hist. Department."[3]

Their honeymoon ended, however, and the cause of the first breach between them was a third party, Charles Girard. Trained by Agassiz, Girard subsequently worked for and with him, but he left following a staff spat in which Agassiz felt that Girard had failed to appreciate his support. Agassiz' biographer, Edward Lurie, states:

> Agassiz interpreted this as patent ingratitude. Annoyance turned to anger when Girard turned up as Baird's assistant in herpetology at the Smithsonian. Girard had found the position on his own, Baird had not consulted Agassiz about the appointment, and from that time on Agassiz would have nothing to do with Girard. When Baird and Girard published any joint paper or book, as they often did, it was bound to receive a slashing review from Agassiz.[4]

Excerpts from a letter Agassiz wrote to Baird in 1853, following the publication of *A Catalogue of North American Reptiles in the Museum of the Smithsonian Institution* by Baird and Girard is illustrative.

> It is not easy for me to trust to paper what I have to say to you, there being seldom a remedy to misapprehensions from writing. If you will however remember that nothing but a sincere interest in you could prompt me to write, my note may not be useless. From beginning I have looked to the Smithsonian Institution as the greatest foundation for the promotion of science in this country, and I have lost no opportunity of securing the election of such an assistant in the department of Natural History as I knew competent to advance such a noble cause. Your paper on Batrachians had satisfied me that you have the requisite qualifications. But now what shall I say of your catalogue of Serpents? It is true that it discloses great industry by the extensive collection you have brought together from the remotest parts of the country; and this will always be very creditable to you. But the scientific part of the work is very crude; I should never have expected that while you are connected with the Smithsonian Instit. such a volume would be issued with its sanction and still less that your name should appear on its title page. To tell you the truth of my impression I do not believe that you have had much to do with it & I hope sincerely for the sake of your scientific reputation that it will turn out so. But why did you not at least look

it over. If you had been willing to listen to my advise [*sic*] before, you should have known that Girard, though capable of sustained work and endowed with considerable ability in distinguishing the peculiarities of animals, has no judgement, and is utterly unable to trace original researches without supervision. Moreover he is as obstinate as a mule, if contradicted, which makes it necessary that he should be led with a high hand and kept in an entirely subordinate position. Now this supervision of his work you have not made; you have not tested the value of the characters upon which he has based his generic and specific distinctions. I recognize his hand both in the style of the language used, and in the scientific character of the work. In the hurry of your many engagements you have entrusted to him a task to which he is not equal; and there goes forward from the Smithsonian Instit. a production which in quality is far inferior to what is done elsewhere, though by the quantity of the materials you had the means of surpassing every work of that kind. And now I ask you what is there left for the friends of the Smithson. to do? To let that pass unnoticed, or to criticize it as it deserves? To let a hasty incorrect performance go abroad as a model or to expose the whole? This language may appear severe. It is so; it is more so to you personally than I would ever use speaking to others but it is plainly deserved.[5]

Baird's prompt response was respectful, but he gave no ground.

My dear Professor,
   I am exceedingly indebted to you for the frankness with which you have criticised the Serpent Catal. and so far from being offended, I am grateful for the interest which prompts you to go into the discussion of the various points involved. It would ill become me, a beginner, to assume everything near perfection, as the result of my work, and it is only by the criticism of friends (among whom I am proud to rank you) that I may hope to improve. I beg that you will always tell me freely of whatever you think is susceptible of improvement in my doings.
   So much by way of preamble. And now if you will allow me to explain some of the inconsistencies and inaccuracies to which you refer, some of them satisfactorily I hope. I must however state in the outset that I am not excusable on the ground of having left the work to my collaborator without proper censor. On the contrary, the rough work was divided about equally, genus by genus, each making out the full descriptions and investigations of his share subject to the criticism of the other. Every line written by Mr. G., however, I carefully read and discussed, in many cases going over the whole subject and comparing and examining all the specimens in connection with the description. The analytical tables I did entirely myself, and you may not wonder at the inaccuracies when you learn that it was an afterthought,

carried into effect in the space of two or three days. I expressly refer to its inaccuracies in the preface and give it merely an analysis, not a natural arrangement.

Baird then proceeded to defend, courteously but firmly, and with reference to well-known authorities, each of the specific points Agassiz had raised, adding in conclusion and obviously with tongue in cheek:

> I have now, my dear Professor, attempted vindication from the charge of carelessness and youthful precipitancy as well as I have time at the present writing as I do by return mail, with the nineteen other letters requiring the same dispatch. I need not assure you again however that it is with the utmost feeling of respect and gratitude for the interest you have taken in me which prompts you to a friendly castigation. I admit my faults, and deficiencies, which I hope time will correct, and hope that you will assist by continuing your kind criticism and advice. I trust you will oblige me by marking on a copy of the catalogue any notice of bad grammar or other errors and let me have it soon. It will be necessary to reproduce the work soon and I wish to make all necessary alterations. Whatever you do in the matter will be gratefully acknowledged.[6]

Baird found it wise to deal cautiously with Agassiz, because the latter was very much admired by Joseph Henry; and particularly in the midst of the Jewett affair, Baird could not afford to clash openly with any close friend of the secretary's. However, it is clear that Henry understood the situation. He commented to Alexander Dallas Bache in July 1853:

> The strictures of Prof. Agassiz on the Catalog of Reptiles will, I hope, do Baird some good though I do not think the criticism in every respect well founded. Baird showed me the first letter of Agassiz, and his answer to it. The answer was written in a very respectful spirit, or at least apparently so, though it met in a number of cases the objections to the work very properly. Agassiz is not without a strong feeling of dislike and prejudice in relation to everything connected with Girard, and is therefore not well conditioned in feeling to give a proper criticism on the catalog. I doubt not, however, that Baird's book will be found to bear the marks (of) hasty production and perhaps of defective judgement in the deductions.[7]

Recognizing the advantage of keeping the peace with Agassiz, Baird noted in a letter to his friend Jared Kirtland in October 1853 that he had visited Agassiz in Cambridge, where "we had a very long talk together which proved satisfactory to both, and we separated with plans for joint operations upon the fishes of North America." The proposed joint publication never saw the light of day, but for the next few years they maintained a fairly active correspondence and cooperated in projects of mutual interest and benefit. Agassiz sent Baird funds for Kennicott's Alaskan adventure in 1861, and Baird loaned specimens from the Smithsonian collections to Agassiz for study. However, according to Edward Lurie: "Agassiz had never really respected Spencer F. Baird, even though he had been partly responsible for that naturalist's Smithsonian appointment. With the passing of time, he came to think of Baird as retarding progress in natural history, an attitude that was intensified as Agassiz demanded more and more government specimens, and Baird became increasingly unwilling to part with them."[8]

Agassiz, together with a number of his fellow scientists, mostly in Cambridge, formed an informal association called "the Lazzaroni" (after the society of the beggars of Naples, Italy), designed to take over the leadership of, and to set standards for, American science. Under Agassiz' inspiration, seconded by Alexander Dallas Bache (who was also no friend of Baird's), the Lazzaroni overreached themselves in 1863. Without the knowledge of Joseph Henry, who, although a member of their group, they rightfully suspected would have objected strongly, and taking advantage of the national focus on the war, they persuaded sympathetic friends in Congress to pass a bill creating the National Academy of Sciences, with a maximum membership of fifty—to be selected by the Lazzaroni. They pointedly excluded Baird on the pretext that he was "only a descriptive scientist" and thus not eligible for membership in an academy created to promote original investigation.[9]

The obvious intent of the Lazzaroni to set themselves up as the arbiters of scientific worth and accomplishment in American science resulted in widespread opposition throughout the American scientific community, and the matter came to a head at the meeting of the academy in New Haven the following year, with the exclusion of Baird as the focal issue.

Shortly after the meeting opened, Baird was nominated for membership. Agassiz began to rally his forces for the showdown vote, thinking he could easily prevent Baird's election. But when the vote was in, Baird had become an academy member with the support of Joseph Henry, Asa Gray, James Dwight Dana, and virtually all the naturalists present. Asa Gray wrote to Baird shortly after the meeting.

[Jeffries] Wyman and I, who had kept wholly aloof before, went on to New Haven to see what the feeling was, and especially to see if there was a disposition to commit what seemed to us an injustice in respect to yourself and one other. We found that in the Natural History Class, which was almost fully represented, every member present but one appeared to feel that it was the clear duty of the Academy to elect you. That one threw every obstacle in the way . . . but all in vain—though great pertinacity was required on the part of the Class to secure an opportunity of expressing its will and purpose. . . . We did our duty, and circumstances made me prominent in the discussion more than I could wish. I regret to add that Mr. Agassiz lost his temper—and as I found next day—took personal offense against me—I am sure without fair reason.[10]

Joseph Henry, who had voted for Baird's admission wrote Agassiz an explanation of his support of Baird and described the event and his feelings about it even more precisely in a letter to Bache dated August 15, 1864.

The meeting of the Academy went off on the whole very well, although our friends from Cambridge were much displeased because they did not succeed in preventing the election of Prof. B. They were right in principle, but wrong in practice. I fully agree with Agassiz that physiological research is a higher order of scientific investigation than the description of species, but the *amount* of labor as well as the *kind* must be taken into consideration, and as all the naturalists, with the exception of Agassiz and one or two others, have made their reputations and were elected into the Academy on account of just such work as B. has done, the opposition of Agassiz, who stood alone, was considered against the whole class, and had he recommended keeping B. out by urging a rule of the Academy, the majority of naturalists would have withdrawn.[11]

Baird was under no illusions regarding Agassiz' attitude. In the letter he wrote in 1866 to Professor A. A. Gould in response to the offer of the Boston Society of Natural History directorship he said, "Prof. Agassiz is very desirous of having a National Museum established in Washington to be separated from the S.I. and I presume would be opposed to my having charge of it & being in any way connected with it. If he succeeds in both (presumed) objects I should certainly leave Washington for any [illegible] place."[12]

Nevertheless, Baird and Agassiz each had something to offer the other in the way of exchanges, and because of Agassiz' membership on the Smithsonian Board of Regents, they maintained civil, if wary, contact and sporadic cooperation for ten years up until Agassiz' death in 1873. Lurie observed in his biography of Agassiz that for all his greatness, Agassiz was unable to accept other naturalists on a level of equality, and he fell out with many of his European and almost all of his American contemporaries.

Joseph Henry, secretary of the Smithsonian Institution from 1846 to 1878. Courtesy of the National Portrait Gallery.

Assistant Secretary Spencer F. Baird, ca. 1860.

Original Smithsonian Institution building, the Castle, north facade, 1858.

The Great Hall of the Smithsonian Castle, ca. 1858, showing cases probably designed by Baird for exhibit of the permanent collection.

Baird's Smithsonian office, his Wooten desk on the left and his black coat hanging on the right.

Baird's Wooten desk, currently on exhibit in the Arts and Industries Building (but unidentified as Baird's). On the desk are personal Baird memorabilia from the national collections, including Baird's portfolio, eyeglasses and case, stationery, field telescope, knife, magnifying glass with handle, measuring rod, two volumes of *A History of North American Birds*, traveling inkwell, and a white cloth napkin reportedly used by Napoleon I at his breakfast on the morning that he left the Island of Elba. How this last item came into Baird's hands is a mystery.

Members of the Megatherium. *Left to right standing*: Robert Kennicott and Henry Ulke; *seated*, William Stimpson and Henry Bryant.

William Healey Dall, Baird's protégé and his first biographer.

Robert Ridgway, student and co-author with Baird of *A History of North American Birds: Land Birds.* He was curator of birds at the United States National Museum after Baird's death.

Jean Louis Rodolphe Agassiz (1807–1873), famous Swiss naturalist and a regent of the Smithsonian.

Asa Gray (1810–1888), botanist and Smithsonian regent from 1874 to 1888. He clashed with Agassiz by supporting Baird's election to the National Academy of Sciences.

Chapter Ten

A Dedication to the Demonstrable

To SPENCER BAIRD, as a dedicated Baconian, ideas and truths were valid to the extent that they could be tangibly demonstrated. Concepts that could not be verified by the study of objects in hand might or might not appear logical, but unless they could stand the test of scientific scrutiny according to his standards, he was, with rare exceptions, simply not interested.

Baird's attitude toward religion is illustrative. In none of his available writings—to Mary, to his close friends, in his private journals, and even when he was well aware that the end of his life was near—did he give the slightest hint of his beliefs with regard to the existence of a deity or a hereafter, or to the fact or the future of his own mortality. Yet he was brought up in a strongly religious home. In the few existing letters between them it is clear that one of his mother's chief preoccupations was with religion, and she devoted considerable effort to trying to awaken a religious interest in her son. A birthday letter she wrote him in February 1850 is characteristic.

> I am thankful, my dear child, to our Heavenly Father that he has made you what you are, that he has restrained you from much sin and wickedness that too many of the young fall into, and I hope that you also feel sensible

for the numberless blessings for which you are indebted to him, health and friends, a good wife, and sweet child are all his gifts, besides innumerable incidents of his watchful Providence over you, and signally shown in your restoration to health last summer, when from all accounts your life must have been in great danger. . . . I must not conclude this part of my letter without saying what I think, my dear son, you are justly deserving of, and that is that you have ever been to me a kind and dutiful child; in this respect you do not have anything to reproach yourself with, and I trust never will.[1]

While living at home in Carlisle, Baird went to church regularly, though often to churches of different denominations. He noted in his journal each church he attended and the name of the minister who had delivered the sermon, but he never included any comment on the content. After the Bairds were established in Washington, they subscribed to a private pew in a Washington church for a few years, and his early journals refer to Lucy's attendance at Sunday school. However, Mary does not appear to have had any more interest in religious matters than her husband, and after a year or two the matter of churchgoing was no longer mentioned.

In opinions attributed to students or Smithsonian employees, Baird was described variously as agnostic or atheist. An unsigned page of notes in pencil among some papers of Baird's contains the following anecdote: "A group of young scientists gathered together in discussion, claiming Prof. Baird as an agnostic. Prof. Baird suddenly appeared. 'What are you doing?' asked he of me. 'Bibliography of ———.' 'Pshaw [said Baird]. Why don't you make some discovery of new truths. Better, I sometimes think, if all the books but two in the world were burned.' 'What are they?' 'Bible and Shakespeare.'"[2] Yet Baird lived and worked at a time when theological and scientific communities were in heated confrontation, and many of his colleagues took sides passionately. Agassiz, for instance, was an unreconstructed creationist; the evolutionists were quite vociferous; and few remained on the sidelines either in America or abroad. But two who did were Joseph Henry and Spencer Baird.[3]

Baird never openly took a position regarding Darwinism. He declared his own pragmatic approach to the evolutionary process in a letter dated November 30, 1869, to H. W. Elliott, one of his collectors.

My object is to define the forms that characterize certain regions, not only as a matter of ornithology, but of physical geography. If *I* can do this to my own satisfaction, it is nothing to me that others say *they* can't. I can with my series convince anyone, un-prejudiced, of the differences, and I don't care whether they constitute varieties, species, or genera. I believe all the small ones [thrushes], [illegible], furescens, swainsonii, et alia, came from one ancestor in the first place, and then that all thrushes had a common origin in the preceding period.

In his memorial to Baird in 1888, Dall commented perceptively:

Unlike some of his contemporaries twenty years ago, the views of Darwin excited in him no reaction of mind against the hypotheses then novel and revolutionary. His friendly reception of the new theories was so quiet and undisturbed that, to a novice seeking his advice and opinion amid the clatter of contending voices, it seemed almost as if the main features of the scientific gospel of the new era had existed in the mind of Baird from the very beginning.[4]

Baird was certainly familiar with Darwin's theory of natural selection. In his paper "The Distribution and Migrations of North American Birds," the arguments he presented on geographic variations within species, and hybridization between similar species with overlapping ranges, were right in line with Darwin's theses. Still, he never expressed his views directly on the subject of Darwinism, and he mentioned Darwin's name only twice in all the writings we covered in our research. Baird noted in his journal on December 27, 1843, that he had visited the Library of Congress and "got out Darwin's Narration of the Voyage of the Beagle." Years later, in 1861, he wrote to his friend Henry Bryant, "I hope you are not crazy too, with the whole world. Don't talk of fighting: there are plenty without you to do this, and we must keep up a few Naturals [*sic*] to keep Darwinism from being forgotten."[5]

Baird did reveal that he had more than a casual interest in the evolution controversy in a letter he wrote on October 26, 1874, to Whitelaw Reid, editor of the *New York Tribune*, in which he recommended publication of a talk he had heard on the subject.

I was greatly impressed at the meeting of the Philosophical society last Saturday evening with an address by the Reverend Dr. Shields, Professor of Natural Theology at Princeton, entitled The Present State of Science. It

kept me awake for an hour and a half, which I can assure you is a very unusual thing in a public address of any kind. It struck me as it did other
members of the Society, as one of the most admirable summings up of the
questions in litigation between science and theology that have ever been attempted, exhibiting an immense amount of learning and a degree of fairness in the whole question that is somewhat marvellous in gentlemen of his
training.[6]

It seems evident that Baird was prepared to take a position, public or
private, only on what he was satisfied could be scientifically demonstrated
by means of comparative study of specimens or artifacts. Such questions
as the existence of God and the purpose of his own existence, whether
speciation of animal life occurred by divine mandate or through a process
of natural selection, and even whether black people should be enslaved or
red people massacred were to him so incapable of scientific demonstration
that he not only took no sides in the controversies of the day, he simply
dismissed them from his priorities and his correspondence.

Baird did share some of the cultural prejudices of his time, one of
which concerned the role of women. In 1885 he wrote to S. H. Scudder in
connection with recruitment for a position in the International Exchange
Service. "I have a full appreciation of the merits, business capacity, and
efficiency of women, as is shown by the fact that our present librarian is a
'female of that sex'; but the place I refer to may grow to be a controlling
one, covering several extensive departments which could not well be sub-
ordinated to a woman."[7]

The major political issue throughout Baird's youth, early manhood,
and first ten years at the Smithsonian was slavery. Despite the intensity of
public concern in which they were steeped in Washington, neither
Spencer nor Mary Baird ever appear to have expressed any opinion on the
subject in writing. In June of 1847 there was great excitement in Carlisle
when a slave owner tried to reclaim a Negro woman who had escaped
some time earlier and had married a free black man in Carlisle. The Reverend John McClintock, professor of mathematics at Dickinson, who had
married the Bairds, was deeply involved with the defense of the woman,
and passions in the town ran high. The situation got out of hand, and in
the ensuing turmoil the slave owner was killed. Baird cryptically noted in

his journal: "Great excitement in town . . . about some runaway slaves. Person badly hurt in fight." And he went on to record his collection of the day.[8]

Baird necessarily became more involved in public concern over the war, and he did express personal opinions about it, although never in terms of his feelings about the issues involved. He deplored the fact that it had not been possible to find a compromise solution to the problem, and he wrote to his colleague, Thomas M. Brewer, in 1861: "Bryant was making fun of you in saying that I was secessionist. It would be a pretty thing for a Pennsylvanian to be so with strong Union feeling. I *was* averse to coercion, and rather in favor of letting the South try its desired experiment." And then he revealed his real concern: "I feared the effect of civil commotion on the Smithsonian."[9]

In a letter to a southern friend, Baird expanded upon his feelings.

> You cannot tell how deeply I deplore the present unhappy condition of affairs, and the fratricidal aspect of all our relations. My heart is sick and sore of the prospect before us. Myself, not personally concerned in any of the public movements, and without any partisan feelings on the subject, and with so many near and dear friends on opposite sides of the border, I do not allow myself to be blinded to the real issues and dangers of the time. All I can do is hope that at the [illegible] hour, some kind providence may interfere to bring all parties to reason, and respect for each others rights and privileges. . . . Whatever be the result, as long as the Smithsonian is in existence and a free agent, there will be no difference in its relations to different parts of the continent. It recognizes no distinctions as between America and the rest of the world, why should it ever, in America. Whatever power may control Washington, it is our hope to be allowed to carry out our sublime mission in the most catholic manner.[10]

Some of his Megatherium assistants volunteered for military duty; the husband of his favorite sister Molly, Henry J. Biddle, was wounded and died in a southern prisoner-of-war camp; his brother-in-law Charles Churchill sought his intercession with the secretary of war in obtaining a commission; and Confederate forces twice threatened Washington; but Baird not only showed no disposition to volunteer, he strongly urged his brothers and friends not to do so either. In a letter to his mother, dated April 27, 1861, he wrote: "I don't like the idea of so many persons leaving

Pennsylvania. The more remote states should form the advance guard, leaving Pennsylvanians to watch the frontier and be ready to repel any northward invasion. Keep Tom at home. He is not wanted here; and I hope won't come." And on May 8 he wrote to Will Baird:

> I think that both you and Tom had better stay at home, and not volunteer, either of you for the aggressive part of the war. If it be as long in continuance as I fear it will, a strong home guard will be needed to defend the borders. At present many more persons insist on going; most of them as well able to go as not. Those who can do better at home should stay there. No harm, of course in drilling and being ready, but there is no reason for all to move."[11]

In March 1863 the federal government passed a draft law, under the terms of which all able-bodied males became subject to conscription, but the law also contained two loopholes allowing a draftee either to obtain an exemption for three hundred dollars or to procure a substitute willing to serve in his place. On June 17, 1864, Baird wrote to his brother-in-law Frank Churchill on business (Frank handled Baird investments), and noted: "In view of the certainty of a draft in this district the present summer and the probable repeal of the $300 exemption clause, I thought it a matter of prudent precaution to procure a substitute for 3 years while I could obtain one, and thus be prepared for any contingency. I therefore yesterday put in a colored substitute, and shall get this morning my exemption papers, the operation costing me $278.00."[12]

After the Civil War came the many punitive actions against Indians in the West, but these, too, excited no comment from Baird, despite the deaths in frontier skirmishes of both his nephew and namesake, Spencer F. Baird Biddle, and a valued collector, Captain John Feilner, and frequent descriptions in letters from other collectors of dangers they experienced on the frontier. He continued to encourage all his collectors to seek out Indian burial mounds or middens, and to obtain all the remains— human and cultural—they could find. His goal was simply to trace the origin of this hominid taxon; he showed no evident interest in or sympathy for the Indians as fellow Americans or as exploited human beings. Nor did he appear to share John Wesley Powell's deep concern over the ruinous exploitation of western lands.

What might seem more curious was Baird's apparent indifference toward the threatened extinction of some of the animal species to which he devoted so much attention and study. In 1876 he wrote to Edward Shepard of Williamstown, Massachusetts, advising him with regard to a proposed exploration by members of the Williams College Society of Natural History and recommending that they focus their efforts in the Hudson Strait area. "The testimony of Captain Hall and other travellers in that region shows the existence of quite a number of species of waterfowl now considered extremely rare, among them especially the famed Labrador Duck, which, though generally supposed to be extinct, is, we have reason to believe, quite abundant there. It is quite likely that enough of these could be secured to meet a considerable proportion of the cost of exploration." In late 1882 Baird sent General William Tecumseh Sherman, by then a regent of the Smithsonian, a stuffed owl that the general had requested, and noted in his accompanying letter, "You are perhaps aware that Owls are very difficult to get at the present time, owing to their enormous demand for ladies' headgear and as ornaments for the parlor and library." And in 1887 he wrote to his friend George A. Boardman, "You have probably heard that Mr. Hornaday secured 23 excellent buffalo skins recently: so that we shall be supplied, even should the species become extinct."[13]

Baird did endorse the idea of game laws in an active correspondence with both Charles Hallock, editor of *Forest and Stream* magazine, and W. F. Parker, a well-known designer and manufacturer of sporting guns, but he declined nomination as federal commissioner of game on the ground that in addition to being too busy he felt that game control was properly a state rather than a federal function. He also declined to speak about the need for game laws at a sportsmen's convention being organized by Parker in 1874, "though I sympathize very much with the movement and will do all I can to aid in its object." And in response to Hallock's invitation to write an article for *Forest and Stream* in support of a movement for national game protection laws, Baird wrote:

> While sympathizing fully with the plan for national action in regard to the protection of game . . . I . . . must decline to have anything from myself published on the subject. It is very necessary for one occupying my position

to be extremely circumspect respecting any interference with subjects not officially committed to his care, & I might prejudice severely the interest of my present functions by going outside of the strict letter of my Commission.[14]

Baird supported the taking of species, however endangered, if it was for the advancement of science, but he did oppose it when done casually by youthful dilettantes. One of his last letters was written to his sister Molly on July 14, 1887.

> You misunderstand my position in regard to bird-nesting.
>
> When I was in the business, I was collecting material for an exhaustive work on the Natural History of the birds of North America, and a set of nests and eggs of each species, in all variations was a necessity. I consequently needed to have as large a variety as possible, so as to complete the ground.
>
> The ordinary bird-egging boy, whose enterprise is not to be frowned at, is not such an individual, he simply wants to make a collection of eggs without an ulterior scientific object. A single egg will answer the same purpose in his case as the one hundred required in the one first mentioned. Unless you have an embryo Audubon with a decided scientific object likely to be carried out, I would frown upon anything more than the taking of a single egg from the nest, and this should be approached with the greatest caution, and the egg taken should be removed with a spoon. By taking out an egg with a spoon the other eggs are not likely to be contaminated. The parent bird detects the touch of human fingers, and abandons the nest immediately.
>
> I am inclined to ascribe the reduction in the number of our home birds as much to the taking of eggs for various purposes or driving away the parents as to actual extermination of the birds themselves; however, the most effectual way of preventing the difficulty is by prohibiting the taking of eggs entirely, which I would earnestly recommend.[15]

Interestingly, Baird appears to have later abandoned his basic requirement of scientific demonstrability when he became the principal and most persuasive lobbyist in Congress for the establishment and funding of a federal commission to investigate and ultimately to promote the conservation of a national natural resource. Baird appears to have accepted at face value claims of some fishermen and state officials that fish populations on the Atlantic Coast were diminishing. He had even less evidence to support his apparent conviction that ocean fish populations might be increased by artificial propagation and release. Yet Baird threw his full support and enthusiastic effort behind both proposals.

It does seem remarkable that, although seemingly unmoved by the threatened extinction of the passenger pigeon, the Labrador duck, and the bison, and begging off even writing an article in support of game laws, Baird showed such concern over a reported diminution in the supply of commercially harvestable ocean fish. A partial explanation may be that by 1871 he felt the need for a new challenge. He had by that time received and classified most of the vertebrate fauna of North America and had published his descriptive works on them. He had trained assistants who were well able to handle the routine sorting and classifying of any collections still coming in from the West and Northwest. During his summers on the Massachusetts coast, he had developed an interest in marine life, and he found in the concerns of his fishermen and fisheries contacts a new and especially appealing area for investigation—one with potentially desirable political benefits. Indeed, political benefits were never absent from Baird's goals, as is evident in a letter he wrote in response to Charles G. Atkins, who had questioned the merit of sending salmon eggs to areas which seemed unsuitable as salmon habitat. "It makes no difference what is done with the salmon eggs. The object is to introduce them into as many states as possible and have credit with Congress accordingly. If they are there, they are there, and we can so swear, and that is the end of it."[16]

As his vision stretched beyond the simple allure of a new field of research and the attendant professional challenge, it seems probable that he may have seen an operation that could be all his own. By 1871 Baird had been in Joseph Henry's shadow for twenty-one years, and no end seemed to be in sight. Even though he had for years been nominal director of the United States National Museum, he still had to explain every expenditure to Joseph Henry and obtain his signature on the vouchers before submitting them to the Interior Department for payment. However, when in 1871 the president appointed him United States Commissioner of Fish and Fisheries, he was his own boss at last, and he found no difficulty in this particular case in sublimating his scientific standards to political expediency, especially as he doubtless saw in it the potential for collecting and scientific research that he was ultimately able to exploit.[17]

Finally, it is worth noting Baird's attitude toward the many lesser scientific controversies that raged around him. They were often intense and often between friends or associates who sought his support. Baird's student and associate, Robert Ridgway, wrote that "a very marked trait of Professor Baird's character was his aversion to personal controversy, which was so decided that under no circumstances could he be drawn into one."[18] Ridgway might better have qualified this statement to the effect that Baird avoided other people's controversies. Baird never avoided controversy when he was the target of it, and he was involved in personal conflicts throughout his public life. Yet in each of the issues affecting him directly, Baird stood his ground with the assurance that he had demonstrable evidence on which to base his position.

Speculation, theories, and concepts that did not directly involve him he scrupulously avoided. Dr. John Shaw Billings called special attention to this facet of Baird's character in the memorial he delivered before the National Academy of Sciences on April 17, 1889. "He had a clear, definite idea of what he wanted, and he did not scatter his energies. He did not meddle with other people's business, and thus avoided one great source of hostility; and unless a matter was in some way actually or prospectively connected with the subjects in which he was interested he had no time to give to it."[19]

Chapter Eleven

Assistant Secretary

1865–1878

I hardly think that I need trouble myself in regard to the question of a succession, as I am confident that a majority of the Board would not listen for a moment to the application of outsiders. I am not so sure of President Porter as I am of some others, and if you can conveniently ascertain his views on the subject it would be a great relief should I learn they are favorable to myself.

—Spencer Fullerton Baird, from a letter to Asa Gray, 12 March 1878

BY THE BEGINNING OF 1866, during the postwar era, Spencer Baird had succeeded in finding a balance between the duties Secretary Henry expected him to perform and the equally demanding tasks of identifying and classifying the blizzard of unrelated specimens and artifacts arriving at the Smithsonian from exploring expeditions and other collectors. He had in his own right earned an international reputation as a leader in American natural science.

The extent of the esteem in which Baird was held became immediately apparent in 1866 when Secretary of State William Henry Seward negotiated a treaty with the Russian government for the purchase of Alaska. Many Senate leaders were wary of "Seward's Folly" largely because of the almost total lack of information available to them on the area and its resources. Senator Charles Sumner, chairman of the Foreign Affairs Committee, turned for help to Washington's foremost natural scientist, Assistant Secretary Baird of the Smithsonian Institution. Since 1864 Baird had been receiving with his collections a series of long and informative reports from his intrepid protégé, Robert Kennicott.

On the basis of his familiarity with Kennicott's reports, and with a recently returned member of Kennicott's expedition at his elbow, Baird was prepared to speak more authoritatively on the natural resources of Alaska than anyone else in Washington. On the strength of Baird's testimony Sumner and his senatorial colleagues were satisfied that the natural resources of the area were sufficiently valuable to justify the purchase, and they ratified the treaty. Baird was then called upon to exercise his persuasive powers before the House Foreign Affairs and Appropriations committees in order to secure the money to carry out the purchase. The final bill was passed by both houses and signed by the president on July 27, 1869.

Baird continued to be thoroughly occupied during these days with his functions at the Smithsonian. Collections were arriving continually from all the government expeditions, and although he did profit from the help of Megatherium members and others, the responsibility for the classification, preservation, and distribution was entirely his, as were the selection, assignment, and equipping of naturalists to accompany the survey teams. Joseph Henry continued to expect Baird to handle the publishing and the distribution of all of the Institution's annual reports, *Contributions to Knowledge* editions, and other publications, and to manage the ever-growing international exchanges with a worldwide coterie of correspondents. Baird was also occupied with his own publications, and the extent of his correspondence was almost incredible. He noted in his journal that his usual annual output was over three thousand letters, written in his early years without stenographic assistance.

Throughout his career a number of Baird's letters were with, or about, family members. Money was always a concern to the Bairds, and when they began keeping house in Washington, they found the cost of living in the city distressingly high in comparison to what they had been accustomed to in Carlisle. However, they also found with the help of family members in Carlisle, they could purchase their staples there more reasonably than in the city and count on prompt delivery in Washington. Baird's younger, unmarried sisters, Rebecca and Lydia, acted as agents for these transactions, and Baird took it upon himself to do the ordering. Many of the letters in his personal file were to Beck, with lists of food items she was to purchase and send to Washington in hampers provided for the purpose.

Beck played an active part in many intrafamily affairs. From the regular and frequent correspondence between her and her brother one may infer that she was capable, straightforward, and the family bulwark. Beck never married, and she accepted as her task in life the care of her close relatives, particularly her unmarried older brother, Sam. She was a frequent visitor in the Baird house in Washington and presumably helped Mary Baird in times of illness. She outlived all her brothers and sisters. Lydia was doubtless quietly helpful to Beck, but she remained very much in the background. She was often mentioned in family correspondence, but briefly and without descriptive detail. She, too, remained a spinster and died at the age of forty-nine.

In 1870 Baird took on an additional role, moonlighting as science editor for a newspaper, the *Philadelphia Public Ledger*, and for the Harper brothers' trio of periodic publications, *Harper's Bazaar*, *Harper's Weekly*, and *Harper's Annual Record of Science and Industry*. He was motivated in part by a desire to find a new source of income to replace his earnings from his work on the *Iconographic Encyclopedia*, which had terminated with the volume's publication a few years earlier, and in no small part by another urge. "As Assistant Secretary of the Smithsonian Institution in charge of some of the important departments under the direction of Professor Henry," he wrote to an English correspondent in 1872, "I feel it a duty to the community to assist in the efforts at popularizing science and increasing the number of its votaries."[1]

Baird discussed some of his new tasks in a letter to Sewall Cutting, a cousin of Mary's.

> You are well aware that my position as Assistant Secretary of the Smithsonian Institution gives me access to the finest collection extant, in America

at least, of the transactions of learned societies & scientific journals, the number of foreign journals alone on our exchange list being over 2000 . . . the result of which is that every year adds some five or six thousand volumes of the freshest investigations, supplying therewith important data, months & even years before they are accessible to the ordinary student or compiler.

My duties in charge of this department render it necessary for me to examine the works as they arrive for the purpose of collating them & ascertaining whether the file is complete; & this forced intimacy with the books makes it an easy matter to ascertain the nature of their contents. For many years I have contemplated a digest of the more important facts in these works, but it was not until forced into it by my friend Mr. Geo. W. Childs, who insisted that I should prepare some articles for the Public Ledger, that I seriously undertook the task. . . . now, in addition to the resources of the Smithsonian Institution, I receive direct by mail, sometimes in advance of their actual publication abroad, some sixty (60) foreign periodicals. . . . In order to render my work the more reliable I have associated with me some of the best physicists & naturalists in the country; among them Professors Newcomb and Harkness of Washington, Professors Joy and Newberry of New York, Prof. Cope of Philadelphia, Prof. Verrill of Yale College, & many others; while several foreign scientists of eminence, render me a similar favor.

My plan is to make an examination of every journal as it is received at the Smithsonian Institution or addressed to me by mail & to mark those articles containing interesting matter, & then to prepare an abstract to include the general results, supplementing these or correcting them by information otherwise obtained, & not infrequently combining the indications of several communications or authors into one paragraph. . . . At the present time I have brought my plans to a satisfactory degree of efficiency, &, continuing my connection with the Philadelphia Ledger, I supply such information of an industrial or practical nature as it requires, while the facts and discoveries in archeology, ethnology, natural history, etc. find a place in the Scientific Record of Harper's Magazine, & the items of general intelligence respecting movements & progress in science are printed in the Scientific Intelligence of Harper's Weekly.

Numerous items relating more particularly to household & domestic economy also appear in Harper's Bazaar. So you know, I have the entire control of the scientific departments of the three periodicals of the Mess'rs Harper.[2]

During his later years in Carlisle, Baird had shifted his collecting and study interests from birds to fish, and this continued to be true for a time after his appointment to the Smithsonian. Whereas his agreement to co-write with Agassiz a catalogue of North American freshwater fishes never came to fruition, Baird directed his collecting efforts on summer trips to acquiring specimens of every species of freshwater fish in the eastern United States and Canada.

As Mary's health deteriorated, the family sought cooler climates for her summer comfort. In 1856 they tried Beasley's Point, New Jersey, and in 1863 they made the fortuitous choice of Woods Hole, Massachusetts. As Spencer Baird was hardly a man to lie on the beach in the sun, it is not surprising that he promptly extended his ichthyological interest to the saltwater fish of the Atlantic coast and that he became concerned with a reported decline of commercial fish stocks.

From the coastal fishermen, whom he had characteristically engaged to send him all the unusual species they brought up in their nets, and from representatives of concerned committees in the coastal state legislatures with whom he had established contact, Baird came to believe that populations of such commercially important food fish species as shad, striped bass, tautog, sea bass, and scup had been steadily diminishing. Presumably his informants produced persuasive statistical evidence to support their claims, for by the late 1860s Baird had become convinced that the problem required serious attention. In December 1870, he sent a report on the situation to the chairman of the House Committee on Appropriations in which he recommended that "an item be introduced in one or another of the bills in your hands, providing the sum of say five thousand dollars, or as much thereof as may be necessary, to be expended . . . in prosecuting investigations into the subject of the food fishes of the Atlantic Coast, with a view of ascertaining what remedy can be applied toward securing the supply against its present rapid diminution." In a communication to the Committee on Appropriations, dated January 3, 1871, Baird added a further thought. "I would, therefore, suggest the appointment of a Fish Commissioner, on the part of the United States, whose duty it shall be to prosecute this investigation, and report upon these points to Congress."[3]

Baird then assisted the influential senator George F. Edmunds of Vermont, whom he had met through George P. Marsh and with whom he had developed a close personal friendship, in drafting a joint bill, which was passed by both houses and signed by President Grant early in 1871. Under its terms the president was authorized "to appoint, by and with the advice and consent of the Senate, from among the civil officers or employees of the Government, one person of proved scientific and practical acquaintance with the fishes of the coast, to be Commissioner of Fish and Fisheries, to serve without additional salary."[4]

There was only one man in government service who fit this job description, and President Grant promptly appointed Spencer Fullerton Baird United States Commissioner of Fish and Fisheries—without additional salary. Baird promptly accepted the appointment, which indeed he had created for himself, and thus took on a considerable new task in addition to his other official duties and his personal interests and concerns.

From 1871 on, the Bairds spent their summers in coastal New England, where Baird could best devote his attention to Fish Commission business. They were in Woods Hole, Massachusetts, in 1871; Eastport, Maine, in 1872; Peake's Island, Maine, in 1873; Noank, Connecticut, in 1874; again in Woods Hole in 1875; and Gloucester, Massachusetts, in 1878.

While Baird had for a time turned his principal research interest to the study of fish and other vertebrates, he had never lost his love for birds, and shortly after beginning work at the Smithsonian, he had written to his friend John Cassin, "I am getting back a little of my old ornithological enthusiasm, and expect to be somewhat of a ornithologist one of these days."[5] He was not exaggerating. By 1864 he had published the catalogue and review of the birds of North America and his distribution and migration monograph, and in 1874 *A History of North American Birds: Land Birds* appeared, co-written by Baird, Thomas M. Brewer, and Robert Ridgway. It was an extensive study providing both the taxonomic description of all American bird species discovered and classified up to that time and their habits and behavior. Planned was a sister volume on water birds, which for economic reasons was not published until years later. Brought out by Little, Brown, and Company, *A History of North American Birds: Land Birds* was the first commercially published book in which Baird had had a hand since the *Iconographic Encyclopedia*. He was obliged to keep up a very extensive correspondence, covering his negotiations with editors, colorers, engravers, and printers. Much of this effort involved his work with Professor Josiah Dwight Whitney on Whitney's volume about the birds of California. These were his final efforts in both birding and publishing, however, as demanding responsibilities in other fields usurped ever more of his time and attention.

In 1872 Secretary Henry turned over to Baird full administrative responsibility for the United States National Museum, and from that time on, much of his time was spent in negotiations with Congress over budgets and funding. (At Henry's insistence, federal appropriations for the museum were handled through the Department of the Interior, although budgets and expenses were prepared and approved by the Smithsonian, a singularly complicated arrangement, but one under which Smithsonian funds were protected from any financial responsibility for the museum.) Comparable but less complicated management responsibilities for the Fish Commission obliged Baird to leave ichthyological research to colleagues as well, although he kept in close touch with all operations in both areas and found time to initiate and actively monitor the practice of fish culture on a major scale.

Baird accepted the Fish Commission assignment not only without salary but also without having any provision made for a headquarters. At first, as his work consisted of just the mandated investigation, working space did not pose a problem. However, as the scope of the commission's operations expanded under his management, and since Secretary Henry was firmly opposed to having non-Smithsonian activities conducted on Smithsonian premises, Baird felt the need for a house large enough to provide both living accommodations and office space for the Fish Commission. Therefore, in 1875 he and Mary purchased a building lot at 1445 Massachusetts Avenue, where they proposed to build a new and more commodious house. Since Baird's salary plus his moonlighting income was just enough to cover their living expenses, money was a problem, but fortunately a source was found within the Baird family.

The youngest of the Baird sisters, Mary—or Molly, as she was generally known—had in 1854 married a distant cousin, Henry J. Biddle, the well-to-do head of a successful investment house in Philadelphia. Commissioned in the Union Army at the outset of the war, he was wounded and taken prisoner in 1862. When he died that year in a Confederate prisoner-of-war camp, he left his widow with three sons and two daughters, and quite well provided for. Spencer and Molly had always enjoyed a warm older brother–youngest sister association, and Molly greatly admired her successful older brother. Now she came to his aid by offering him a loan of twelve thousand dollars to build his new house, which he gratefully accepted. Furthermore, on his recommendation, she bought the adjacent lot and built a house as an investment. This brought them into a very close relationship, and Molly became Spencer's closest sibling contact after Will's death in 1872.

Molly never remarried after her husband's death, and she devoted herself to raising her lively family. She inherited her grandmother's business acumen, managing her affairs skillfully, and spent much of her time in Europe with her daughters. Her three sons frequently called on their uncle Spencer for help with various problems and activities, from an application to the dean at Princeton to reinstate the eldest after suspension for a student prank to participation in western exploring expeditions. (It was Molly's second son, Spencer, who was killed on the frontier in 1877.)

In 1876 the United States celebrated the centennial of its independence with an international commemorative exposition in Philadelphia. Baird took on a new role in this connection. On Secretary Henry's recommendation he was appointed a member of the Interdepartmental Board, charged with presenting the government exhibits. His responsibility was the organization and display of the exhibits of the Smithsonian Institution, the United States National Museum, and the United States Commission of Fish and Fisheries. Congress appropriated monies "as a loan" to cover the government participation in the exposition, subject to the interesting proviso that should receipts be sufficient to enable the exposition directors to repay the loan, Congress would authorize the use of part of the reimbursement for construction of a new building to house the United States National Museum.

The need for additional space to accommodate the steadily growing collections now straining the Smithsonian's facilities had become imperative, and both Henry and Baird had been appealing to Congress regularly for help. However, with the Civil War debts hanging over their heads, few members of either house were disposed to vote for major expenditures for a museum. It may well have been that the attachment of this proviso to the exposition loan was a ploy to get Baird and company off Congress's back and that no one seriously expected the exposition to pay for itself. If so, Congress failed to reckon with Spencer Baird.

Baird and two assistants whom he personally selected, Professor William P. Blake, an innovative mineralogist, and Colonel Thomas Donaldson, whom the *New York Times* described some years later in an obituary as "having had a larger acquaintance with public men than any other man in the country," had already begun in 1874 to put together what were ultimately rated as the most popular exhibits in the immensely successful exposition. Baird and his assistants organized a two-part display. The first part was an exhibit on the Smithsonian itself with emphasis on its research role. The second part offered a dramatic representation of the natural history of the United States, covering its ethnology and its animal and mineral resources, including displays on the economic values of those resources. The editor of a popular and respected journal of the time wrote, "The Government exhibit was considered by all visitors as decidedly the best part of the International Exhibition, in view of the extent and exhaustiveness of the collection and the method and order of its display."[6]

Baird spent most of the hot summer of 1876 in Philadelphia, until the heat became unbearable to Mary. He monitored and continually improved his exhibits, and served on committees and judging panels. In addition, he spent much of his time quietly persuading representatives of the American states and of foreign countries participating in the exposition to donate to the Smithsonian the contents of their exhibits instead of going to the expense of shipping them home at the end of the exposition. He later circulated to all exhibitors a letter introducing Colonel Donaldson, who as agent for the United States National Museum was "to secure for the same various articles illustrating the technical Arts and Industries. . . . He will explain more fully the plan of the Smithsonian Institution in connection with the National Museum, and show in what way the contribution desired may be of benefit to yourself as well as to the cause the Smithsonian has at heart."[7]

The exposition was a tremendous success. It broke even, the directors repaid the congressional loan, and two years later Congress allocated funds to build the promised museum building. Hardly soon enough, however, since the persuasive efforts of Baird and Donaldson had resulted in enough donations after the close of the exposition to fill sixty freight-car loads, which, as Baird noted, was "a quantity far beyond the storage capacity of the Smithsonian building." He noted further that in anticipation of needing storage for these donations Congress had already authorized the transfer to the Smithsonian of the Armory building on the square between Sixth and Seventh streets, where the bulk of the collections were stored until the new building (the present Arts and Industries Building) was opened in 1881.[8]

Baird enjoyed nearly six months of relative quiet after the work of packing up and shipping to Washington the exposition exhibits. However, his reputation as the official with the widest knowledge of American fisheries had come to the attention of Secretary of State William M. Evarts, who called for his expertise in a difficult negotiating session with the British and Canadians over fishing rights in Canadian waters. The Treaty of Washington, signed in 1871 between the three countries regulating these rights, was expiring in an atmosphere of tension over differences of interpretation between American and Canadian fishermen. United States boats were being harassed and in some cases seized by Canadian authorities, who had also, with British backing, raised a substantial damage claim against the United States.

Secretary Evarts appointed Baird a member of the United States delegation to the negotiating session, scheduled to convene in Halifax, Nova Scotia, in the summer of 1877. The diplomatic members of the delegation relied on the professional knowledge of the United States fish commissioner to support their defensive position. Consequently, the Baird family was obliged to spend the summer months in Halifax. While Baird was universally praised for what delegation member Richard Henry Dana described as "the clearness, fairness, and weight of authority with which he delivered himself," the position of the United States was weakened because neither Baird nor his colleagues had the Canadians' grasp of detailed statistical information on their country's commercial fishing industries or their scientific knowledge of the populations and movements of mackerel, the fish species of most direct concern. In a decision which

SPENCER BAIRD OF THE SMITHSONIAN

shocked all Americans, the arbitration panel levied a heavy judgement against the United States and awarded operational concessions to both sides.[9]

On Baird's return to the Smithsonian in the fall of 1877, he found himself in the role of acting secretary. Joseph Henry's health was rapidly failing, and he was increasingly less capable of running the Institution. Inevitably, the succession question loomed ever larger in Baird's thoughts. He had a clear concept of the role he felt the Smithsonian Institution should fill in America, and he nursed troubling premonitions of what might happen if some unqualified political favorite should be appointed to the secretaryship after Joseph Henry's death. He saw himself as the one person who could reliably carry on the policies established by Secretary Henry and himself. Furthermore, he wanted the job. It was the target of his entire life's ambitions.

Consequently, he wrote confidential letters to two of his particular friends on the Board of Regents, James D. Dana, his first sponsor for the assistant secretaryship, and Asa Gray, his principal supporter in the National Academy membership fight, soliciting their intercession on his behalf with their fellow regents. In two letters to Gray, both dated March 12, 1878, the depth of his concern is evident. He described Henry's decline and noted that applicants from many areas of the country, including his cousin Professor John LeConte of Philadelphia, were already contacting some of the regents. In the second of these letters he added:

I need hardly say that in the event of the very great misfortune of the loss of Prof. Henry, that if chosen by the Board of Regents to fill his place, I should endeavor to carry out his policy and the traditions of the Institution to the best of my ability, feeling that having myself assisted to evolve and determine most of its directions of a [illegible], I have a right to look forward to the succession, even though I may be unfit to occupy in all respects Prof. Henry's chair. I doubt whether there is anyone who has a poorer opinion of myself than I have in many respects; but I think I can continue in the future as well as in the past, the general routine of the Smithsonian. I am now very nearly the age that Prof. Henry was when I joined him in Washington, and I can ask, I think, no better fortune than to have some young man associated with me who would discharge his duty to me and to the Institution as honestly as I am conscious of having done, or at least endeavored to do in my time. The discussion of the succession to Prof. Henry was one that I hoped would be repressed as long as possible, but as it is being brought up all over the country I think it proper to take some action in my own behalf. May I ask you to confer with President Porter and ascertain what his views are on this subject, and whether he may be inclined from what he may know or from what you can tell him to put aside without affecting any efforts that may be made by rivals to supplant me in the Institution.[10]

On May 13, 1878, Joseph Henry died. On May 17, the day following Henry's funeral, the Board of Regents unanimously elected Spencer Baird to be secretary of the Smithsonian Institution. In his first annual report as secretary, in 1878, Baird wrote, "Honored by the Board in being selected to succeed Professor Henry, it was with the greatest diffidence, and with an unaffected distrust in my ability to administer worthily the operations of the Institution, that I accepted the trust."[11]

Chapter Twelve

Secretary
1878–1887

Thou hast it now: King, Cawdor, Glamis, all.
—William Shakespeare
Macbeth

As MACBETH MIGHT HAVE WARNED HIM, Baird found the anticipation of becoming secretary of the Smithsonian Institution more satisfying than the fulfillment. He soon learned that the administrative chores and kindred burdens of the position obliged him to pass entirely to others the collecting, the classifying, and the study of natural history, in which he had found his greatest satisfaction throughout his life.

When Spencer Baird wrote to Asa Gray requesting his intercession with the chairman of the Smithsonian Board of Regents to assure his accession to the secretaryship on Joseph Henry's death, he assured Gray that he would "endeavor to carry out his [Henry's] policy and the traditions of the Institution to the best of my ability."[1] Baird did continue a number of the programs which meant so much to his predecessor. He continued to make Smithsonian funds available in support of explorations (with the assurance that resultant collections would come to the United

States National Museum), he maintained and even increased the system of international exchanges, he supported the publication of scientific papers in each new volume of *Smithsonian Contributions to Knowledge*, and in the annual reports, and he followed Henry's practice of allowing none of the associated agencies under his control to draw on the Smithson funds, which he reserved scrupulously for expenses directly identified with the Smithsonian. At the same time, however, Baird initiated changes which totally altered the character of the Institution. Since his time the Smithsonian has followed the course that he charted, progressively becoming a complex of national museums of the United States' scientific and cultural achievements, managed by the Smithsonian Institution as its policy-making and administrative headquarters.

An essential key to Baird's success in this development was his outstanding managerial talent. He had an extraordinarily systematic memory in which he kept every administrative detail accessible—a capability he had already demonstrated in both his taxonomic work and his management of the Smithsonian's international exchange program. As secretary, his demonstration of this talent proved awesome as he kept the funding and accounting for four diverse and complex entities separate and in order. The interest on the Smithson fund, supplemented on occasion by private donations for special purposes was the source of the financing for the Smithsonian Institution. The United States National Museum was funded by congressional appropriations channeled through the Department of the Interior. Federal appropriations covered the operations of the Fish Commission and were allocated directly to the commission. And after 1879 congressional funds were directed to the Smithsonian for the Bureau of American Ethnology and routed through the United States National Museum. Baird accepted direct personal responsibility for each of these entities and handled all their complexities with such precision that he was never questioned on his administration of any account for which he was responsible.

The changes in the focus of the Smithsonian under the Baird administration are evident in its annual financial statements. In a memoir, which he read before the National Academy of Sciences two years after Baird's death, Dr. John S. Billings called attention to some major changes in the use of Smithsonian funds which took place soon after Baird's assumption of the secretaryship.

> The average annual expenditure for original research for 1850 to 1877 was a little over $2000 a year. After Professor Baird took charge, in 1878, it fell to $802.80 for each of the next three years, and then ceased entirely. In like manner the expenditures for apparatus and for laboratory were soon cut off after 1878, while, on the other hand, the expenditures for collection and for explorations more than doubled, being in the main for the benefit of the National Museum. The character of the publications also changed; the cost of the Smithsonian contributions to knowledge, which from 1870 to 1877 averaged $8,140.71 per annum fell to an average of $3,270.83 annually during the next ten years, while the cost of the annual reports more than doubled in the same time.[2]

What Billings failed to note was that reductions in many Smithsonian activities and expenditures were more than counterbalanced by a rise in comparable efforts at the United States National Museum, through which original research continued to be conducted and which published its own annual reports beginning in 1886. In addition, research activities and resultant publications which in Joseph Henry's time might well have been attributed to the Smithsonian Institution were now being produced under the aegis of the Fish Commission. Baird's predominant interests were in these two Smithsonian stepchildren, and under his management the Institution itself became largely an executive headquarters monitoring its operating divisions.

In 1879 a new operating agency was placed under the Smithsonian's administrative roof. In that year the four major surveys of the trans-Mississippi region, which had up to then been supported by separate congressional appropriations, were consolidated into a single bureau, the United States Geological Survey, headed by Clarence King and administered by the Department of the Interior. At the same time, Major John Wesley Powell, who had directed one of the surveys, arranged to have all of the anthropological work brought together in a separate agency, the Bureau of American Ethnology (BAE).

Powell felt that the Department of Interior would be too vulnerable to political pressures to be a safe repository for his long-term scientific work. At his urging Congress placed the BAE under the administration of the

Smithsonian Institution, where it was allied with the United States National Museum but funded in its own name, thus adding to Baird's administrative responsibilities an important and semiautonomous new organization. Baird promptly called on Powell to assume its direction.

During his nine years as secretary, Baird had the good fortune to have capable and reasonably congenial assistants as directors of two of these entities—George Brown Goode as assistant director of the National Museum, and Powell as director of the BAE. Nevertheless, he chose to bear the entire supervisory load himself and deliberately appointed no assistant secretary until the last year of his life. Furthermore, for as long as he could, he held all these organizations on a very tight rein, never allowing any of his subordinates even the degree of independence he had enjoyed under Henry.

Consequently, from 1878 on, Baird was obliged to devote almost all of his attention to administrative management. He wrote that he devoted his mornings to Fish Commission affairs and his afternoons and evenings to the Smithsonian and its two adjunct bureaus. He had little time for scientific researches or publication. By mutual agreement with *Harper's* and the *Tribune* he brought his science editor functions to an end, and his direct association with collection acquisition and collector recruitment became a thing of the past.

There were compensations, however. Many prestigious societies at home and abroad elected him to honorary membership, he received honors and awards from many other societies, admiring followers named a host of newly discovered animal species for him, and Harvard University awarded him an honorary degree of doctor of law at the commencement ceremony commemorating the university's bicentennial.[3] Baird's Fish Commission work brought him notable international recognition in 1880. Profiting from the experience he had gained at the 1876 exposition, he designed and put together with the assistance of George Brown Goode the United States exhibit that received the First Honor Prize at the International Fisheries Exhibition in Berlin. Although Baird did not attend the exhibition himself (he sent Goode as his representative), the emperor of Germany and king of Prussia personally announced the award of the grand prize "to Spencer Fullerton Baird, in recognition of his efforts as the official head of the American Department, and especially of his personal attainments and service as a scientific investigator of the fisheries, and as a fish culturist." In further endorsement, the president of the prestigious Deutsche Fischerei Verein (German Fisheries Union) stated in a banquet speech that Baird was "recognized throughout Europe as the first fish culturist of the world."[4]

Baird was at last his own boss. His senior scientific critics, Agassiz and Bache, had died; the honor accorded him in political and social circles in Washington had never been higher; Congress granted almost any request he made; and he derived real pleasure from his summers in Woods Hole. Yet, in other areas, Baird faced troubling difficulties. By the end of 1880 all of his old friends had died, Mary's chronic illness was a constant trial for him, and his own health began to cause him serious concern. Moreover, Baird's relations with several of his closest subordinates caused him continual worry.

His administrative dealings with John Wesley Powell were never easy after the BAE came under Baird's administration. Although their personal relationship was friendly, they differed strongly on methods, and perhaps even more strongly on the use of funds. Baird and Powell had known and cooperated with each other for a number of years before 1879. In 1871 Congress had provided funds through the Smithsonian for Powell's famous Colorado River survey, and Baird had had an active interest in the results. Powell had proposed to Baird that he would collect for him in the Grand Canyon the nests and eggs of three species of swift which he had observed there, and in 1873 Baird furnished him with collecting instructions and his desiderata for the Colorado River exploration of that year.

In October of 1875 Baird wrote Powell requesting a summary of his activities for inclusion in *Harper's Annual Record of Science and Industry*, and in 1876 Powell's report of his 1873 exploration was published "with the concurrence of the Secretary of the Smithsonian Institution" in a new Smithsonian series entitled Contributions to North American Ethnology. Also, both Baird and Powell shared a strong interest in the work of a young anthropologist named Frank Hamilton Cushing, whom Baird had employed to help with the Indian exhibits at the Philadelphia exposition in 1876 and who subsequently reported to both Baird and Powell on his spectacular work among the Zunis in New Mexico. In 1879 Powell stepped down as acting president of Washington's illustrious Cosmos Club (of which he had been chief organizer) to permit the election of Baird, the club's first formally elected president. Each respected the other's professional achievements. In 1880 Clarence King resigned as head of the United States Geological Survey and nominated Powell for his successor. It is reliably reported that President James Garfield consulted only Baird on the nomination and, after hearing Baird's endorsement, promptly sent Powell's name to the Senate for confirmation.[5]

Baird, however, believed that the way to find basic truths in scientific research was to assemble large collections of physical specimens and to develop conclusions from careful comparisons of tangible artifacts. Powell felt equally strongly that the study of linguistics and cultural behavior was the key to understanding primitive peoples. Baird pressed for the collection of Indian artifacts and their study by his people in the United States National Museum's Department of Anthropology, while Powell's Bureau of American Ethnology staff focused their attention on the development of Indian language dictionaries and the study of mythologies and cultural behavior. But Baird, as congressionally appointed director of the National Museum, was Powell's boss. He thus had control over the allocation of BAE funds, and this brought them into conflict.

Early in their association, Baird had advanced National Museum funds to Powell for an exploration in the Sandwich [Hawaiian] Islands by Captain Clarence Edward Dutton. As repayment, he demanded that Powell turn over to the museum a part of the annual BAE appropriation, and he made further demands, as he explained to Assistant Director Goode in a letter on August 10, 1882.

> I have asked Major Powell to arrange for the payment of the salaries of Dr. Rau and Dr. Foreman [both National Museum anthropologists] from the Ethnological appropriation, and also to reserve $5000 to be expended under the special direction of the Smithsonian Institution in archeological research. I do not know whether he will kick against this or not, but I think I shall insist upon it.
>
> I have also told him that he ought to pay the salaries of all persons connected with the Geological and Mineral work. It is true he pays them now,

but that is simply for the purpose of making up the advance by the Smithsonian Institution to Capt. Dutton during the explorations in the Sandwich Is. It does not help the appropriation of the Museum in any way. I think it will be necessary for him to add some additional names to his rolls, at least for the few months necessary to settle the entire account.[6]

There were other disagreements on this score, and in August 1883 Powell did "kick" politely but heatedly in a long letter to Baird.

I beg permission to state that I think it unwise that the fund should be diverted from the purpose for which the appropriation was made, namely for research, and devoted to the building up of the Museum.

I also wish to express a regret that the Secretary of the Smithsonian should take a part of the fund from under my control, and should further employ assistants in the Museum who are not under my direction. . . .

I beg leave to suggest that the Bureau of Ethnology is an institution created by myself, that its plans are my own, and that whatever success it has achieved has been through my labors: that to this work I have devoted the larger share of my time for the last 13 years, and that I cannot see it gradually taken from me without some feeling of disappointment.[7]

Baird stood his ground. He insisted in a response to Powell that as long as the Smithsonian was responsible for the BAE, he would control and approve its budgets and estimates. He reminded Powell firmly that the BAE had been transferred to the Smithsonian at his (Powell's) request, not the Smithsonian's, and he added that if Powell would prefer to move to another department or to set up his own independent bureau, the Smithsonian would not stand in the way. But his most telling argument was that there was little sympathy or understanding in Congress for philology. He asserted that the only sure way to secure appropriations for anthropological research was, in his experience, to stress that if Americans did not hurry to collect the valuable Indian artifacts in the West, Europeans would get them, and Americans would then have to go to Europe to study the origins and cultures of their own native peoples.[8]

Powell gave in, but not without a final protest.

I have expressed my opinions about the work of the Bureau freely, as it has been my practice to consult with you about matters more freely than with any other person for many years. In this matter of the Bureau I am immediately under your instruction and hold myself subject thereto. I shall therefore interpret your letter as instructions to continue Mr. Palmer and Mr.

Walther upon the rolls of the Bureau. In order to do so I must cut off some other work in progress and discharge men in my employ whom I trust; and retain one at least who is personally objectionable to myself. . . . Please understand me. I think the work should be done, that it is important for the Survey and the Museum alike; but I do not wish to be put in the attitude of doing work that properly belongs to the Museum and have it considered a favor to myself.[9]

Baird carried his exercise of control even further. On August 20, 1883, he instructed the Smithsonian's chief clerk, William J. Rhees (whom he had left in charge during his summer absence in Woods Hole), to confer with F. W. True and BAE administrators regarding some difficulties with handling BAE mail, about which Powell had protested. "I want you to start . . . with this postulate: that we require a record of everything that comes within our building, and also, a statement of its disposition. If Maj. P. receives certain packages, we want the fact noted, and also that they have been transferred to him. We have nothing to do with the senders or the contents; but there can be no divided sovereignty in this matter."[10]

Baird had reason not to alienate Powell, as he noted in a letter to True near the time of the preceding exchanges. "I do not want anyone to think that Major Powell is in antagonism to the National Museum. I wish to cooperate with him in all respects, and think that an arrangement will be made of mutual benefit. It will require the concurrent efforts of both to get the new building, and if I press him too hard, he may manage to have it assigned exclusively to himself, which would not suit our purpose at all."[11]

That a compromise was reached is evident, for the BAE remained attached to the Smithsonian, although Powell had let it be known that he was considering a change (as Baird mentioned in a letter to Colonel Donaldson dated March 28, 1884). It is equally clear that friction remained. Baird wrote to Goode on July 1, 1884:

Major Powell entirely mistakes the theory of the transaction between us. The understanding was that in view of my relinquishing control of the $5000 of the Ethnological appropriation he was to pay $5000 of any salaries I chose to designate. The original arrangement had nothing to do with any question between the Geological Survey & the National Museum. I certainly cannot consent to give up, in any respect, control of any gentlemen we may transfer to his payroll. I think upon the whole you had better say that there is probably some misunderstanding, & suggest his writing to me on the subject.[12]

Baird and Powell must have reached an amicable settlement; after 1884 there are no further written evidences of dispute. On January 11, 1888, the Meeting Commemorative of the Life and Scientific Work of Spencer Fullerton Baird was held under the joint auspices of the Anthropological, Biological, and Philosophical Societies of Washington. The most moving of the papers delivered on that occasion was entitled "The Personal Characteristics of Professor Baird." The speaker was John Wesley Powell.[13]

Baird's disputes with Powell were undoubtedly irritating, but to a large extent bad feelings were mitigated by their agreeable social relations. More troublesome were the continual problems Baird confronted in his work with the two senior members of the administrative staff of the Smithsonian: William J. Rhees, chief clerk, and Daniel J. Leech, correspondence clerk and next in line to Rhees. Joseph Henry had hired Rhees in 1853 as general assistant and had promoted him to the post of chief clerk two years later. In this role he was the principal administrative officer of the Institution, with ever-growing responsibilities as the Smithsonian increased in size and activity. Thus by the time Baird became secretary of the Smithsonian, he and Rhees had worked in close proximity for twenty-five years, although in separate areas and with little evidence of close interaction.

During the summer months, when both Henry and Baird were away from Washington, Rhees was frequently the senior officer present, and consequently in charge. At those times, on matters requiring prompt decisions he often corresponded with Baird, who was easier to reach than the peripatetic Henry. And Baird often requested from Rhees information on what rearrangements the secretary was making with Baird's collections when Henry was in town and starting one of his periodic housecleaning rampages. Otherwise, there appear to have been relatively few direct interactions between the assistant secretary and the chief clerk while Joseph Henry retained his tight hold on Smithsonian administration.

Trouble between Baird and Rhees began soon after Baird became secretary. It apparently stemmed from three principal sources. First was the fact that Baird held Rhees (and indeed all of his immediate subordinates) on a much tighter rein than had Joseph Henry. Within limits Henry had delegated considerable authority, giving his employees a free hand to run their divisions as long as he was satisfied that he could rely on them to stay within bounds. His fiscal responsibility was almost entirely centered on the Smithson fund, for which he was accountable primarily to the regents. He took seriously the claim that since he was not a federal official, he could not legally be in charge of federal funds, and he saw to it that congressional funding for the United States National Museum was therefore channeled through the Department of the Interior.

Baird, on the other hand, had two federal appointments, one as United States Commissioner of Fish and Fisheries and the other as director of the United States National Museum. Although the secretary of the interior continued to be accountable for National Museum funds during Baird's years as secretary, Baird was responsible directly to Congress for Fish Commission funds and, after 1879, for BAE money, and he took these responsibilities very seriously. Hence he maintained even tighter control than his predecessor over all expenditures and disbursements, including Smithsonian accounts, to Rhees's outspoken dissatisfaction.

A second source of unhappiness for Rhees was what he regarded as Baird's neglect of the Smithsonian as he focused his attention on its newly attached elements. Rhees was intensely loyal to the Smithsonian and to the dominant role the Institution had been playing under Joseph Henry— a role to which he had himself devoted twenty-five years by the time of Baird's accession to the secretaryship in 1878. He was clearly distressed by the change in the role of the Institution which he saw taking place under Baird. In a long memorandum of general unhappiness, which he delivered to Baird in 1884, Rhees wrote, "It has been impracticable to establish from the Smithsonian fund a large *Library* . . . or a *Museum*." After noting that even the early studies in meteorology had been abandoned, he observed: "There is at present no distinctive and well-defined scientific object to which the Institution gives its attention. Its work is mainly and almost exclusively 'Administration.'"[14]

A third cause of unhappiness for Rhees was undoubtedly that even as assistant secretary, Baird had maintained a distance in their relationship of superior toward employee of lesser social status. Baird's attitude became even more evident after he became secretary, but while still assistant secretary, he wrote a letter to Rhees from the Philadelphia exposition that illustrates his peremptory tone. "In a letter written to you some weeks ago to which you paid no attention, I sent a bill to be paid from the Montana appropriation for mineral cases, and asked you to give me a statement of the expenditures on that fund. Please let me have this at once."[15]

Rhees could hardly have been other than sensitive to the distance Baird kept between them in comparison to the Bairds' social acceptance of Powell, Goode, Donaldson, Thomas B. Ferguson, and the many scientists, students, and collectors who worked in proximity to one another and to Baird. The Baird home was always open to these assistants, yet there is no indication in Baird's journals or correspondence that Rhees or his family were ever invited by the Bairds socially, or that Baird ever invited Rhees to take part in any of the excursions by land or sea in which he regularly included other colleagues.

On Baird's side it must be noted that throughout his administration, squabbles between Rhees and his subordinates and the administrators of the other three agencies were ceaseless and inevitably required Baird's intervention. Rhees and Daniel Leech, the correspondence clerk, were constantly at odds with each other, and each regularly appealed to Baird to intercede. To one such appeal from Rhees in 1880, Baird replied: "I do not know what I shall do if I have another touchy gentleman on my hands requiring to be continually pacified. Mr. Leech is a pretty good load to carry and I do not crave an additional element of the same character." In 1884 when another spat between the two surfaced, Baird wrote Rhees, "You may rest assured that knowing the feelings entertained by yourself and Mr. Leech towards each other, I shall not take sides, but where any action on my part is necessary, hear both parties before coming to a conclusion."[16]

During Baird's summer absences in Woods Hole, when Rhees was in charge of daily activities in Washington, there were frequent differences between Rhees and Charles W. Smiley, the administrative officer of the Fish Commission, over the handling of mail that went to the Smithsonian but related to the commission; between Rhees and Goode, with regard to administrative overlap; and between Rhees and Powell, also regarding administrative matters. One cannot but wonder at Baird's reluctance to appoint a deputy who might have relieved him of at least some of these annoyances, but he seemed determined to keep all administrative and operational matters under his direct personal control.

In 1884 Baird appears to have sensed some employee dissatisfaction, for he sent a personal memorandum to all Smithsonian staff members in which he requested descriptions of their duties, together with their comments and suggestions. Most of the members of the staff submitted one- or two-page replies, with general expressions of satisfaction. Rhees, however, seized this opportunity to express his concern over what he regarded as the secretary's intrusions into his prerogatives as chief clerk and a senior officer of the Institution. He returned two long memoranda, listing in the first memorandum sixty-six specific duties that he regarded as the proper functions of the chief clerk. To these he added nine pages of more generalized functions, including work he was called upon to do with the National Museum and the Fish Commission, and drew the strong conclusion that for these he merited a substantial increase in salary. Rhees's second memo was entitled "Memorandum of Some of the Work That Ought to Be Done." He noted another sixty-six items of administrative and logistic nature, ranging from filing systems to building maintenance. And to this memorandum he appended a thirteen-page paper entitled "Remarks Relative to the Organization of the Smithsonian Institution," in which he stated his principal complaints. After describing his long experience and broad qualifications as chief clerk, he added:

> Not only the theory but the practice has been, until recently, to entrust the Chief Clerk with ample powers to act on all matters of routine . . . where no new line of policy or unusual expenditures were involved. . . .
>
> The Secretary, however, has thought it proper to deprive the Chief Clerk of the power to make any expenditures whatever, even for the simplest and most necessary articles, or to exercise many of the functions hitherto believed to pertain to his office.[17]

The only answer from Baird to be found among the Rhees papers in the Smithsonian Institution Archives is a brief and hastily scribbled note (partially illegible) in Baird's handwriting on what seems to be a piece of scrap paper. In it Baird rejected Rhees's description of the Smithsonian's work as "purely Administrative" and insisted that since the secretary alone is responsible to Congress, he cannot delegate authority over the expenditure of Smithsonian funds.

There are numerous additional examples of Baird's firm, even unsympathetic, treatment of Rhees. It is not surprising that when a memorial ceremony was held to honor Baird the year after his death Rhees was not a contributor. Instead, a favorable account of Baird as an administrator was presented by William B. Taylor, who had served a relatively short time as administrative officer of the National Museum.

Chapter Thirteen

United States Fish Commissioner

On a June day in 1871, a large, well-dressed, distinguished man in his fifties stepped briskly from the coach that brought the passengers of the Old Colony Railroad from Monument Beach to Woods Hole. The face of the newcomer, with his well-trimmed slightly curly beard and shaved upper lip, was familiar to some of the local residents gathered to watch the daily arrival of the coach. They recognized him as an important person from Washington who in 1863 came here to spend part of the summer fishing and resting. . . .

The newcomer was the famous zoologist and naturalist, Spencer Fullerton Baird, Assistant Secretary of the Smithsonian Institution and newly appointed, by President Grant, first U.S. Commissioner of Fisheries.[1]

Baird's arrival on this occasion caused little stir in the tranquil fishing village of Woods Hole, Massachusetts. Yet it was an event that was to change the character of the area fundamentally. Within a very few years, Woods Hole would become one of the world's great marine biological and oceanographic research centers, a direct result of its selection by Baird as an ideal location for the pursuit of his congressionally assigned research mandate.

Yet if Spencer Baird's arrival in 1871 could be said to have changed the destiny of Woods Hole, certainly no less can be said of its effect on the destiny of Spencer Baird. His appointment as fish commissioner projected him into an entirely new role—a role in which he became an experimenter, a seeker of solutions to two riddles for which neither the collection and classification of specimens nor any other previous experience could have fitted him.

First of these riddles was the question which Congress had, at Baird's urging, created the Fish Commission to find an answer to: What was causing the reported depletion of commercially valuable fish stocks on the Atlantic coast? And the second was a question Baird himself raised after he was in Fish Commission harness: Can depleted ocean fish populations be restored and even increased by release of fish propagated in hatcheries and raised to a suitable size?

Not that Baird abandoned his interest in collection and classification, or that his skill at museum and laboratory development did not come into play. Indeed, his spectacular success in both of these fields at Woods Hole has obscured the fact that he was notably unsuccessful in fulfilling his assigned mission. He expended his energy and his political persuasiveness in pursuit of what proved to be false leads as to the cause of the reduction of food fish, he failed to persuade any of the coastal states to take the action he promoted, and he never came up with any scientific explanation of the decrease—or indeed any proof that there was a decrease of a permanent character. He did investigate and eliminate some of the suspected causes of the decline, but his idea for a remedy, marine fish culture, was altogether speculative and without any scientific basis, and it proved to be as ineffective a restorative for ocean fish populations as Thomas H. Huxley had predicted it would be when the subject was considered in England.

By 1870, when Baird became directly interested, fishermen, fisheries officials, and fish dealers in New England were already divided into opposing camps with regard to the cause of reduced harvests of scup, a particularly popular food fish; of menhaden; and of the anadromous fishes shad and salmon, which leave the sea and enter freshwater rivers and estuaries to spawn. The so-called dory fishermen, who fished from small boats near the coast, and the sport fishermen insisted that a relatively small group of entrepreneurs, who had larger capital resources and thus could afford to put up fish traps and weirs in coastal waters and across the mouths of rivers and estuaries, were responsible for a depletion in populations of the fish in question. They reasoned that the commercial fishermen not only caught an unfairly large number of these fish but also prevented the anadromous fish from entering their spawning grounds, thus interfering with their annual reproduction. The trap owners and the dealers who profited from their abundant harvests argued in turn that there was no proof of this claim, and fought any effort to restrict their style of fishing.

In the coastal states of New England, debate waxed hot on this issue during the early 1870s. Baird accepted the views of the dory fishermen, as did many of the state fish commission officials. Connecticut had, as early as 1868, passed restrictive legislation calling for the elimination of fish traps by 1871. It is curious that without any scientifically demonstrable evidence of either depletion or presumed cause, Baird accepted the existence of both and did his best to persuade the fish commissions and the legislatures of Maine, Massachusetts, and Rhode Island to restrict the use of these devices at least to alternate days of the week. The Rhode Islanders seriously considered restrictive legislation along the lines he urged, but dropped the idea when they found that their neighbors in Massachusetts were continuing to let their fishermen fish in the usual way. Even Connecticut made no effort to carry out its restrictions, and soon repealed them.

Baird then sought an alternative solution in fish culture, which was being developed (under far more controllable conditions) by several newly established private trout hatcheries. However, so great was its faith in his expertise that in 1872 Congress made an initial appropriation of fifteen thousand dollars to permit Fish Commissioner Baird to initiate a program for the propagation of food fishes—an amount which by the time of Baird's death in 1887 had grown to two hundred thousand dollars annually. With these funds Baird made extensive efforts to establish viable populations of anadromous fish: shad, salmon, and striped bass (rockfish), in particular, in eastern rivers, as well as whitefish in the Great Lakes, and cod and halibut in the sea. On the Atlantic coast his efforts were a total failure, as were the endeavors of his Midwest agent, James W. Milner, to increase whitefish populations in the Great Lakes. Baird did, however, accomplish the extraordinary feat, considering the technical capabilities of the time, of shipping several tank-car loads of young shad and striped bass all the way across the continent for release in the Pacific, where both species are now well established and of some commercial value.

Baird's efforts had one practical success. Impressed by European reports of the value of carp (*Cyprinus carpio*) as a food fish, Baird successfully imported stocks of carp, established several carp ponds near the base of the Washington Monument, and engaged in a highly productive program of raising and distributing carp. Now plentiful in the ponds, rivers, and lakes of North America, carp are generally regarded as a noxious pest, "being of low grade as food, rooting like a pig in the bottom of lakes and ponds, thereby keeping the water turbid."[2] Their abundance is regretted by freshwater sport fishermen.

In fairness to Baird, his intent was admirable. The carp is an accepted food fish in Europe, easy to raise and highly prolific, and Baird anticipated its becoming a cheap and abundant source of protein for the American masses. However, the American masses never took to carp meat, and Baird appears to have violated his own scientific principles in this case, too, by having evidently neglected to make a scientific study of the habits of this fish before launching a major propagation and distribution of it. Baird's enthusiasm for this program was evident in all his writings of the period. He walked to and from the Smithsonian via his carp ponds nearly every day he was in Washington, and he spent many hours escorting members of Congress and other government officials on promotional viewing excursions. So great was the interest he stimulated that he could hardly keep up with the demand; virtually every congressman seized the opportunity to send a free shipment of carp fry to deserving constituents.

Baird's arrival in Woods Hole in 1871 did not result at once in the establishment there of the Fish Commission's program. He spent succeeding summers at Eastport, Maine; Noank, Connecticut; and Gloucester, Massachusetts, before settling on Woods Hole in 1875. By that time he had concluded that the choice was between Woods Hole and Newport, Rhode Island, both south of Cape Cod in areas where he had found a greater variety of fish species and warmer weather for fish culture. Baird described the basis for his final choice of Woods Hole.

The water is exceptionally pure and free from sediment, and . . . a strong
tide, rushing through the Woods Hole passage, keeps the water in a state of
healthy oxygenation especially favorable for biological research of every
kind and description. The entire absence of sewage, owing to the remote-
ness of large towns, as well as the absence of large rivers tending to reduce
the salinity of the water, constituted a strong argument in its favor.[3]

To acquire the property for the station, Baird was obliged to seek subscriptions, offering potential supporters among scientists and universities
(particularly Princeton, Johns Hopkins, and Williams) use of the station
and its facilities. Baird wrote to John M. Forbes, a major contributor,
"The colleges in question and Mr. Agassiz [Alexander Agassiz, son of
Louis] made their contributions with the understanding that, as far as
possible, they were each allowed to send one specialist to the station for
the purpose of carrying on scientific research." Congress promptly responded to Baird's persuasive appeals with substantial appropriations for
major harbor improvements and the construction of laboratory and residence buildings. Baird's influence with and acceptance by Congress was
such that he was never called to account for his original mandate, nor was
he ever given "the specific authority to undertake the ambitious study of
coastal and oceanic waters that was actually under way."[4]

In a congressional debate regarding the continuance of the Fish Commission after Baird's death, Representative Poindexter Dunn stated:

> I presume that members generally know that it [the Fish Commission]
> originated at the instance of Professor Baird in the institution of a mere in-
> quiry in 1871, and that it has grown now to be one of the most important
> bureaus of the Government in the estimation of a great many thoughtful
> and considerate people. Appropriations have been made from year to year
> and placed at the disposal, practically, of Professor Baird almost without
> limitation, and I believe during most of the time without detailed report as
> to the manner of their expenditure, so great was the confidence which
> Congress and the country had in his wisdom and in his integrity, and the
> results have justified that confidence.[5]

Within a few years after his appointment as fish commissioner, Baird's
interest in censusing fish populations had expired, and he had shifted his
focus of interest back to his old loves, collecting and classifying. By the

time he became secretary of the Smithsonian Institution in 1878, he felt that he and his collectors had accounted for most of the land and fresh-water fauna of North America. Now he found in the ocean and along the coastline a huge and unstudied new taxon waiting to be discovered and revealed to the world of science by someone with the knowledge, skill and requisite physical and financial assets to take on the task.

Baird noted as early as February 24, 1871, in a letter to a correspondent who had asked if the Fish Commission appointment would not unduly divert him from his Smithsonian work, "All that is involved is that it en-ables me to carry on a favorite branch of investigation under better condi-tions than otherwise." Dr. John Shaw Billings made the same point in a memoir of Baird, written in 1895. "The Fish Commission was precisely suited to his tastes; it gave him the opportunities of making immense col-lections, of which he was not slow to avail himself, and there was enough utilitarianism in the work, that could be appreciated by everyone, to make it easy to secure ample appropriations from Congress for carrying it on."[6]

As soon as he had settled on Woods Hole as the permanent field head-quarters and future laboratory for the Fish Commission, Baird placed Professor Addison E. Verrill of Yale University in charge of operations. Verrill's ostensible function was to survey the mollusk beds of Vineyard Sound in order to determine whether depletion of these food items was the cause of coastal fish shortages. However, Verrill was as dedicated to basic science as Baird himself, and he soon extended his activity to the collection and description of all marine invertebrates of the coastal area. The study that he ultimately produced on this subject became a classic in the field.[7]

Baird had little time to spare from his organizational and administra-tive duties to participate in the collecting work. However, he directed and monitored the trips of his research vessels; took students and distin-guished visitors, including on one occasion President Chester A. Arthur, aboard for one-day excursions; and personally checked over the collec-tions the vessels brought in. And whenever he had a little spare time, he enjoyed wading or boating, collecting shallow-water species with seines or hand nets.

Two important activities in which Baird played a leading role demonstrate the extraordinary breadth of the man and his phenomenal attention to every detail of his work. The first was the design of the laboratory. The historian of the Bureau of Commercial Fisheries Biological Laboratory in Woods Hole has described how Baird and Verrill collaborated in drawing up plans for the arrangement of the laboratory and in designing all of its equipment, from aquaria and water tables to storage cabinets. And he adds, "The actual construction and materials used by the contractor for laboratory benches, chemical and office tables, and of other equipment were meticulously scrutinized and personally approved by Baird."[8]

Second was the major part Baird played in the authorization, design, and construction of the research ship *Albatross*. During the first twelve years of Fish Commission work, Baird had obtained the loan of a succession of yachts and navy tugs for dredging and trawling, the best of which was a fully equipped steamboat, the *Fish Hawk*, on which the commission depended from 1880 to 1883. In the latter year, however, Baird obtained from Congress money to permit the construction of a ship designed and equipped especially for deep-sea research, and he participated intimately and knowledgeably in every aspect of its design. Baird saw to the inclusion not only of staterooms and laboratories for the scientists who would be aboard for lengthy research cruises but also of dredges, traps, trawls, and other devices for collecting at various depths. Dean Allard, the author of an important and discerning study of Baird's Fish Commission work, expressed his opinion that "if (Baird) had done nothing more than secure the construction of *Albatross* his name would deserve a prominent place in the history of biology; for this ship, which continued to serve science until 1921, probably did more significant work in oceanic research than any other vessel.[9]

An order which Baird issued on April 10, 1883, to the commanding officer of the ship reveals the extent of his personal interest in every detail of the operations at Woods Hole.

> Sir: As soon as you can be ready for the service (of which you will give me a week's notice), you will go to sea for the purpose of investigating the conditions which govern the movements of the mackerel, menhaden, bluefish, and other migratory species along the coast of the United States in spring, commencing your investigations off Hatteras, or in the region where these

fish usually make their first appearance, and following up the schools in their movements.

The special work to be performed will be to determine the rate of progress of the fish along the coast, their comparative abundance and condition, the places where they first show themselves, the physical condition of their surroundings as to temperature and currents of the water, its chemical and biological peculiarities, etc.

You will endeavor to ascertain whether the appearance of the fish at or near the surface depends upon the condition of temperature, wind or sky, and also by the use of the apparatus at your command, what character of food in the water seems to determine their movements. You will cause examination to be made of the stomachs of such of these fish as you can capture and carefully preserve a portion at least of the contents of the stomach for immediate or future examination.

Should you deem it expedient you will cruise off the coast a sufficient distance to determine the outward line of motion of the fish, and you will communicate to such fishing vessels as you may meet any information that may enable them to prosecute their labors. The time of this work is left to your discretion. You will whenever you touch at any port of the United States send a telegram to me and await instructions as to further operations, if there be nothing to detain you.

You will give to the naturalists of the expedition all Possibilities for collecting and preserving such specimens as you may meet during the cruise.[10]

Another aim which Baird tried to pursue, though without notable success, was to find new fishing grounds for American fishermen and new marketable fish species. He thought he had indeed found a new food fish when one of the cruises discovered the tilefish, but these fish unaccountably disappeared from the area where they were first caught in relative abundance, and they never proved to be reliably harvestable.

As the work at Woods Hole developed, Baird nurtured a dream of its future as a great educational center for marine biological study. In December 1882 he wrote to President Daniel Gilman of Johns Hopkins University:

I do not know whether I have mentioned the extension of my plan in connection with the establishment of special laboratories and summer schools of natural history. I am about securing quite a large tract of ground in addition to that required for the immediate purposes of the Commission, on which may be erected the buildings for the establishment of laboratories and schools. I shall probably be able to give the ground, or the privilege of using it; leaving it to each university or college desiring to establish a school only the expense of erection of a suitable building, to include dormitories for the students, lecture room, and laboratory. I will be able to furnish the pure salt water to each building. . . . Some arrangement may probably be made for a common mess to reduce the expense, and in that direction leaving to each component of the scheme simply the matter of lodging and instructions. Supposing that from 10 to 15 persons represent the force of each establishment, we can easily find accommodations for say 100. It is probable that the occupant of each table in the Fish Commission laboratory will have more particular charge of the class in the side establishment. A course of lectures may be improvised to be delivered by the different specialists to a combined class of students.[11]

Lack of funds prevented the participant universities from bringing this plan to fruition during Baird's lifetime, but in 1888 and 1889 Alpheus Hyatt, a former friend and colleague, successfully promoted the establishment of the present Woods Hole Marine Biological Laboratory, for which he acknowledged Baird's idea as his source.

Baird had a relatively tempestuous career as administrator of each of the three major institutions he headed. He never appointed a deputy who might have taken part of the responsibility off his shoulders, and none of his administrative subordinates were easy to deal with. The Fish Commission had its full share of personnel squabbles, besides the frequent tiffs between Rhees of the Smithsonian and Charles Smiley, principal administrator of the commission. Baird's two closest and most important assistants, James W. Milner and Thomas B. Ferguson, disliked each other intensely. And Baird had to deal with charges against the commission that were brought to the secretary of the navy by a disgruntled navy officer named Wood. The charges were leveled principally at Ferguson, who was a frequent source of trouble for Baird. In December of 1886 Baird responded sharply to a note from Ferguson expressing criticism of the administration of the commission. "I was a little startled to have you refer to looseness in the way of [illegible] the matter of correspondence and records of the Commission during our interview this morning, and must ask you to formulate this charge a little more definitely."[12]

In this instance Ferguson came readily to heel, but there are a series of feisty letters from him to Baird criticizing Baird's friend Eugene G.

Blackford, the owner of the Fulton Fish Market in New York (who was a source both of new specimens and of personally selected fish for Baird dinner parties), and demanding changes in the command and the missions of some of the Fish Commission boats. In turn, there are letters from Baird chastising Ferguson for using an employee of the commission to perform personal services.

When Baird was obliged to stop work entirely in early 1887, he wrote to Ferguson, placing him in charge of Fish Commission operations. He received a reply, dated May 7, 1887, which tells much about Ferguson and the problems Baird had to deal with in working with him.

> It is with the greatest misgivings that I attempt this work, even temporarily, with the present organization and system; and for this reason I will be very glad if you would express as *specifically* as possible the course of conduct which you wish me to require of each member of the Commission whom you desire to hold to an individual responsibility. . . . whereas, your eminent abilities and the universal respect in which you are held, make it a comparatively easy matter for you to regulate the duties and smooth over the difficulties which may arise from time to time among the members of the Commission, especially as it is composed of men who are indebted to you for their appointments and for the many kindnesses they have received— On the contrary with myself, not being on the most cordial terms with some of your more prominent employees and disapproving the course of some, it is quite different, and there cannot be that same feeling of dependence and gratitude with the employees, for with a single exception not an appointment has been made to the office of the Commission on my request or recommendation. . . . During your absence, as it is only temporary, I feel it my duty to carry out any definitely expressed wishes whether I approve of them or not, and in the absence of any instructions, I, of course, will act as I may think best, but I sincerely trust that in the interests of peace and accord, you will leave as little as possible, especially where the employees of the Commission are involved, to my determination.[13]

However capable an operations officer Baird may have considered Ferguson to be, he clearly added a heavy burden to Baird's many difficulties during his final days.

Another serious aggravation with which Baird had to cope as his health deteriorated was the Chenowith case. In 1884 J. D. Chenowith, a newly appointed auditor for the Treasury Department and eager to achieve distinction as an investigative reporter, called for an investigation of the Fish Commission on the ground that the commissioner had improperly used federal funds for the erection and staffing of a building to house and feed both government and nongovernment people working for the Fish Commission. Chenowith also appears to have passed hints to the press, implying other illegal activities on the part of the commissioner and his staff, and these innuendos were widely published.

Baird responded at once, and characteristically, with a deluge of lengthy and detailed defensive letters to the secretary of the treasury (Chenowith's boss); members of Congress; the editor of the *World* (the paper which featured the story); a contact in the Treasury Department, Major George H. Hobbs; and particularly his influential friend, Senator George F. Edmunds. In addition to his protestations of innocence of intentional wrongdoing, Baird asked that an impartial committee be appointed by the president to investigate the affairs of the Fish Commission; but none of the officials to whom Baird appealed seems to have taken Chenowith's reports seriously. Treasury Secretary Daniel Manning declined to call for an investigation, and Baird and the Fish Commission received a clean bill of health from Congress. In an ironic and rather sad denouement of the affair, Chenowith later appealed to Baird to help him gain confirmation of his appointment and thus keep his job. It is also characteristic of Baird that he did so.

In summing up the significance of Baird's achievements as fish commissioner, the following passage from Dean Allard's study is most apt:

> He was the instigator and founder of the Commission which provided money, facilities, and an occasion for exhaustive research in the seas surrounding Woods Hole. Through his annual report printed at government expense he published important scientific papers, including Verrill's elaborate monograph. In an era when the outlet for such scientific papers was severely limited, this was no mean contribution in itself. Above all, Baird created an environment at Woods Hole in which gifted scientists could undertake significant research in the highly profitable new field of marine biology. In effect, he established a marine biological laboratory which, though temporary in nature, was accomplishing what Anton Dohrn planned for his distinguished institution at Naples. In brief, Baird once again played the role of an organizer and promoter of science.[14]

Adolf Cluss, architect, supervising the construction of the first United States National Museum.

Building Commission inspecting progress at the United States National Museum, 1880. *Left to right*: General M. C. Meigs, U.S. Army; General William Tecumseh Sherman, regent; Peter Parker, regent; Baird; Adolf Cluss, architect; William J. Rhees, chief clerk; D. J. Leech, correspondence clerk.

Portrait of Baird on a cigar box, indicative of the popular esteem and recognition accorded him during his career.

The United States National Museum, shortly after its opening in 1881. It is now the Smithsonian's Arts and Industries Building.

Major John Wesley Powell (1834–1902), explorer of the Colorado River and first director of the Bureau of American Ethnology.

William Jones Rhees (1830–1907), chief clerk of the Smithsonian under Secretaries Henry, Baird, and Langley, and historian of the Institution's early years.

Baird in 1871, United States Commissioner of Fish and Fisheries.

Laboratory at Woods Hole, Massachusetts, designed by Baird and Addison E. Verrill. Photo courtesy Marine Biological Laboratory.

Research ship *Albatross*, built and equipped according to specifications by Baird. SS *Albatross* was an ironhull, twinscrew vessel of 234 feet overall length and with a displacement of 1,034 tons. It was built by Pusey and Jones, Wilmington, Delaware, in 1882. Designed and equipped for oceanic investigations anywhere in the world, *Albatross* was the United States' principal oceanic research ship from 1883 to 1921, when it was finally retired from service. Photo courtesy National Archives.

Spencer Baird, *far right*, and George B. Goode, *far left*, seining in the shallows in Woods Hole harbor. Photo courtesy Marine Biological Laboratory.

Wagonload of carp fry containers en route to the control station at the carp ponds on the Washington Monument grounds. Photo courtesy National Archives.

Sorting carp fry at the carp ponds for shipment throughout the United States. Visible in the background is Tiber Creek, which ran along what is now Constitution Avenue. Photo courtesy National Archives.

Masks of two indians, Chief Nock-O-Yo-Uh, a Cheyenne, *left*, and Oscar Brown of the Sioux tribe, aged 13, *right*. The masks of these and other Indian prisoners in the custody of the United States were made with their permission as the result of a request from Baird to Captain Richard H. Pratt, who was in charge of the camp. Pratt later founded the Carlisle Indian School in Carlisle, Pennsylvania. Photo courtesy Department of Physical Anthropology, National Museum of Natural History.

John Cassin (1813–1869), ornithologist at the Academy of Natural Sciences in Philadelphia and a close friend of Baird's.

Three of the many natural history species named in honor of Baird by appreciative students and followers. *Top*: Baird's beaked whale (*Berardius bairdii*), a pelagic species found in the north Pacific and named by Baird's colleague Leonard Stejneger in 1881. Photo by Larry Foster, courtesy Dr. Stanley M. Minasian. *Bottom left*: Baird's tapir (*Tapir bairdii*), named for Baird by zoologist Theodore N. Gill in 1865. These animals are common and fairly tame on Barro Colorado Island in the Panama Canal, where they go frequently in search of handouts to the kitchen of the Smithsonian Tropical Research Institute. *Bottom right*: Baird's sandpiper (*Erolia bairdii*), identified and named for Baird by Elliott Coues. Photo courtesy Claudia Wilds.

Left: First Honor Prize, awarded to the United States at the International Fisheries Exhibition in Berlin in 1880 in recognition of the world leadership in fisheries research and fish culture achieved by the United States Commission of Fish and Fisheries under the organization and direction of Commissioner Spencer F. Baird. The trophy is on exhibit in the Arts and Industries Building, Smithsonian Institution, although without attribution.

Bottom: Granite boulder with bronze tablet commemorating Baird. Erected in 1902 at Woods Hole, Massachusetts, by the American Fisheries Society.

George Brown Goode (1851–1896), assistant director of the National Museum under Baird, and his successor as director.

Secretary Baird in 1882 at the peak of his responsibilities as secretary of the Smithsonian Institution and United States commissioner of fish and fisheries.

The Baird Family: Mary, Spencer, and Lucy, 1887.

Bust of S. F. Baird by William Couper, located in the American Museum of Natural History, New York.

Chapter Fourteen

Friends and Associates

LONGFELLOW ONCE SAID OF EMERSON

> that he used his friends as he did lemons—when he could squeeze nothing
> more from them, he threw them away; but this, while in one sense true
> does Emerson a radical injustice. He had no vanity, no self-importance;
> truth and philosophy were so supreme in their hold on him that neither
> himself nor any other self was worth so much as the solution of a problem
> in life. To get this solution he was willing to squeeze himself like a lemon,
> if need were; and why should he be otherwise disposed to his neighbor?[1]

Baird has been criticized on similar grounds, and with some justice. Like
Emerson, Baird was possessed of a near total dedication to his goals, and
almost all the professional associations in his life were founded on mutual
sharing of those goals. With rare exceptions, Baird had little time to offer
to any of his collectors once they ceased for any reason to share in his pursuits. We see a different side of Baird in his relationships with four people
with whom he had established close personal friendships, most of which
had begun in his Carlisle days. With one exception, these friendships
lasted as long as both participants lived. These friends were George P.
Marsh, John Cassin, Henry Bryant, and Thomas M. Brewer.

Marsh was a good deal older than Baird. Although he had come to know Baird through Mary Baird's family, he soon developed a close, almost paternal relationship with Baird. As a congressman and a regent of the Smithsonian, he promoted Baird's candidacy for the assistant secretaryship; and later on, Baird appealed to his uncle, Charles Penrose, to aid Marsh's appointment as United States minister to the Ottoman Empire. Since Marsh alone of Baird's active correspondents was not a naturalist, their letters were comparatively personal, though while in the Turkish Empire, Marsh did make a continuous effort to collect and ship to his friend specimens of Near Eastern fauna.

Marsh continually expressed concern over two facets of Baird's early work at the Smithsonian: the pace and pressure of his working schedule and what he considered the extent to which Baird was obliged to "waste" his time in "menial tasks." He once wrote, "Two counsels I give thee. Don't work yourself to death, and don't work yourself to death in nothings. 'Tis as good *ne faire rien* as *faire des riens*, and the labels on box covers and addresses on envelopes are *des riens*." And in a later letter, he declared:

> I grieve at the exiguity of thy salary, but more at the loss of thy time. What a pity that Mr. Henry, Mr. Jewett, and thou (I do observe order of rank and precedence in naming you) all men specifically calculated to *increase* in your respective ways the sum of human knowledge, should have all "shot madly from your spheres" . . . and insanely devoted yourselves to the answering of foolish letters, directing of packages to literary societies, reading of proof sheets, and other mechanical operations pertaining to the *diffusion* of knowledge! When I am Emperor, I'll turn you all out, put clerkily thick-headed men in your place, and set you to work at your old vocations again.[2]

He teased his young friend on the subject of his letter writing. "I'm glad you have so much money in your hands, & I advise you to run away with it & travel eastward. You'll do more for science that way than by writing 1060 letters in six months, and fifteen that evening. Even I, with my surprising abilities, can't write 1060 *good* letters in six months, and, if so, what drivelling *must yours be*."[3]

To the first of these letters Baird replied:

> Don't fear for my health, I never was so stout, and perhaps well in my life. Although I work hard (from five A.M. till I fall asleep spontaneously P.M.)

yet I take so much exercise as to keep me up. . . . As to the nature of my business, I sometimes feel as if I were wasting time attending to these details; but then again I become reconciled in a measure, on knowing, as I do, that if I do not attend to them no one will, and I flatter myself that the publications of the Smithsonian Institution could not go on without me.[4]

To Marsh, as to no one else, Baird confided his plans and ambitions. In a letter dated July 2, 1853, he described the abundance of materials arriving at the Smithsonian and the difficultly of preserving and storing them in the limited space available, and he added, "I expect the accumulation of a mass of matter thus collected (which the Institution cannot or will not 'curate' efficiently) to have the effect of forcing our government into establishing a National Museum, of which (let me whisper it) *I* hope to be director. Still even if this argument don't weigh now; it will one of these days and I am content to wait." The following November he touched on this subject again. "The coming session of Congress is going to be a stirring one. I would not be much surprised to hear of attacks being made on the Smithsonian by persons dissatisfied with the administration of its funds. The great question of a National Museum will probably be brought forward. . . . numerous . . . plans are talked of. I don't much care how they manage it, so that *I* can have charge of the Nat. Hist. collections."[5]

When the Democrats came to power in 1854, Marsh's appointment in Constantinople came to an end, and he was obliged to look for a job at home. He became a Republican in 1856, but Buchanan and the Democrats won again in 1856. Marsh wrote Baird with characteristic humor: "Well, exit Pierce, enter Buchanan! Which is the poorer creature of the two will soon be known to those who are able to dive low enough for such investigations as this. I wish they may both be rewarded according to their works."[6]

Meanwhile, Marsh had solicited Baird's help in his job search, and Baird devoted considerable time and effort to trying to help his friend. In April 1859 he advised Marsh that he had proposed him for the vacant post of president of the University of Pennsylvania, but he added that an objection had been raised "on the score of your religious beliefs being tinctured with German mysticism, pantheism, or something of that kind, to which in reply I insisted on your being the stiffest kind of an old straight up and down Congregationalist who goes to church like a good boy when his wife's health would permit (my own case exactly, you know)."[7]

They exchanged several letters on the subject of a study Marsh had written on the natural history of dromedary camels and their potential for useful introduction into the southwestern United States. The study was based at least in part on Marsh's experiences astride a camel while crossing the Sinai desert. Baird obtained books on camel morphology which his friend had requested, helped him in the search for a publisher, and rejoiced with him when the study was published simultaneously in New York and Boston in 1856.

In 1861 President Lincoln appointed Marsh U.S. minister to the newly created government of Italy. Baird still kept an eye out for attractive job possibilities, however, and in 1866 wrote in his letters to Marsh that Professor Othniel C. Marsh had been in Washington observing Smithsonian operations in connection with a plan to found what became the Peabody Institute in Baltimore. He noted that he had suggested George P. Marsh as director. However, he wrote again ten days later that since the salary was to be no more than three thousand dollars, he had instructed Professor Marsh to withdraw Minister Marsh's name from consideration.

They also corresponded at some length about schools for Marsh's son, George, who had been expelled from a New England prep school. When Marsh returned from Constantinople, his efforts to collect zoological specimens for Baird ended. However, after Marsh went to Rome, he and Baird continued a regular exchange of letters. Marsh worked steadily to obtain from the Italians their official publications on matters of interest to the Smithsonian, and Baird reciprocated by forwarding Smithsonian annual reports and other scientific publications. In lieu of zoological specimens, Marsh sent his friend sets of postage stamps—collecting them was one of Baird's hobbies—and archaeological journals and studies for Lucy, who had at that period expressed intense interest in archaeology.

After Marsh's death in 1882 Baird never again corresponded so intimately with anyone; however, his relations with his three closest naturalist friends also offer examples of special warmth. His friendship with John Cassin dated from his visit as a young man of twenty-one to the Academy of Natural Sciences in Philadelphia and continued until Cassin's death. Cassin, although not a professional scientist (he worked much of his life at the Philadelphia Custom House), was a keen and knowledgeable ornithologist by avocation. For many years he was closely associated with the academy, where in time he became vice-president and curator of ornithology. His fondness for Baird is well illustrated in a letter he wrote on December 24, 1853.

> A good many Christmases now have passed, Professor, since you and I have been cronies—more than will again probably—and yet ye're a' the same to me, Professor—rather more so,
>
> So it goes—one has in this world many acquaintances, but few friends and those few afford to any man, who is at all considerable of a man—in the exercise of the friendly feelings and duties, gratification of the highest and most ennobling character—One cannot overestimate long tried and faithful friends—
>
> So, professor, wishing you again—and all yours—a happy Christmas and many—for ourselves, hoping it may never be worse with us—I am
>
> Yours as ever
John Cassin[8]

Baird and Cassin kept up a close relationship for twenty-seven years. They corresponded regularly and frequently, almost always on natural history topics but often in a vein of intimate bantering that is rare in Baird's other correspondence. Indeed, Cassin's affectionate good humor may have saved the association in 1852, when Baird bristled at what he regarded as criticism by Cassin of the catalogue of reptiles, written by Girard and himself.

On April 22, 1852, Cassin had written Baird "essentially at the suggestion of LeConte and Leidy—about the papers by you and Girard—they say that the descriptions are too brief and they think you had better revise them—LeConte says that he and Woodhouse have not been able to identify species by them at all—could only arrive at a presumption—Wilson and [illegible] are also of the same opinion." A notable characteristic which Baird demonstrated throughout his life was that he never took lightly direct criticism of his own actions or work, and to this letter he responded at once and sharply. After noting that the paper in question was carefully described as a catalogue and was never intended to be an identification guide, he barked: "I must confess to be a little 'mad' at the criticisms of the paper, which is fuller than [illegible] appears in the Proceedings. If it don't suit them, let them send it back, and I won't offend their taste and feeling any more." Cassin replied on April 26: "Well now—that beats cock fightin'—I'd like to see the man that found any fault or criticised your paper—who said anybody did? . . . There was not the slightest intention to criticise or in any way to disparage you—not a word of it—for you are an universal favorite, and deservedly so certainly in our establishment."[9]

More than once Cassin tried at Baird's request to find jobs for both Sam and Tom Baird. Sam, Spencer's next older brother, appears to have been a kind and caring person but shy and lacking self-confidence. He never married, was devoted to the family, and served all the Bairds, particularly his mother, with legal and financial advice. Spencer was never as close to Sam as he was to Will, but he had frequent occasion to try to find jobs for Sam, which the latter often had to leave because of an eye problem.

In 1867 Sam Baird had been laid off from his job in the naval office in Philadelphia. At the same time a senior position in that office became open and Cassin was an applicant for it. We see an unexpected side of Baird—and happily a rare one—as demonstrated in the following letter to his brother Will in Reading, Pennsylvania:

> We are having a big race for Naval Office at Phila. Ancona is to be nominated by the President; if rejected, then Cassin will come next who will restore Sam. I am working therefore for Ancona's rejection. Will you send me at once any memoranda concerning any special Copperhead doings in Berks [County] [illegible] to resistance of draft, or any [illegible] 'peace' operations. Send general statement, with printed extracts from papers, speeches, or anything you can find. Better not under your own name, but that of some other Republican.
>
> With such matter I can easily fix him as I know well several members Senate [illegible] Committee, to whom [illegible] will be referred.[10]

Baird had clearly been in Washington long enough to learn a few dirty tricks, but in this case his manipulation did not work for Cassin, although he did succeed in having Sam reinstated.

Many years earlier, in 1846, Baird had supported his friend Cassin in a more orthodox way in a letter to Thomas B. Wilson, then president of the Academy of Natural Sciences, relative to the identification and classification of the birds in a large collection the academy had purchased in France.

> I know of but one individual in the country—and I believe I am well acquainted with all the Ornithologists—who is at all capable of doing what is necessary. This is Mr. John Cassin of Philadelphia. Years ago, when I first commenced the study of Ornithology, I found him well versed in it, and now he is the only person I have yet seen who knows foreign specimens as well as American. Familiar with the use of ornithological books, and there are few here now who are so, he is in every way competent to continue on a large scale what he has been doing for many years on a smaller. You will, I hope, pardon me, dear Sir, for saying that it would be of the highest importance to the interests of science to secure his services, if not for permanency, for a few years at least.[11]

When Baird wrote the above letter, Cassin's association with the academy was informal, but he was sufficiently involved to be able to have the academy pay Baird's expenses for a trip to Boston on a study project related to the academy's collection. It was on this trip that Baird met and began close friendships with two colleagues with whom he had been for some time a correspondent—Thomas M. Brewer and Henry Bryant.

Brewer was a doctor and professor of medicine who left his profession and went into business as a publisher and bookseller. He was also active in Boston politics in matters relating to public education and was for many years an elected member of the school board. Ornithology, particularly the study of birds' eggs, was a serious avocation for Brewer. He became America's leading oologist and was ultimately coauthor with Baird and Robert Ridgway of *A History of North American Birds: Land Birds*, for which he wrote most of the species descriptions. His friendship with Baird was intimate and mutually supportive for nearly forty years and ended only with his death.

The Baird-Brewer correspondence in the Smithsonian Institution Archives is voluminous and mostly related to birds, but it is often entertaining, as the two friends teased each other on subjects of mutual interest. An example appears in a letter Baird wrote Brewer in 1872.

The North Fork of the Canadian River . . . is a stream with which an eminent educational man ought to be familiar. If one of the girls of the Normal
School ever asked where the Canadian R. is and could not tell [several illegible words] a severe reprimand for not knowing. Please take your map
and find the Canadian R., about latitude 35 and longitude 96, & see where
the North Fork of the Canadian comes into the Canadian R. proper, & be
enlightened.[12]

Baird had particular sport with his friend Brewer in 1877, during the
fierce and often bitter debate among ornithologists over the introduction
of the house sparrow into America—a debate which became known as
"the Great Sparrow War." Brewer was the most vociferous champion of
the sparrows, and a Baird protégé and colleague, Elliott Coues, was chief
protagonist for their extermination; the exchanges between the two became so insulting that they ended up bitter enemies. Baird maintained a
low profile on the matter, although he yielded a polite view in a letter to a
Kansas correspondent. "The controversy as to the relations between the
European House Sparrow and the native birds is one that has [illegible]
many reliable contestants on each side that I do not dare express any deci-
sive opinion, though I confess to some incredulity as to the evil consequences some of my colleagues see on account of their presence in the
United States."[13]

Still, Baird could not resist needling Brewer a little. On March 4, 1878,
he suggested enlisting the entomologists in war against the sparrows,
since they were eating the larvae of the insects the entomologists were
trying to study. And the following day he wrote again. "As the sparrows
are so formidable in driving away everything around them, why would it
not be well to introduce them into the Indian country to clear out the Indians. They might have a very powerful influence in that direction."
However, after Coues had published a particularly virulent attack on
Brewer, Baird wrote his old friend:

> I think it may be worth your while to write some sort of a letter to Mr.
> Twining [editor of the *Washington Gazette*, in which Coues' article had ap-
> peared] protesting this action, and against his assumption that the natural-
> ists agree with Coues in his impressions.
>
> I do not like to interfere myself as my position may have to be somewhat
> judicial, but if you choose to address the letter to me, I will forward it.[14]

The closeness of Baird's friendship with Brewer was illustrated with particular clarity on the occasion of the great Boston fire of 1872. The bookstore of Brewer and Tileson burned to the ground and all stocks of books with it. Baird immediately wrote to express his deep concern and, when he learned that Brewer and his family were safe, wrote again to offer fifteen hundred dollars to help with the restoration. Happily Brewer's losses were covered by insurance, but Baird's gesture was a significant one, since money was a scarce commodity for the Bairds at any time.

One other link between Baird and the Brewer family occasioned some correspondence of an extracurricular sort—stamps. Spencer Baird was an avid stamp collector, as was Brewer's daughter, Lucy, and Brewer himself to a lesser extent.[15] A good many letters between Baird and Lucy's father included such paragraphs as the following amongst the ornithologia:

> Lucy is delighted with her new p.o. stamps. . . . She has one duplicate not in yours of papal stamps [illegible] which she wishes me to enclose for you, and she also wishes me to send you for examination and return a stamp which none of us can decipher or find described. Frank Storer says it is Belgian, but we cannot find it so put down.
>
> I bought . . . a copy of John Edward Gray's illustrated catalog of postage stamps, which is the latest and best put out. I shall go to work at once in re-arranging my collection and in finding out what I have and what I have not. In the course of a week I will write you a list of my desiderata.[16]

Thomas M. Brewer died on January 23, 1880. He was the last of Baird's really close naturalist friends, and Baird felt the loss deeply. None of his subsequent letters to or from professional associates reveal any comparable degree of warm intimacy.

Baird's other intimate friend in Boston was Henry Bryant, M.D., a pillar of the Boston Society of Natural History and, according to Lucy Baird, her father's closest friend among his ornithologist associates. Baird himself always addressed Bryant as "Dear Old Doc," and in a letter of introduction that he wrote in 1865 to P. L. Sclater, secretary of the British Zoological Society, he described Bryant as "my Patroclus and Achilles, my Damon and Pythias, my Siamese twin, my brother-in-arms, my friend . . . one of the most accomplished of American ornithologists, and specially devoted to the North American and West Indies birds, whose species no one knows better than he."[17]

Unfortunately, just before Bryant's death in February 1868, their close relationship came to grief as the result of a misunderstanding over money. Bryant was well-to-do, and on several occasions he put up funds to support collectors or expeditions organized by Baird, in return for which Bryant received a share in the resultant specimens. In 1865 Baird and George N. Lawrence, a prominent New York ornithologist, organized an expedition to South America, to be led by H. Behrendt, a specialist on Latin American birds and a frequent contributor to the Smithsonian collections. At Baird's request, Bryant agreed to put up three hundred dollars to cover the estimated expenses for supplies and equipment.

As the preparations neared completion, it developed that the costs would run substantially higher than three hundred dollars. Bryant, who was never in good health, fell ill at this crucial stage, and neither Baird nor Lawrence was able to contact him. Apparently confident of his friend's generosity, Baird authorized the additional expenditures. When Bryant received the bills, he was very angry indeed, and wrote Baird a strong protest.

> I have also waded through Lawrence's bills and Behrendt's letter—which I dislike to do very much as it was bad enough to know generally that I had been made a fool of without the facts of each [illegible] being thrown in my face. . . . I have marked some of the things the use of which I cannot conceive of with a [illegible]—such for instance as 1 lb. [illegible] potash—the remedy for secondary syphilis. I have taken the trouble of calculating the number of doses contained in a pound and find it amounts to 3608, which I should think might be reasonably expected to cure them both. The supply of French capsules (I presume [illegible]) for gonorrhea does not seem quite an extension—from which fact I infer that B[ehrendt] does not expect to get that Disease as often as the other.[18]

Baird sent a long response, explaining that both he and Lawrence had attempted on several occasions to contact Bryant and, failing to get a reply, had gone ahead with the program, since departure time was imminent. Bryant replied on December 25, 1865.

> Your impudence is so excessive that it is almost amusing.—I have just advanced $1211, all of which may very likely go to the bottom of the sea or be lost by many mischances.—I am if everything goes right to put up $300 additional for a collection which may be worth $600 at the very outside. You

wish me to advance $300 gold for the pleasure of your handling a few more new species which Lawrence will describe.

I am glad you wrote as it seems Grayson did not accept your offer of $150. I wish you to write that you can not now furnish it if desired. [Bryant had evidently offered this money for an expedition by Colonel Andrew Jackson Grayson, an ornithologist, bird artist, and active collector in California.]

I do not say that I shall never be willing to give money for collecting again—but I certainly shall not without there is a little more equality between the means furnished and the probable return.—Every time it has been worse than the previous.

For my most important venture—the $500 for Xanthus—I got some specimens of the Cape St. Lucas birds after they had all been picked over twenty times—and the Mexican birds which I should never have got if I had not accidentally found them in your room.—I wrote in my last that I wished you not to [illegible] again to the Peten expedition as far as money matters went.—I now ask you not to ask me to contribute anything more for collecting any where or anyhow—I am at present open only for purchasing at *precise* rates such birds as I want.[19]

Baird's responses in this situation again reflect his defensiveness when confronted with direct criticism. He never acknowledged any fault on his part, never apologized. Instead, he acted as if he were the aggrieved. On January 1, 1866, he wrote: "I felt much hurt by the way in which you wrote me. . . . Some of your letters I kept unopened for hours, dreading to read what might be in them. . . . I don't blame you for I know very well you thought, and probably still think you were right and just. . . . you will excuse me for saying that I trust you will one day see that in all I did in the matter, I had solely in view your interest." Bryant finally closed out the affair in a letter written the next day. "I feel quite pleasant about the whole affair now that I find I have a fellow sufferer who feels so much worse than I do. In fact I have chuckled inwardly since I read your letter. I don't see but what as we have both been wounded it is a fair Drawn battle and we must cry quits.—So I will wish you a happy new year which you had not the grace to wish me."[20]

There were only one or two letters between them after that. Bryant went on an expedition to the West Indies shortly after this exchange. He became sick and died in Puerto Rico in January of the following year.

Baird was of some help to his widow and son in disposing of Bryant's collection.

Baird refers in letters to George Marsh to a close friendship with Senator George F. Edmunds of Vermont, with whom he had become acquainted through the Marsh family. The Bairds and the Edmundses were near neighbors in Washington, the Edmundses visited the Bairds in Woods Hole, and on one occasion Baird joined the Edmunds family on a trip to Florida. Edmunds was one of the most influential members of the Senate and appears to have been of considerable help to Baird on both National Museum and Fish Commission matters. However, since they were in direct contact both officially and socially, there was very little letter writing between them, and nothing else of a revealing nature can be found.

Baird's relationships with some of his younger associates were close but followed a very different pattern. To such protégés as John H. Clark, Caleb Kennerly, Robert Kennicott, William Stimpson, Elliott Coues, Frank Cushing, George Brown Goode, and Robert Ridgway, Baird was the affectionately regarded but respected senior professor, and their extensive individual correspondence with him is uniformly reflective of just such a relationship. He came closest to intimacy with three of them—John H. Clark, Elliott Coues, and in Baird's final days, George Brown Goode.

Clark had been one of Baird's students during his teaching days at Dickinson. The Bairds always referred to him by his student nickname, Adam, and although he had to leave college for reasons of health and did not graduate, his interest in natural history was so stimulated and his fondness for his professor so lasting that in 1851 he joined Baird in Washington as a volunteer collector. Baird had Clark appointed naturalist on the United States and Mexican Boundary Survey Commission, and Clark had meanwhile so endeared himself to all the Bairds that he became virtually a member of the family. In a letter Baird wrote in December 1855 to his brother-in-law, Henry Biddle, he referred to Clark as "my son," and Lucy Baird noted in her memoirs that "during his winters in Washington [Clark] was usually a member of our family."[21]

While in the field, Clark entrusted his money to Baird. Baird noted in a letter to Clark on October 3, 1852, while Clark was still on the commission expedition, "I find the $650 you sent on here in good condition. $500 I will send to Frank Churchill [Mary's brother] to invest. He already has a dividend on the first of $35.00, from which is to be deducted $20 on the original $1000." Clark returned to Washington in 1854, and his relationship with all the Bairds became more intimate. Mary's letters to Spencer during his trips often included references to "Adam." In March of 1854 Mary wrote, "Adam says to tell you that the Boundary Commission to be broken up. . . . Hope this doesn't mean losing Adam."[22]

On March 10, 1855, after Clark had returned to Texas, Baird wrote him:

> Mrs. Baird has doubtless written all about our new house. . . . One room has been furnished with special reference to your accommodation and tastes in blue, and the only drawback to the full enjoyment of the new quarters is your not being here to share them.
>
> . . . I do not know that I have anything more to say just now. There are sundry items of general news I might impart, but I do not wish to anticipate Mrs. B. who talks of writing in a day or two. Hoping to hear often from you while absent, and to see you back again among us in your home, I remain, dear Adam, your sincere friend.[23]

References to Clark continued to appear in Baird's correspondence and journal. Spencer wrote Mary that when she returned to Washington from a trip to Philadelphia, Adam would meet her. Later he wrote that he was short on cash and would have to borrow money from Adam to pay a board bill he had just received. In 1861, as Washington was felt to be threatened following the Union defeat at Bull Run, Baird noted in his journal, "*Monday, Apr. 22.* At 2.45 P.M. Father, Mother and Lucy . . . left to try and reach Carlisle by way of Frederick under escort of J. H. Clark." In August 1863 Spencer wrote Mary that Adam cut the grass, and later that month he advised her that Adam was on his way to be with the family at Woods Hole [Baird was back in Washington] and would comfort Lucy in her fear of thunderstorms. "Have baby and Adam go out often in row boat. It all makes for amusement and variety."[24]

Even more indicative of the extent to which Baird had come to rely on

Adam is a note in Baird's diary on June 26, 1865, only days after the serious fire which had partially destroyed the upper floors of the Smithsonian building. "M. very ill all day in agony of pain. Could go to S.I. only for an hour. Telegraphed for Adam."[25] Clark, who was in New York on business, arrived the following day and helped to spell Baird at Mary's bedside until she was again mobile, at which time he returned to New York.

However, in 1866 the boundary commission terminated its work and Clark moved to Illinois, where he bought a farm and directed his energies to farming. When he ceased to be directly associated with Baird's interests, the relationship cooled rather swiftly. He and the Bairds continued to correspond, but less and less often and strictly about personal news. In 1872 he joined another expedition and wrote to Baird from Denver, but this was not a Smithsonian-sponsored expedition, nor one in which Baird had any direct interest. The following year his letter was written on stationery of the United States Engineer Office in Salt Lake City. On February 1, 1873, Baird wrote Mary, "Adam and Mr. Poesche [an unidentified companion] called. Adam is Adam. Says he's going to resign."[26]

There are no letters in the Smithsonian Institution Archives files to or from Clark for the next ten years. Then a rather sad letter appears which Clark wrote from his farm in Illinois to "Dear Professor." Dated April 1882, it tells that he has been seriously ill, and notes: "I am married now [illegible] have a boy nearly two years old and a girl as many months. . . . I would like to know where you are going to spend the summer and fall. If I do not recover beyond my expectation I must try like some of the big folks of our land to sojurn on the seashore for a while this season—if wife and babies can be left behind." Baird's reply was affectionate but cool. He issued no invitation, only an explanation that accommodations at Woods Hole were few and filled up by Fish Commission staff. And he closed, "hoping that you will not fail to keep us advised of everything that concerns you, with love from all, I am affectionately yours, Spencer F. Baird."[27] There appear to have been no further communications between them, and Clark died shortly thereafter.

Another of Baird's students and protégés, Elliott Coues, over the years became one of the country's best-known ornithologists. Yet this association also came to an end—in this case a bitter one (at least on the part of

Coues)—as Baird's regard for the younger man cooled.

After receiving an enthusiastic letter from Coues, then seventeen years old but demonstrating serious interest in and knowledge of birds, Baird arranged for him to join an expedition to Labrador in 1860. He then brought the young man to the Smithsonian, where Coues further distinguished himself when he discovered a new species of sandpiper in a collection which had arrived in one of Kennicott's shipments from the Northwest. In publishing his finding, Coues wrote:

> In presenting to the scientific world this, my *first* new species, I should do violence to my feelings did I give it any other name than the one chosen. To SPENCER F. BAIRD, I dedicate it, as a slight testimonial of respect for scientific acquirements of the highest order, and in grateful remembrance of the unvarying kindness which has rendered my almost daily intercourse a source of great pleasure, and of the friendly encouragement to which I shall ever feel indebted for whatever progress I shall hereafter make in ornithology.[28]

On Baird's advice, Coues studied medicine and became an army surgeon, in which capacity he was able to devote much time to the collection and study of zoological specimens. Coues served at a number of posts during the next several years, in Arizona and North Carolina and at Fort McHenry (of "Star-Spangled Banner" fame), from all of which he and Baird kept up a very active and intimate correspondence. As he had with Clark, Baird acted *in loco parentis* with Coues, who sought his advice on even his most personal problems. Coues' biographers noted that "for close to thirty years, from about 1854 when Elliott Coues probably met Baird, until the mid 1880s, Baird served as Coues' mentor, friend, and confidant, and in those years, far more than any other individual, influenced and shaped his career." In 1872 Coues named his firstborn son Elliott Baird Coues and explained in a letter to Baird, "I wanted Spencer Baird, but wife had set her heart on Elliott, so we compromised."[29]

Coues was not an easy person to deal with. He was feisty and independent, had a powerful ego, and led what was for that time a rather licentious sex life. He was married three times. His first marriage was annulled by consent of both parties shortly after its consummation, the second ended in a very nasty divorce, and his biographers note evidences of several extramarital adventures. He had a bitter dispute with Baird's closest friend, Thomas M. Brewer, in "the Great Sparrow War," and he fought with Baird's principal student and assistant in later life, Robert Ridgway.

In 1884 Coues came under the influence of Madame Helen Blavatsky, a spiritualistic medium, through whom he entered into the active practice of theosophy. He founded and presided over the Gnostic Theosophical Society of Washington. Although he did not stick with theosophy for long, and in fact even ended up publicly attacking Madame Blavatsky as a fraud, this interlude did not improve his standing among the nation's naturalists, or with Spencer Baird.

In 1881 Coues pleaded passionately with Baird to help him obtain a transfer back to Washington from Arizona, where he claimed that his wife—by this time "my chief enemy"—had used her influence with the secretary of war to have him "exiled." Failing to receive a transfer, Coues resigned from the army and became a professional naturalist, author, and lecturer. He did not reproach Baird for failing to intercede for him, however, and included the following dedication in his highly regarded *Key to North American Birds*:

TO SPENCER F. BAIRD

NESTOR OF AMERICAN ORNITHOLOGISTS

THIS WORK

BEARING TO OTHERS THE TORCH RECEIVED FROM HIM IN EARLIER

YEARS[30]

Although their association and their exchange of letters continued, it was evident that Baird had begun to have doubts about Coues' stability. At the height of "the Great Sparrow War" he wrote to his friend George Lawrence: "I have seen Coues' article on the American Sparrow [*sic*] in 'The American Naturalist.' It is a disgraceful piece of petty spite."[31] Then in 1884, after his theosophy adventure, Coues wrote to Baird requesting a job at the Smithsonian. For a time Baird simply did not respond, but when Coues wrote him a second time in rather petulant terms, he replied in a very formal and almost legalistic style that he could offer neither position nor money which would be commensurate with Coues' abilities and reputation as a naturalist.

The feisty Coues was highly incensed by what he considered Baird's unsympathetic attitude, and he turned against the man whom he had for so long admired. He wrote to his associate J. A. Allen, another distinguished ornithologist, "It is B's policy never to have one of his peers or betters about him—so that this establishment is simply a hatching house of henchmen who make an honest living by doing what they are told to do."[32] By that time Baird had evidently concluded that despite his earlier affection for Coues, he would be more of a problem than an asset as a member of the staff, and thus the relationship ended, regrettably on a very sour note.

Baird had perhaps his closest and most satisfying association with a younger colleague, George Brown Goode, during the last ten years of his life. Goode was an ichthyologist who had received his training under Louis Agassiz at Harvard, and through Agassiz he had become acquainted with Baird in 1872. He worked with Baird at Woods Hole on an informal basis for several years and so impressed him that Baird employed him at the National Museum in 1877.

David Starr Jordan notes that as early as 1873 Baird had provided Goode with openings in both the National Museum and the Fish Commission. "For several summers," he adds, "Goode was employed in the Atlantic Coast explorations of the Fish Commission, and in the winters divided his time between Wesleyan [Goode was curator of the Wesleyan College Museum] and the National Museum." Baird entrusted Goode with the organization and supervision of the Smithsonian and Fish Commission exhibits at the Centennial Exposition of 1876 in Philadelphia, sent him to Berlin in his place as United States commissioner of fish and fisheries in 1880 and to London in the same capacity in 1883. As Baird's health deteriorated and his doctors insisted that he slow down, he wrote a formal letter to Goode, dated June 29, 1886. "I write to authorize you to complete any business connected with the National Museum that does not positively require my attention."[33] This was as close as Baird ever came to a delegation of responsibility.

Finally, in January 1887, just a few months before his death and when he had become too ill to carry out his own functions, Baird appointed Goode assistant secretary of the Smithsonian and received the informal agreement of the Board of Regents to have Goode succeed him as director of the National Museum in the event of his death.

Goode, too, had become almost a member of the Baird family. His health was frail (he was obliged to withdraw from his position at the Philadelphia exposition and leave to Baird the supervision of the Smithsonian exhibits), and the Baird ladies frequently expressed concern for his well-being and urged him to rest and take care of himself, as did Baird. A closeness and sense of partnership shines clearly and continuously through the curricular topic matter of the correspondence between Baird and Goode, though their relationship remained formal. Baird always addressed his assistant as "Mr. Goode," and Goode always addressed Baird as "Dear Professor." It was in George Brown Goode that Spencer Baird finally found the junior partner that he had told Asa Gray in 1877 he would wish for if he became secretary of the Smithsonian Institution.

Chapter Fifteen

The Manner of the Man

GEORGE BROWN GOODE wrote of Baird that

> his industry was phenomenal: he seemed never to waste a moment; he had
> a wonderful head for details and was an ideal business man. All the innu-
> merable ramifications of the practical work of the Smithsonian Institution
> were not only known to him, but were controlled by him; every moment of
> his time was occupied and he worked with singular speed and efficiency;
> yet he was never hurried or flustered and never so engrossed in his work but
> that he had a pleasant word for strangers, and an open ear to all the wishes
> and complaints of his numerous assistants and employees.[1]

The most striking outward aspect of Baird's personality was his seemingly
total self-assurance. There is no indication in any of his abundant correspondence, in his daily journal entries, or in the letters he received that he
ever asked for help or expressed the slightest self-doubt. An important
facet of this characteristic was his self-containment. He never shared his
inner thoughts, even in his letters to Mary, nor did he ever expose a hint
of introspective thinking even in his journals and personal diaries.

With rare exceptions his letters were entirely on business, and some of
his correspondents protested. In an early letter, Kennicott wrote, "I found
so little of the egotist in you that I could learn nothing of yourself from

your letters," and he added that he was obliged to seek information about his mentor from mutual acquaintances. Even in Baird's youth in Carlisle his letters were often cryptic. A cousin, William Lauber, wrote him in September 1846, "You are always very sparing of words when you write to me, no news, not a word of anybody or from anybody, all cold, dry, dull business. . . . do sprinkle a little fun or such like with the sober text."[2] Similarly, in correspondence with his closest friends and associates—Thomas M. Brewer, Henry Bryant, John Cassin, and George N. Lawrence—Baird revealed little of himself. What they discussed in after-dinner chats when visiting each other one can only surmise; but there was evidently nothing which ever generated any follow-up in later exchanges of letters.

In Baird's correspondence with his brother Will and with George P. Marsh, he offered no clues to his thinking on philosophic matters, but he did often expose a refreshingly informal side of his personality. It is an unexpected Baird who wrote to Will in 1858, after a description of Mary's latest illness and the time he had to spend nursing her, that "these are the only things that keep me from working myself . . . to skin and bone. I am always fresher and better after she has had an attack as it allows part of my mind a rest which it can't have otherwise." And in a typical letter to Marsh, he wrote: "I always have a ravenous appetite. And besides I *talk* a great deal about going fishing, and doing other foolish things; and at any rate I hope to have a good run next summer. . . . It is a fact I have scarcely done a single hour's work of original investigation since my arrival, of aboriginal I will not speak, on account of that modesty which should characterize juveniles. Still, I trust a better day is coming."[3]

Another facet of Baird's self-assurance was his personal charm and magnetism, which endowed him with an extraordinary ability to patronize persuasively. Baird never invited any of his collectors, or indeed his coauthors, to share in the planning or direction of the projects on which he solicited their help, but most felt honored and benefited simply by being permitted to work for him. There was never any question that Baird was patron and boss, but like Tom Sawyer with his whitewashing, Baird generated only gratitude and affection from the many collectors and volunteer assistants to whom he gave assignments.

Elliot Coues described a case in point in Baird's winning over of Captain Charles Bendire,

> who was a man to take strong likes and dislikes on very small provocation, [and] had a falling out with Dr. Brewer and Prof. Baird. . . . He fancied himself slighted by them, or misused in some way. . . . So I determined to tell Prof. Baird about the doughty captain's state of mind, feeling confident that Bairdian suavity, sagacity and tactfulness would easily set matters aright. . . . I never knew exactly how Baird conducted his diplomacy; but he smoothed Bendire's ruffled plumes effectually, soon had him well in hand, and in due course thereafter the Bendire collection was in Baird's hands also, becoming the nucleus of the present unrivalled oological cabinet in the National Museum, of which Bendire was honorary curator until his death. . . . few persons whom Baird ever got hold of escaped him afterward, chiefly for the reason that few ever desired to get away from what he could and would do for them.[4]

An additional facet of Spencer Baird's self-assurance was his possession of a pigeonhole memory. Goode mentions his ability to deal with "all of the ramifications of the practical work of the Smithsonian Institution." At the same time he kept equally close personal control over the Fish Commission, the National Museum, and the Bureau of American Ethnology, and there is no evidence that he ever confused or misapplied any operational or administrative detail of any of the four.

Yet Baird's character possessed an altogether different and childlike aspect, evident in his capacity for enjoyment of the lighter side of life. Besides his interest in stamp collecting, some of his correspondence with the captain of one of his research vessels reveals an interest in purchasing ship models for his collection.[5] He noted in his journal his pleasure in waltzing with Mary at an inaugural ball, and he made many references to "riding out" with Mary and Lucy to points of local interest. Charles W. Smiley, the administrative officer of the Fish Commission, told in a memoir of Baird: "Barnum's Circus was the only large gathering which he loved to frequent. 'I don't care what the rest of you do, I am going to the circus this afternoon,' he exultingly exclaimed one day a few summers ago. The way he threw off care that day was grand."[6]

Lucy Baird reminisced about her father's reading tastes,

. . . his favorite recreation being novel reading. He . . . had no taste for the problem novel; but aside from this, he could read and enjoy almost anything from *King Solomon's Mines* to Miss Yonge, and he particularly delighted in children's stories. He could read the veriest trash with zest as long as virtue was triumphant and vice did not make itself too prominent. He was charmed with *Treasure Island* . . . *Little Lord Fauntleroy* took his heart from the time it was published in "St. Nicholas." On one occasion I remember his being missed during the busiest hours of the morning's work in the office. His secretary sat there with notebook in hand, to take down the morning letters, and several people were waiting to see him on business. . . . I found him seated in a room upstairs with the new number of "St. Nicholas" which had come that morning. He was taking a slight peep, 'only skimming' the pages of the latest installment of the little nobleman's history. He even went so far as to persuade Dr. Burnett [father of Frances Burnett, author of *Little Lord Fauntleroy*] one day at the Cosmos Club to tell him, in strict confidence, how it ended, because he really could not wait until the end.[7]

Baird was also something of a gourmet. Many of his letters to family members or suppliers include comments on the quality of food or wines he had received, and in one series of letters he firmly threatened his local butcher with loss of his custom unless he furnished better quality meats. Many of his letters to Eugene Blackford, the proprietor of the Fulton Fish Market in New York, related to requests for special fish for upcoming dinner parties, and he frequently had friends and assistants in New England send him barrels of local fish or fruits.

But his special favorites were oysters, peaches, and ice cream. In 1854 he wrote to Mary, "We got up about 5 o'clock, and went to an oyster cellar, and eat [*sic*] stewed, fried and roast in the shell till we could eat no longer." Mary wrote on another occasion that she and Lucy ate oysters as a memorial to him on his birthday. In 1849 he wrote to Mary, "Peaches are abundant, and I find about a half a peck a day just give me an appetite." (Recall his honeymoon comment, "Nothing to do but loaf and eat peaches.") His love for ice cream amounted almost to an addiction. He wrote in 1851 to Mary, "Table at Mrs. Wise's . . . oh, glorious thought! delightful contemplation! This is ice cream day." In a later letter during Mary's absence he acknowledged that his only vice had been to go every evening to a local ice cream parlor for a treat.[8]

Nonetheless, there were suspicious chinks in Baird's armor. Beginning with his teenage days in Carlisle, when he noted in his journals formidable walks of from twenty to forty miles in a day (at speeds which, according to his precise notes of starting and finishing times, averaged four miles per hour) and when he imposed on himself an exhausting individual study schedule, it is hard to avoid the impression that Baird was challenged by an insistent need to prove himself to himself, or to achieve total mastery over himself. His response to this challenge, which haunted him throughout his life, was to become a compulsive worker.

Baird had what would for most people be a full schedule in meeting the demands of Joseph Henry for the publication and the organized dissemination of Smithsonian-sponsored and other scientific information. Baird met the secretary's exacting requirements while he continued to develop his network of collectors; trained assistants and protégés in sorting, identifying, and classifying the flow of specimens arriving from exploring groups and other contacts; wrote and edited a total of 1,060 published books, articles, and reports; devoted his afternoons and most of his summer months to the direction of the Fish Commission; acted as science editor for one newspaper and three magazines; and kept up an annual correspondence averaging over ten letters per day.

In 1875 he wrote to one of the Harper brothers, "I have made my usual summary of work done in the year. You will, I know, consider the egotism pardonable when I mention that the letters written amount to 5500 & fill 4615 pages of quarto letter copy book. . . . The count does not, of course, include any formal reports, [illegible], articles, etc." And still he sought more. Writing to Mary's cousin Sewall Cutting in February 1868, he noted:

> Making it my business to cover, as nearly as I can, the entire field of science and its applications I prepare a large amount of matter upon agricultural & domestic & rural economy generally. These articles I would be glad to dispose of to some first class journal that has the means of paying what I would demand. It seems a pity to waste the matter, but there is no space in the Harper's periodicals, & I have therefore been in the habit of setting a portion of it aside for the 'Annual Record,' for which, however, it may have to wait a year. For a time I supplied some of these articles to the [illegible] of the Agricultural Department; but when they made a general reduction in

the price paid for Scientific Communications I was unwilling to accept their offer, & since then have had no connection with them.[9]

Considering the time that Baird necessarily devoted to his working schedule, one can sympathize with the suggestion that part of Mary's troubles stemmed from a feeling of neglect, and one is inspired to search for an explanation deeper than simple dedication to professional goals. It is difficult not to suspect in Baird's work pattern a strong element of sublimation, which bordered on a fixation. Baird had been brought up in a female-dominated Victorian family, with the example of widowed mother and grandmother who had clearly sublimated their own physical instincts in attitudes and behavior suitable to the cultural prudery of the time. As the physical distractions inevitably attendant on reaching adolescence beset him, Baird began to engage in the long walking excursions, self-assigned study programs, and spare-time busyness. His and Mary's courtship was evidently quite proper, and although their letters after they were married were filled with affectionate endearments, there was no semblance of passionate intimacy in any of them. Mary's physical troubles may well have been a contributing factor, but as Dr. Greenlee noted, neither gave any hint that sexual difficulties were a feature of her problem. These hints are more evident in her loneliness. One is tempted to surmise that Spencer Baird was for a number of reasons fearful of his physical instincts and that many characteristics of his adult behavior had their source in a powerfully disciplined effort to repress them.

Compulsive work was only one of the special characteristics that cast a shadow over Baird's apparent self-possession. Another was his well-known reluctance to speak in public. On May 7, 1868, he wrote to J. B. Bowman in Lexington, Kentucky, in response to an invitation to address a group there, "Any kind of public speaking is . . . entirely out of my line, & I would not know how to conduct myself or what to say before an audience of about three people." Again, in 1872 he wrote to Senator Rufus King, "Please to find an alternate, as I may be out of town, & it is equally true that I do not believe, at any rate, I could muster up courage to attend & go through the ordeal of a lecture." Garrick Mallery, president of the Anthropological, Biological, and Philosophical Societies of Washington, expressed his curiosity at this characteristic of Baird's in a memoir published in the Smithsonian annual report for 1888. He described meeting Baird and walking with him to a society meeting,

> and during the walk he spoke of the struggle at that moment between the sense of duty requiring him to take his part in the proceedings of the Society and his repugnance to making any formal address. This modesty—indeed timidity—in an eminent writer and thinker, whose lightest words were sure of eager attention in a society composed mainly of his personal friends and wholly of his admirers, was the more remarkable because his address, presented a few minutes later, was most pleasing in its delivery as well as instructive in its substance. He spoke without notes, and though his style was conversational and by no means oratorical, his appropriate words in their rapid flow expressed his thoughts clearly, completely, and in orderly sequence.[10]

This characteristic seems the more remarkable in one who as a college professor must have lectured to his classes regularly. Before congressional committees or in sessions with other governmental associates his powers of persuasion were legendary. George Brown Goode wrote in this connection:

> His ability as a talker and organizer was never better than when . . . in the presence of Congressional committees, before whom he was summoned from year to year to give reasons for his requests for money to be used in expanding the work of the Fish Commission or the National Museum. He was always received by the members with the heartiest welcome; and it seemed that always these pushing, brusque men of business, who ordinarily rushed with the greatest of haste through the routine of committee work, forgot their usual hurry when Professor Baird was before them. They listened attentively as long as he could be induced to talk about his plans for the development of the organization whose success he had at heart.[11]

Another trait which appears to dilute the concept of Baird's unalloyed self-possession was his lifetime unwillingness to go beyond curious, self-imposed physical and intellectual limits. He claimed that deference to his mother's concern for his health was the reason he had not gone with Audubon to Yellowstone, but he turned down another proposal from Audubon to accompany his son to Texas and Mexico, and an opportunity offered by Cassin in 1843 to collect in Brazil and Paraguay. Baird did go on one collecting expedition as far west as Wisconsin and on others to upper New York state and eastern Canada. However, he showed no interest in travel to Europe, even to attend the Berlin fisheries exhibition of 1880, at which he was lionized *in absentia*. And although he had many contacts in California with whom he was in close and continuous communication, he would not accept any of the many invitations he received from them.

Baird shot most of his birds sitting, caught most of his fish in nets and seines, devoted his major scientific work to classification and description of specimens in hand, and confined his public activities to meetings with small groups on topics about which he was knowledgeable in depth. He did take on two untried experiments with his attempt to explain the diminution of fish stocks along the Atlantic coast, and his enthusiastic foray into fish propagation, but perhaps with ulterior motives in both cases. In short, he gives the impression of a man comfortably self-assured within his own intellectual territory but unwilling, perhaps fearful, to strike out into unfamiliar areas.

Two further characteristics that lead one to wonder about Baird's underlying self-assurance were his instant defensiveness in the face of any criticism which he regarded as directed at him, and the fact that he was clearly unwilling to appoint and share responsibility with a deputy in any of his major activities. Baird was a man of great complexity. Of almost childlike simplicity in many aspects, he was clearly subject to powerful inner drives as well as inhibitions, which in combination gave impetus to his important achievements but which he never attempted to account for even to himself. Spencer Baird possessed great charm and was at ease in his relationships within all social ranks. In part this ease may be attributed to the circumstances of his birth and upbringing in an upper-level and self-confident social class, and in equal measure to his own diligence in informing himself and accepting personal responsibility for his decisions. He carefully restricted himself to areas and subjects in which he was better informed than any of his associates or listeners, and his knowledge—acquired through hard work and an outstanding ability to retain what he had learned—covered many wide and varied fields. He was a man of great abilities and of many, carefully controlled parts.

Chapter Sixteen

Ave Atque Vale

All that live must die—passing through nature to eternity.
—William Shakespeare
Hamlet

THERE WERE FEW OCCASIONS in Spencer Baird's early life when his health caused concern to him or his family. In Carlisle he had reportedly suffered some strain on his heart, on the basis of which he claimed that his mother had objected to his accompanying Audubon to the West. However, he made no mention of medical examinations or treatments in his journals of the period, and there is no indication that he modified his rigorous schedule of long daily walking excursions for anything more serious than an occasional bad cold.

In July 1849 Baird became seriously ill with dysentery during an expedition in western Virginia. He was out of action for less than two weeks on this occasion, and no aftereffects were ever reported. The next mention of anything graver than an occasional cold was in July of 1852, when Joseph Henry noted in a letter to Alexander Bache that Baird had "suffered several pretty severe attacks this spring of an affliction of the heart, and looks very badly."[1] No Baird journals exist for this period (the early stage of the Jewett controversy), and he made no reference to any further heart problems for the next twenty years.

In 1872 Baird stated that he was obliged on orders of his doctor to give up plans to attend the funeral of his colleague and protégé William Stimpson, who had died in Baltimore. He gave no indication of his problem, simply noted in his letter of May 29 to Stimpson's father-in-law, R. N. Gordon. "No ordinary impediment could have prevented my embracing the opportunity to [illegible words] but the refusal of my physician to allow it was imperative." In January of the following year he wrote to Mary from Philadelphia that he had "stopped in to see Dr. Meigs" about some palpitations of the heart. The doctor had assured him that "there was no organic trouble—merely a nervous affliction," and prescribed exercise.[2]

Twelve more years passed during which Baird's principal attention was focused on his wife's illnesses, but in 1885 his own health, which must have been deteriorating for some time, although he had made no reference to it, became his predominant concern. Beginning in November 1885, Baird started keeping separate and very detailed notes regarding the four areas of his anatomy in which he was experiencing disturbing symptoms. These notes began with a summary:

Nov. 18, General Symptoms

Heart. Irregular in beating sometimes intermitting every ten or fifteen beats then starting again with a throb, not violent. Occasionally slight feeling of lightness in lower region of sternum. Sometimes a little pain about heart. Oedema of feet.

Head. Pain on left side above mastoid proces [*sic*]. Intermittent for several seconds or longer; then returning, not continuous, occasionally slight dizziness or unsteadiness. Such headaches rather frequent.

Kidneys. Flow varying very much. Sometimes 48 oz. for twelve hours of night; then usually clear and light colored. Next day perhaps 24; and once 12 oz. In latter cases thicker and turbid, depositing a red tinge on chamber. Usually decidedly less during 12 hours of day.

Legs. More or less oedematous at night, especially feet. Disappears mostly by morning.[3]

For the next eighteen months he added almost daily notes on his symptoms, on the medications he took and their effect, if any, and on the doctors he visited and their diagnoses and prescriptions. For example:

> Nov. 23: Dr. Kidder made examination of urine / 30 oz. clear / Report no glucose no albumen. Feebly acid. Sp. Gr. 1.019.4 . . .
>
> Dec. 22: Dr. Hammond ordered 100 grains Bromide Sodium as relief for sick headache in morning in NY. Could not keep it on stomach. Dr. Goldthwaite ordered calomel and soda which met same fate. Seems as if an attack of sick headache was premonished [*sic*] by excessive urine in night. Twice noticed that this beginning about midnight, and yielding 48 to 50 ounces by morning was thus followed. . . .
>
> July 20: a.m. undefined pains about base of tongue and region of heart. Heart beats regular but steadily about 100 to the minute. Eyes better than when left Washington; about as usual before attack. Urine copious about 50 oz. at night, clear and yellow.[4]

It was during this period that he was further stressed by difficult relations with his principal subordinates in both the Smithsonian and the Fish Commission, and he noted the degree to which these affected his well-being.

> Aug. 19–20: Talked over with Mr. Atkins matter of his taking charge of Station and with Mr. Rhees. Result, apparently increased palpitation and headache and lay awake an hour or two. . . .
>
> Nov. 27: . . . Heart beat more violently, and frequently, though no special oppression. Apparently symptom intensified, a result of somewhat exciting interview with Mr. Leech a few days ago.[5]

The correspondence clerk Daniel Leech created a particular trial for Baird at this time. Baird was obliged to write a series of letters to Leech in early 1887 protesting his continuing complaining and troublemaking, and firmly rejecting the latter's demand to be appointed acting chief clerk. In May, Baird wrote one of his last letters, informing Leech that he had drafted but not sent several letters to him, "although I may conclude to bundle them all up and give them to you in a bunch. . . . I must honestly and conscientiously say that the greater part of my indisposition has been caused by the many controversies in which you have taken part."[6]

Chiefly in response to the urging of his old friend Asa Gray, Baird made the very considerable effort to travel to Cambridge to receive in person the honorary degree awarded him by Harvard at its bicentennial. He then attended the Boston meeting of the National Academy of Sciences, which was in effect his last official public appearance.[7] In May of 1887 Baird's doctors demanded that he cease work altogether and rest for at least a year. He had already, in December 1886, arranged with Samuel Pierpont Langley, a distinguished astronomer and physicist, director of the Allegheny Observatory in Pittsburgh, to join the Smithsonian staff as assistant secretary in charge of Library and Exchanges. This was arranged with the tacit understanding that Langley would be Baird's successor, and Baird had secured the regents' endorsement of the appointment. He had already made George Brown Goode director of the United States National Museum and had given Thomas B. Ferguson charge of Fish Commission operations under Goode's supervision.

In May of 1887 the Bairds went to Elizabethtown in the Adirondacks, where they had spent summers previously and where Mary's cousins, the Hales, were able to arrange comfortable accommodations for them. However, Baird complained in letters of the unexpected heat and the abundance of mosquitoes, which in combination rendered their stay far from restful. Accompanied by Lucy, Baird returned to Washington in June, then proceeded to his beloved Woods Hole.

For a short time his condition seemed to improve, and he even showed some interest in Goode's reports of activities at the museum. But by August he began to fail rapidly, and on August 18, 1887, he passed quietly away. In his memorial tribute to Baird, John Wesley Powell told how on "Thursday, before he died, he asked to be placed in a chair provided with wheels. On this he was moved around the pier, past the vessels he had built for the research, and through the laboratory where many men were at work at their biologic investigations. For everyone he had a word of good cheer, though he knew it was his last. . . . Then he was carried to his chamber, where he soon became insensible."[8]

Dr. Thomas L. Hartman, an internist presently practicing in Washington, D.C., generously agreed to read and comment upon Baird's notes about his health.

> It would be my opinion that Mr. Baird suffered with coronary artery disease manifested by palpitations (? atrial fibrillation, an irregular heart

rhythm), heart pain (angina pectoris), swelling of the legs (peripheral edema) and progressive shortness of breath (congestive heart failure).

His headache complaints are difficult to label but could be due to tension headache related to stress of his work and family situation.

The most difficult symptom to accurately explain would be that of his varying amounts of urine output. This could be related to his fluid accumulation secondary to his heart failure and leg swelling with mobilization of fluid at night. There might have been a form of kidney disease, diabetes, or other disorder that might have caused these symptoms; but it is not easily explainable from the information as related to his notes.

His fatigue, weight loss, and respiratory infections could be part of his terminal decline and its attending complications.[9]

Mary Baird wrote to William Rhees on August 23, "We thank you for your kind dispatch. You will be glad to know that death came gently, and as a fitting end to his calm and peaceful life."[10] According to news reports in the *Washington Post*, funeral services were conducted on August 20 at the Bairds' official Fish Commission residence in Woods Hole, after which Baird's casket was conveyed to Washington by special train, accompanied by Ferguson and other members of the Fish Commission staff. Flags in the Capital were lowered to half-mast, and all businesses were closed in mourning from 3:00 to 4:30 P.M. Mary Baird was too ill to return to Washington for several months, and Lucy remained with her in Woods Hole, with the result that no public funeral or memorial service could be held in Washington until November 30, 1887. The final memorial service was held without fanfare in the small chapel of the Oak Hill Cemetery, attended by the family and the official and personal friends of Baird. According to a magazine account of the funeral:

> After the burial service of the Episcopal Church had been read, eight men, dressed in the long blue uniform blouses of the cemetery, entered and bore the coffin, on which a bunch of lilies of the valley was resting, to the vault. . . . The body of Professor Baird was placed in the niche immediately below that containing the remains of General Churchill. Just as the tablet was being put in position a lady hurried to the vault, which was not visited by the mourners, and asked the workmen to wait until she had placed on the coffin a bunch of calla lilies. Just then an official of the Smithsonian Institution arrived, bearing a handsome wreath of white roses surmounted by palms, which had been sent, through the German legation, by Herr von

Behr, the President of the German Fisheries Verein. This was placed inside the vault. The tablet was then quickly placed in position.[11]

A year later, in August 1888, Baird's close friend Senator George F. Edmunds of Vermont introduced a bill proposing that Congress appropriate the sum of fifty thousand dollars to be "donated" to Mrs. Spencer F. Baird in recompense for her late husband's services to the country as commissioner of fish and fisheries, for which he had received no compensation from the government, either for his work or in reimbursement for the out-of-pocket expenses he had personally incurred in the job. This bill was debated at length, opponents emphasizing the point that while they could support a legitimate claim against the government, Baird had made no claim, and that what was being requested was a donation of government funds to a private citizen, which they felt they had no right to grant. Some senators also considered the amount excessive.

House and Senate conferees finally agreed on September 24, 1888, to compromise wording of a resolution to provide the sum of twenty-five thousand dollars to Mrs. Mary C. Baird and daughter "for services and expenditures of said Spencer Fullerton Baird during his administration of the office of Commissioner of Fish and Fisheries, including rent of rooms for the use of said Commission, from February 25, 1871, to the time of his death in August 1887."[12]

Mary and Lucy Baird left Washington shortly after the funeral and settled in Philadelphia, where Mary died in 1891 and Lucy in 1913.

Chapter Seventeen

The Baird Heritage

We used to call him 'Grandfather of us all,' for in his day there was
no struggling naturalist to whom in one way or another he had not
given assistance.

—D. S. Jordan
The Days of a Man

WHEN BAIRD WAS NO LONGER at the helm, people saw clearly
that he was more than the sum of his many parts. His was the influence
that had given both the Smithsonian Institution and the United States
Marine Biological Laboratory their emphasis and direction. Baird's
influence was dominant for nearly a century, especially in the field of natural history. Change would come, but the center, the heart of the enterprise as Baird saw it, still holds firm.

During his lifetime Baird achieved almost all his professional objec-
tives. From his earliest youth he aspired to become curator of a major natural history collection. He wished to institute a survey of marine fisheries
and to become its independent commissioner. His particular goal as assis-

tant secretary of the Smithsonian Institution was from the beginning to make its natural history collections the most complete in the United States and the equal of any in the world. When Joseph Henry's declining health made it evident that he would not live much longer and that a successor would soon have to be chosen, Baird set his sights on becoming secretary of the Smithsonian. These goals he achieved.

He created the highly successful Smithsonian–Fish Commission–National Museum exhibit at the Centennial Exposition of 1876; he obtained for the Smithsonian at the end of the exposition the valuable exhibit materials of most of the other exhibitors; he created the exhibits that earned for himself and for the United States at the Berlin and London fisheries exhibitions international recognition as the world leaders in fish culture; he persuaded Congress to provide financial support for almost all his plans and programs, and he won private backing for the rest; he persuaded the president to appoint his choice to be director of the Bureau of American Ethnology; and when he realized that his own life was coming to an end, he personally selected his successor and induced the regents to honor his choice.

All these achievements were important to Baird and to his contemporaries. But impressive as they were, these were lifetime achievements, not heritable by future generations, not the stuff of immortality. The achievements for which his name deserves a prominent place among America's great are those which have outlasted all of the above and which constitute Baird's heritage to his nation. These he achieved as a collector, a naturalist, a monument builder, and an educator.

Baird's personal collections constituted the seed stock from which have grown the Smithsonian's world-famous collection of zoological taxonomy and the equally notable National Philatelic Collection. As a collector of collectors he personally made and nourished the contacts whose additions in their turn contributed so importantly to Smithsonian greatness in the fields of anthropology and zoology.

Baird's most important contribution as a naturalist was the introduction into American scientific description of a degree of precision which had not been there before. Robert Ridgway noted in his memorial to

Baird that Leonard Stejneger, a professional zoologist who collected for Baird in the Pacific Northwest, named

> the Bairdian School of Ornithology, a school strikingly characterized by peculiar exactness in dealing with facts, conciseness in expressing deductions, and careful analysis of the subject in all its bearings. . . . Mr. Stejneger has in substance said [that] the European School requires the investigator to accept an author's statements and conclusions on his personal responsibility alone, while the Bairdian furnishes him with tangible facts from which to take his deductions.[1]

David Starr Jordan, a distinguished ichthyologist and first president and chancellor of Stanford University, described his own experience under Baird's tutelage.

> His influence on American Systematic Zoology exerted in the direction of frank exactness was predominant and lasting, so that writers both in America and in Europe often spoke of the "Baird School of Naturalists." For example, he taught us to say, not merely that "the birds from such and such a region show such and such peculiarities" but that "I have examined several specimens of the horned lark, which indicate the presence of such and such peculiarities. The first was taken by John Doe at Medicine Bow, April 12, 1890, and is numbered 25001 on the National Museum records." Thus he would always have it possible for others to distinguish (by reference to the actual material on which one based an opinion) between what one really knew and what one only surmised.[2]

Few of today's students or practitioners of natural history refer to the Bairdian school as the foundation of their systematic work—perhaps many are not aware of it—but the importance of this aspect of the Baird heritage has been recognized by two noted later scholars. In a memorial read before the National Academy of Sciences in 1889, Dr. John S. Billings wrote:

> Classification, description, and naming of the different forms are the essential foundations of scientific biology, for until this has been done identification of particular forms is either difficult or impossible, cooperative work on the part of scattered students is greatly restricted, and broad generalizations can only be put in the form of theories and conjectures. Such work as was done by Professor Baird in this direction gives a starting point to many observers and investigators in different localities, stimulates further inquiry, and when done on the extensive scale on which he did it,

based on the examination and comparison of a large number of specimens from widely different localities, exercises a powerful influence for years to come on lines of exploration, collection, and critical research.[3]

And for a modern opinion, Richard C. Banks of the United States Fish and Wildlife Service and president-elect of the American Ornithologists' Union commented as follows: "Value of Baird's works—The early major reports of Baird et al. are still important departure points for our knowledge of the distribution of North American birds. As such their value will never diminish. All those who work with systematics or distribution today refer to Baird's books of the 1800s at least occasionally."[4]

Practical evidence of Baird's heritage for naturalists is to be found in the nomenclature of genera and species which still bear his name. It has been noted that his name was given to one genus and over a dozen species of fish, and over twenty-five species of mammals, birds, fishes, mollusks, and other forms of life have at one time or another borne his name, together with several fossil or extinct forms of life.

Some of the species initially named *bairdii* have over time been found to be races or subspecies, but many still retain their original identifications. According to Banks, eight species and eight subspecies of birds are still recognized as *bairdii*. Baird's tapir, indigenous to Panama, is a familiar freeloader at the Smithsonian Tropical Research Institute on Barro Colorado Island, where one or more of them come to the kitchen door each evening for a handout, and Baird's beaked whale is a not uncommon denizen of the north Pacific. Several reptiles and large numbers of invertebrates have also been named for Baird, and they add to the testimony of the esteem in which Baird's associates and followers held their "Professor."

The education of others began to play a major role in Baird's life shortly after his graduation from Dickinson, when he started classes for his sisters and their friends. Moncure D. Conway, a student of Baird's at Dickinson, noted in his autobiography that Baird was "the beloved professor" who "possessed the art of getting knowledge into the dullest pupil."[5] An education component was part of all his subsequent activity, including his work in natural history and his museum and institution building. But his greatest contribution as an educator was reflected in the group of major scientists who were educated in the Bairdian school by the master and who in turn passed his educational system on to their many students and successors. Their names are legion, and the works of most are still widely known. Ornithologists, ichthyologists, herpetologists, mammalogists, and archaeologists—all students and followers of Spencer Fullerton Baird.

Theodore Cockerell gave an example of the influence Baird exerted on the careers of so many young scientists of future distinction in the story of the first meeting between Baird and Otis T. Mason, who became a distinguished anthropologist and was the first curator of ethnology in the National Museum.

> The Smithsonian had received some Semitic inscriptions which had lain without being unpacked for some time, nobody taking much interest in them. Mr. Mason, hearing of their arrival, went to the museum to examine them; for he had already become much interested in Semitic ethnology, and expected to make it the chief study of his life. Professor Baird received him most cordially, and placing his hand on his shoulder said, "These things have been waiting for you for six months." So they were unpacked and set out where they could be seen; Professor Henry came in, and the three went over them carefully, the young man explaining them as well as he could in the light of his studies. When it was all over and Mr. Mason turned to go, Baird turned to him and said, "Now I want you to give all this up." While the young man almost gasped in astonishment, Baird continued, "If you devote your life to such a subject as this, you will have to take the leavings of European workers. It will not be possible for you here in America to obtain the material for important researches; but—I give you the two Americas!" And Dr. Mason said to me, "I was born again that day." [6]

C. Hart Merriam, another of Baird's students, summed up Baird's educational bequest in the memorial he delivered in 1923 at the centennial anniversary of Baird's birth.

> Nor can we measure the results of his encouragement and helpfulness in shaping the careers of the younger naturalists, some of whom, no longer young, are present this evening. For no matter how busy—and he was always overwhelmed with work—Baird never begrudged the time given to the encouragement of young men who were really in earnest. Most American naturalists of the generation now too rapidly drawing to a close owe to him at least a part of their training and much of their success, and realize how great a privilege it was to have been enrolled under his leadership. . . .

it was Baird who gave me every facility for work in the Smithsonian building, and in the spring suggested a collecting trip to Florida, which I made early in 1873. This was in part an offset, for Baird knew that I had set my heart on accepting a position on the Wheeler expedition. . . . Baird had dissuaded me from going, insisting that if I went I would probably continue to go year after year and remain a *collector* of natural history specimens rather than become a trained naturalist. Instead, he urged me to go to the Sheffield Scientific School of Yale, where I would have the advantage of laboratory work and lectures on zoology under Verrill, and in botany under Eaton. His advice, in which my father concurred, was followed, and in 1875, while I was still at Yale, he appointed me an assistant in the invertebrate laboratory of the U.S. Fish Commission at Woods Hole. [7]

Baird played a role in the founding of another educational institution which lasted for several years after his death, the Carlisle Indian School. Captain Richard H. Pratt, the founder and for many years the director of the school, had been one of Baird's longtime military collectors. In 1875 Pratt had charge of a group of Indian prisoners at a camp in Florida. At Baird's urging, he persuaded several of his prisoners to permit casts to be made of their facial characteristics and other parts of their bodies. These casts still form part of the collections of the Department of Physical Anthropology in the National Museum of Natural History. It was Pratt's dream to found a school where Indians could be educated in white ways and thus equipped to take their place in the national culture which had displaced them. Evidently Baird encouraged him in this objective, and it may be assumed that Baird exercised some influence in securing authorization and perhaps funding for Pratt. In September 1879 Pratt wrote to Baird, "Carlisle 'is ours and fairly won.' We begin the work this fall. . . . I have you to thank for no small part of the beginning successes. Hope to make it so valuable an addition to our efforts for the Indian race that you will remember with pleasure your endorsement of it in the start." [8]

However, it was in his capacity as monument builder that Baird created the most publicly identifiable element of his legacy. Today's assemblage of museums and galleries, devoted to memorializing our national achievements and resources and constituting the Smithsonian Institution, is essentially the bequest of Spencer Baird to the millions who visit them annually. Obviously, each of the secretaries who have succeeded him have added elements extending the scope of the Institution far beyond even Baird's dreams. However, the American people are the direct heirs of Spencer Fullerton Baird in their cultural and educational enjoyment of this great national museum complex. This would not have been true had the development of the Smithsonian followed Joseph Henry's interpretation of James Smithson's intent.

The present Arts and Industries Building and the National Museum of Natural History Building may be considered Baird's own. Through his great success with the Centennial Exposition, he called Congress's hand and ensured the appropriation for the National Museum, and he personally monitored the planning of both museums and the actual construction of the first.

In Woods Hole stands another perpetual monument to the work of Spencer Baird. Baird's Fish Commission was reorganized after his death into the United States Bureau of Fisheries under the newly created Department of Commerce and Labor, and the laboratory he had founded, designed, and directed for so many years became the Bureau of Commercial Fisheries Biological Laboratory and Aquarium under the Department of the Interior. Scientists at the laboratory worked together with those at the United States Marine Biological Laboratory and after 1930 with those at the Woods Hole Oceanographic Institution. Yet the very concept of marine fisheries research was Baird's, and it was he who selected the ideal site to undertake such research. As Paul Galtshoff notes, "At the time of Baird's death the scientific work of the Woods Hole Laboratory was already on a sound foundation."[9] In recognition of the importance of his initiating role in all that had developed at Woods Hole, the American Fisheries Society placed at the station in 1902 a granite boulder with a bronze tablet as a lasting memorial.[10]

Baird was a great American whose memory deserves far better recognition from his countrymen than it has received to date. His achievements were the greater and the more memorable because, as James Smithson wished, they were altogether in the service of man. Baird was a worthy secretary of Smithson's institution. He contributed throughout his life to the increase and diffusion of knowledge, and his contribution both supplemented and complemented that of Joseph Henry, since, as a museum builder, he made this knowledge far more accessible to all of mankind than Henry ever thought appropriate.

The international fame of the Smithsonian's natural history and social collections; a lasting system of definitive natural history study; the conversion of the Smithsonian Institution from a "think tank" to the policy guide and administrative headquarters of a great complex of museums; the contributions of his students and "missionaries"; widely recognized genera and species of American fauna bearing his name—all contributed to the progress of American science and scholarship and are the heritage of Spencer Fullerton Baird to the nation of which he was such a distinguished representative.

Appendix

Notes

Bibliography

Index

Appendix

Awards, Honors, Membership Certificates, and Diplomas of Spencer Fullerton Baird

These certificates and diplomas, together with associated correspondence, are located in the Smithsonian Institution Archives in Collection Division 5. Those marked with an asterisk are located in the Map Case, Drawer 13.

Academia Germanica Naturae Curiosorum, Jena, Germany: honorary member, 1860*

Academy of Natural Sciences, Philadelphia, Pennsylvania: correspondent, 1842; member, 1867

Adirondack Club, New York: honorary member, no date

American Academy of Arts and Sciences, Boston, Massachusetts: fellow, 1848

American Archeological and Asiatic Association, Iowa; life member, 1895*

American Association for the Advancement of Science, Cambridge, Massachusetts, secretary, ca. 1852

American Exhibition of Foreign Products, Arts and Manufacturers, Boston, Massachusetts: memorial certificate, 1883; visitor, 1883*

American Fish Cultural Association and American Fish Culturists' Association, New Hampshire: honorary member, 1872

American Oriental Society, New York: corporate member, 1858

American Philosophical Society, Philadelphia: member, 1855*

American Whig Society, Princeton, New Jersey: honorary member, 1874

Audubon Club, Detroit, Michigan: honorary member, 1868

Berlin Improvement Society, Pennsylvania: honorary member, 1845

Boston Society of Natural History: corresponding member, 1844; honorary member, 1869

Buffalo Society of Natural Sciences, New York: honorary member, 1874

Burlington County Lyceum of History, New Jersey: corresponding member, 1859

California Academy of Natural Sciences, San Francisco: honorary member, 1855

Centennial and Memorial Association of Valley Forge, Pennsylvania: stockholder, 1878

Chicago Academy of Sciences: corresponding member, 1859

Cleveland Natural History Society, Bowdoin College: honorary member, 1859

Columbian University, Washington, D.C.: honorary doctor of laws, 1875*

Congrès International des Americanistes, Brussels, Belgium: delegate, 1878

Corcoran Gallery of Art, Washington, D.C.: trustee, 1878

Cosmos Club, Washington, D.C.: president, no date

Davenport Academy of Natural Sciences, Iowa: corresponding member, 1877; honorary member, 1879

Department of Fish Culture of the Lower Seine, Paris, France: gold medal, 1883

Der Deutsche Fischerei Verein, Berlin, Germany: corresponding member, 1871

Deutschen Ornithologen Gesellschaft, Radolfzell, Germany: member, 1856*

Dickinson College, Carlisle, Pennsylvania: honorary professor, 1845; honorary doctor of physical science, 1856

Die Naturhistorische Gesellschaft zu Nurnberg, Nuremberg, Germany: honorary member, 1847; honorary member, 1878*

Elliott Society of Natural History, Charleston, South Carolina: corresponding member, 1854

Entomological Society of Pennsylvania, corresponding member, 1845, 1859

Essex Institute, Salem, Massachusetts: corresponding member, 1859

Geographical Society of Quebec, Canada: honorary member, 1878

Harvard University, Cambridge, Massachusetts, honorary doctor of law, 1886

Henry Institute of Science, Philadelphia, Pennsylvania: honorary member, 1857

Historical Society of New Mexico: corresponding member, 1860

Historical Society of Pennsylvania: corresponding member, 1846

Historical Society of Tennessee: honorary member, 1858*

Imperial Medical Society of the Caucasus, Russia: corresponding member, 1887*

Indiana Academy of Sciences: member, no date

International Fischereis Austellung, Berlin: First Honor Prize, 1882

International Fisheries Exhibition, London, England: diploma, 1883

Iowa Historical and Geological Institute: honorary member, 1855

Iowa Lyceum and Museum, Des Moines: honorary member, 1853

Kirtland Society of Natural Sciences, Ohio: corresponding member, 1869, 1870

Kaiserliche Konigliche Zoologische u. Botanische Gesellschaft, Vienna: member, 1870*, 1878*

Kongelige Norske Sanct Olafs Orden, Norway and Sweden: knight of the Royal Norwegian Order of Olaf, 1875

Koninkljke Naturkundige Vereeniging, Nederlandsch-Indie, Batavia: corresponding member, 1861*

Koninkljke Zoologisch Genootschap, Netherlands: honorary member, 1885

Leeds Philosophical and Literary Society, Pennsylvania: honorary member, 1847

Linnaean Society, Lancaster, Pennsylvania: corresponding member, 1862

Linnaean Society of London, England: foreign member, 1870

Linnaean Society of Pennsylvania College: honorary member, 1844, 1845

Literary and Historical Society of Quebec: corresponding member, 1853, 1854

Lyceum of Natural History, New York: corresponding member, 1846; honorary member, 1865

Magyar Fudomanyos Academia, Pest, Hungary: corresponding member, 1863*

Massachusetts Anglais Association: honorary member, 1874

Minnesota Academy of Natural Sciences: honorary member, 1873

Museum fur Volkerkunde, Leipzig, Germany: representative, 1874, 1876*

National Academy of Sciences: member, 1864*

National Institute for the Promotion of Science: corresponding member, 1842; resident member, 1851

Naturforschende Gesellschaft zu Halle, Germany: member, 1879*

New Orleans Academy of Sciences: corresponding member, 1854

New-York Historical Society: corresponding member, 1873

New Zealand Institute: honorary member, 1867

Norfolk and Norwich Museum, England: honorary member, 1859

Norske Fiskeriers Fremme: honorary member, 1884*

Numismatic and Antiquarian Society, Philadelphia: honorary vice-president, 1878, 1879

Nuttall Ornithological Club, Cambridge, Massachusetts: corresponding member, 1876; honorary member, 1878

Parthenian Society of the Baltimore Female College: honorary member, 1856

Philadelphia Medical College: honorary doctor of medicine, 1848

Philadelphia Sportsmen's Club: nonresident member, 1874

Physicalische-Medizinische Gesellschaft, Würzberg, Germany: corresponding member, 1884

Pottstown Library and Literary Association, Pennsylvania: honorary member, 1851

Reading Society of Natural Sciences, Pennsylvania: corresponding member, 1870

Scientific Society of Dickinson College: honorary member, 1872

Shakespeare Club, Carlisle, Pennsylvania: corresponding member, 1848

Sociedada de Geographia de Lisboa, Portugal: corresponding member, 1878

Société d'Acclimation: gold medal, 1879*

Société Nationale des Sciences Naturelles de Cherbourg, France: corresponding member, 1878

Société des Sciences, des Arts, et des Lettres du Hainaut, Mons, Belgium: corresponding member, 1854*

State Historical Society of Wisconsin: honorary member, 1854

Toner Lectures, Washington, D.C.: trustee of fund manager, 1878

Union Club of Santa Barbara, California: honorary member, 1878

Union Literary Society of Cassville Seminary, location unknown: honorary member, 1853

United States Centennial Commission, Philadelphia, Pennsylvania: judge of Group 5, 1876; bronze medal, 1876; award for food fish exhibit, 1876*

Verein fur vaterlandische Naturkunde, Wurtemberg, Germany: corresponding member, 1879

Zeeuwsch Genootschap der Wetenschappen, Middelburg, Netherlands: honor unknown, 1855*

Zoological and Acclimatisation Society, Melbourne, Australia: silver medal, 1878

Zoological Society of London: foreign member, 1860

Notes

The authors have drawn much of the information herein from unpublished diaries, journals, and correspondence of Spencer Baird, Joseph Henry, William J. Rhees, George Brown Goode, and many others in the Smithsonian Institution Archives' extensive collections, or Record Units (each one cited in the notes as RU). The most valuable of the forty-six RU's into which we probed was, of course, the Spencer F. Baird Papers (RU 7002), consisting of 9.6 linear meters of papers. Other collections are specifically identified in the notes when quotations or direct references have been used.

Introduction

1. SFB to Levi W. Mingle, 9 November 1885, RU 7002, Box 11.
2. Dall, *Spencer Fullerton Baird*, 22. See also a draft biological sketch of Baird by Mrs. M. D. Lincoln (Bessie Beech), RU 7002, Box 68.
3. Samuel P. Langley to George B. Goode, 28 February 1890, RU 7063, Box 38.
4. Ellis Yochelson wrote, on the Baird Auditorium: "The room had its moment of glory in 1971, a year that marked the 100th anniversary of the founding of the Fish Commission by Spencer Fullerton Baird, as well as the 125th anniversary of the Smithsonian Institution. In connection with the celebration of the role of fisheries, a bust of Baird and a brief account of his work were

installed directly in front of the auditorium. On November 16, 1971, in a ceremony honoring Baird, the auditorium was named for him. When the installation of the escalator obscured the bust, it was moved inside and to the rear of the auditorium, where, unfortunately, not many people saw it. Subsequently, the bust was put in storage, but it has been returned. Visitors seldom see the plaque on the low pedestal of the bust" (Yochelson, *National Museum of Natural History,* 180).

Chapter 1. The Smithson Bequest

1. Langley, "James Smithson," 20.
2. Hellman, *Smithsonian,* 13.
3. Carmichael and Long, *James Smithson and the Smithsonian Story,* 55.
4. Langley, "James Smithson," 19; Oehser, *Sons of Science,* 3.
5. Rhees, ed., *The Smithsonian Institution,* 1879 edition, 1:2.
6. Carmichael and Long, *James Smithson and the Smithsonian Story,* 150.
7. Richard Rush to John Forsythe, 24 September 1836, in Rhees, "James Smithson and His Bequest," 10.
8. Oehser, *Sons of Science,* 22.
9. Rhees, ed., *The Smithsonian Institution,* 1879 edition, 1:799.
10. Ibid., 1:300.
11. Goode, "Founding of the Institution," 37–48; Kohlstedt, "A Step toward Scientific Self-Identity in the United States," 362.
12. Goode, "Founding of the Institution," 19.
13. Ibid., 54.
14. In the Smithsonian files, which form a part of the Rhees collection in the Huntington Library, San Marino, Calif., there is an interesting letter from Col. Thomas E. Donaldson to SFB, dated 4 July 1878: "I propose at my own expense to bring from Europe, when place of interment is found, the body of James Smithson, the founder of the Institution, and to place over it in the grounds of the Institute at Washington a suitable monument.—In an interview we can further consider the matter" (MS RH3058; reproduced by permission of the Huntington Library).

    Apparently Donaldson did discuss this proposal with Baird, but the only follow-up is in a letter in the Smithsonian Institution Archives from Baird to Donaldson, dated 24 August 1878, in which, among other matters, he wrote, "Mr. Rhees tells me that he has suggested to you to stir up de la Batut and get from him some more mementos of Mr. Smithson. This would, of course, be very desirable" (RU 7002, Box 8).
15. *Annual Report . . . Smithsonian Institution . . . 1904,* 8.

Chapter 2. The World of Spencer Baird

1. Daniels, *American Science in the Age of Jackson*, 3.
2. Dupree, *Science in the Federal Government*, 27–28.
3. Daniels, *American Science*, 65. For an excellent account of the professionalization and organization of American science in the nineteenth century, see Bruce, *Launching of American Science*, chap. 3ff.
4. Hinsley, *Savages and Scientists*, 7.
5. SFB, Journal, 1836 and passim, RU 7002, Box 68.
6. Greene, *Washington*, 211.
7. SFB to George A. Boardman, 8 March 1873, RU 7002, Box 5.
8. SFB, 10 November 1866, RU 7002, Box 3.

Chapter 3. The Early Baird

1. SFB, Journal, 31 December 1842, RU 7002, Box 68.
2. *Annual Report . . . Smithsonian Institution . . . 1850*, 42–43.
3. Dall, *Spencer Fullerton Baird*, 15.
4. Ibid., 9.
5. Lydia S. Biddle to SFB, 14 August 1837 and 24 July 1844, RU 7002, Box 38.
6. Robert Ridgway wrote that Baird informed him "that he had once in a pedestrian contest walked forty miles in eight consecutive hours" (*Annual Report . . . Smithsonian Institution . . . 1888*, 706).
7. SFB to Churchill Cutting, 30 July 1884, RU 7002, Box 10.
8. Deane, "Unpublished Letters of John James Audubon and Spencer F. Baird," 198–99.
9. Ibid.
10. SFB, Journal, 8 September 1852, RU 7002, Box 68.
11. Deiss, "Making of a Naturalist."
12. SFB, Journal, 23 January 1841, RU 7002, Box 68.
13. Deane, "Unpublished Letters," 53.
14. Lydia S. Biddle to SFB, 25 July 1845, RU 7002, Box 38.
15. SFB to Lydia S. Biddle, 9 July 1846, and Lydia S. Biddle to SFB, 15 February 1848, RU 7002, Box 38.

Chapter 4. Years of Change

1. Mary Helen Churchill to SFB, 25 December 1844, RU 7002, Box 37.
2. Dall, *Spencer Fullerton Baird*, 144.

3. SFB to William M. Baird, 4 August 1846, RU 7002, Box 38.

4. William M. Baird to SFB, 5 August 1846, RU 7002, Box 38, and SFB, Journal, RU 7002, Box 68.

5. Dall, *Spencer Fullerton Baird,* 150–51.

6. SFB, Journal, RU 7002, Box 68.

7. SFB to James D. Dana, 3 January 1850, RU 7002, Box 2.

8. SFB to William M. Baird, 7 November 1850, RU 7002, Box 2.

9. SFB to George R. Bibb, 1 March 1852, RU 53, Reel 2, Box 2.

10. James D. Dana to SFB, January 1847 and 7 February 1847, RU 7002, Box 19.

11. Joseph Henry to SFB, 3 March 1847, RU 7002, Box 25.

12. Dall, *Spencer Fullerton Baird,* 165.

13. In a letter to the Iconographic Publishing Company dated 12 March 1887, expressing his thanks for a complimentary copy of the 1887 edition, Baird wrote, "It was my first literary venture, and gave me experience in book-making and publishing that, perhaps more than anything else, had to do with my selection for the position of Assistant Secretary at the Smithsonian Institution" (RU 7002, Box 11).

14. George P. Marsh to SFB, 14 June 1846, RU 7002, Box 29.

15. SFB, Journal, 1847, RU 7002, Box 68.

16. Dall, *Spencer Fullerton Baird,* 187–88.

17. SFB to Mary Baird, 1849, RU 7002, Box 37.

18. Joseph Henry to SFB, 11 December 1849, RU 7002, Box 25.

19. Joseph Henry to SFB, 8 July 1850, RU 7002, Box 25.

Chapter 5. Spencer and Mary and Lucy

1. Cockerell, "Spencer Fullerton Baird," 68.

2. Goode, "The Three Secretaries," 195.

3. Allen T. Greenlee, M.D., to E. F. Rivinus, 8 June 1989.

4. All passages quoted here from correspondence between Spencer and Mary Baird, RU 7002, Box 37.

5. SFB to Safford Hale, 17 February 1887, RU 7002, Box 11.

6. SFB to Rebecca Baird, 20 October 1884, RU 7002, Box 10.

7. SFB to Lydia S. Biddle, 10 February 1848, RU 7002, Box 38.

8. SFB to Lucy Baird, 1 January 1855, RU 7002, Box 37.

9. SFB to Molly Biddle, 6 June 1877, RU 7002, Box 12.

Chapter 6. Assistant Secretary, 1850–1865

1. See SFB to the Iconographic Publishing Company, 12 March 1887, RU 7002, Box 11.
2. SFB, Diary, 3 June 1852, RU 7002, Box 68.
3. SFB, Journal, 1 January 1861, RU 7002, Box 43.
4. SFB to George P. Marsh, 9 February 1851, RU 7002, Box 2.
5. Memo from Brigadier General Churchill to military collectors, RU 7002, Box 39.

Chapter 7. The Baird-Henry Relationship

1. John Torrey to SFB, 17 May 1854, RU 7002, Box 34.
2. Dall, *Spencer Fullerton Baird,* 159.
3. Ibid., 187; Joseph Henry to SFB, 13 June 1849, RU 7002, Box 25.
4. SFB to Joseph Henry, 3 November 1849, RU 7002, Box 2.
5. Various letters from SFB to Mary Baird, April–December 1849, RU 7002, Box 37.
6. Joseph Henry to SFB, 23 and 24 April 1850, RU 7002, Box 2.
7. SFB to Mary Baird, 6 October 1850, RU 7002, Box 37; SFB to George P. Marsh, 5 June 1851, RU 7002, Box 2.
8. Rhees, ed., *The Smithsonian Institution,* 1879 edition, 2:942.
9. All following testimony in *Report of the Select Committee of the Management of the Smithsonian Institution,* Rpt. 141, 33d Cong., 2d Sess.
10. Baird's diary for 1853 contains entries only from November 1 through November 6. He kept no diary in 1854, made only a few sporadic entries in 1855, and made none during 1856, 1857, and 1858. He resumed his customary daily journal keeping in 1859. Note: The books in which he recorded his daily activities are listed archivally as journals from 1838 to 1851, as diaries from 1851 to 1855 and from 1859 to 1865, and as journals again from 1866 to 1887.
11. John Torrey to SFB, 13 May 1854, RU 7002, Box 34.
12. Joseph Henry to Alexander Bache, 11 July 1853, RU 7053, Box 3.
13. Joseph Henry to SFB, 14 August 1856, RU 7002, Box 25.
14. Joseph Henry to SFB, 14 August 1868, RU 7002, Box 25.
15. SFB to A. A. Gould, 14 April 1866, RU 7002, Box 3.
16. SFB to Peter Parker, 13 February 1873, RU 7002, Box 5.
17. SFB to George P. Marsh, 13 December 1870, RU 7002, Box 3.
18. *Annual Report . . . Smithsonian Institution . . . 1877,* 8.

19. Washburn, "Joseph Henry's Conception of the Purpose of the Smithsonian Institution," 145.

Chapter 8. A Collector of Collectors

1. *Annual Report . . . Smithsonian Institution . . . 1855,* 31.
2. SFB, Journal, 1841, RU 7002, Box 41.
3. SFB, draft of circular signed by Joseph Henry, 1850, vol. 1, p. 277, RU 7002, Box 2.
4. Dall, *Spencer Fullerton Baird,* 237.
5. SFB to Charles C. Jewett, 19 February 1850, RU 7002, Box 2.
6. Greg Thomas, "The Smithsonian and the Hudson's Bay Company," 291.
7. Ibid., 296.
8. Ibid., 298, 297.
9. *Annual Report . . . Smithsonian Institution . . . 1863,* 53–55, 38.
10. Lieutenant Darius N. Couch to SFB, 16 February 1853, RU 7002, Box 18.
11. SFB to Mrs. Robert L. Stuart, 7 May 1873, RU 7002, Box 34, and SFB to T. C. Dickinson, 13 January 1876, RU 7002, Box 12.
12. Deiss, "Spencer F. Baird and His Collectors," 639.
13. SFB to Captain Stewart van Vliet, 28 September 1851, RU 53, Box 1.
14. SFB to Thomas M. Brewer, 18 December 1871, RU 7002, Box 4; SFB to John Burroughs, 12 February 1873, RU 7002, Box 5; SFB to Burroughs, 5 October 1876, RU 53, Reel 72; Burroughs to SFB, 27 March 1872, RU 7002, Box 16.
15. Dall, *Spencer Fullerton Baird,* 238.
16. George P. Marsh to SFB, 23 August 1850, RU 7002, Box 29.
17. SFB to George P. Marsh, 2 May 1852, RU 7002, Box 2.
18. Dall, *Spencer Fullerton Baird,* 230.
19. Viola, *Exploring the West,* 147.
20. Billings, "Biographical Memoir of Spencer Fullerton Baird, 159.
21. SFB to Molly Baird, 25 December 1875, RU 7002, Box 38.
22. Saxon, *Selected Letters of P. T. Barnum,* 270–76.
23. Ibid.
24. Joseph Henry to SFB, 23 August 1864, RU 7002, Box 25.

Chapter 9. Spencer Baird and Louis Agassiz

1. Agassiz and Agassiz, *Journey to Brazil,* 8.
2. Dall, *Spencer Fullerton Baird,* 187.

3. SFB to William M. Baird, 6 December 1849, RU 7002, Box 2, and Louis Agassiz to SFB, 9 October 1849, RU 7002, Box 13.
4. Lurie, *Louis Agassiz*, 341.
5. Herber, *Correspondence between Spencer Fullerton Baird and Louis Agassiz*, 53.
6. Ibid., 59–60.
7. Joseph Henry to Alexander D. Bache, 11 July 1853, RU 7053, Box 3.
8. SFB to Jared Kirtland, 3 October 1853, RU 7002, Box 2; Lurie, *Louis Agassiz*, 341–42.
9. Bache's antagonism toward Baird seems to have stemmed from an incident in 1859 about which Bache wrote to Henry: "I beg to inform you that your promise that I should read the proofs of the paper on magnetic variation has not been kept, and that the (1st) form has been struck off with many verbal inaccuracies which I should have desired to correct. I have concluded there-fore not to read the proof at all, but to leave the whole responsibility with Prof. Baird and Mr. Schott, who have been the cause of the this `contre-temps'" (RU 7081, Box 31).

    The bitterness and animosity that Agassiz, Bache, and some of their asso-ciates in the Lazzaroni felt toward Baird are exemplified in a letter from Bache to a friend in 1863. "I have been obliged to admit in reply [to com-plaints about the membership list] that there are some men too mean to bring into our Academy, thus slightly intimating that I so class George P. Bond and Spencer F. Baird. I have had favorable opportunities for inductions upon them in parts of their lives and have come to distinct conclusions" (Reingold, *Science in Nineteenth-Century America*, 205–6).
10. Asa Gray to SFB, 27 August 1864, RU 7002, Box 23.
11. Lurie, *Louis Agassiz*, 334; Reingold, *Science in Nineteenth-Century America*, 217.
12. SFB to A. A. Gould, 14 April 1866, RU 7002, Box 3.

Chapter 10. A Dedication to the Demonstrable

1. Dall, *Spencer Fullerton Baird*, 205–6. His mother is referring to a serious bout of dysentery that Baird suffered while on a collecting trip in Virginia during the summer of 1849.
2. RU 7002, Box 68.
3. Louis Agassiz to SFB, October 1849, Ru 7002, Box 68. Joseph Henry "main-tained a sphinx-like silence" (Coulson, *Joseph Henry*, 294) on Darwinism, but he ultimately wrote to Asa Gray, "I have given the subject of evolution much thought, and have come to the conclusion that it is the best working hypoth-

esis which you naturalists have ever had" (Goode, "The Three Secretaries," 150).

4. SFB to H. W. Elliott, 30 November 1869, RU 7002, Box 3; Dall, "Memorial," *Annual Report . . . Smithsonian Institution . . . 1888*, 736.

5. SFB to Henry Bryant, 27 April 1861, RU 7002, Box 3.

6. SFB to Whitelaw Reid, 26 October 1874, RU 7002, Box 6.

7. SFB to S. H. Scudder, 17 March 1885, RU 7002, Box 10.

8. The Bairds' apparent unconcern with slavery may not have been atypical. In her description of mid-nineteenth-century Washington, Constance Greene notes that for Washingtonians in general, slavery and states' rights issues were almost by universal tacit consent excluded from public and unguarded private discussion. "The fiercer the storm blew roundabout, the greater the quiet at the center" (Greene, *Washington*, 179–80). For a full account of the incident in Carlisle, see Wing, *History of Cumberland County, Pennsylvania*, 177–78.

9. SFB to Thomas M. Brewer, RU 53, Reel 24.

10. SFB to W. J. Allen, 11 May 1861, RU 7002, Box 3.

11. SFB to Lydia M. Baird, 27 April 1861, RU 7002, Box 3; SFB to William M. Baird, 8 May 1861, RU 7002, Box 38.

12. SFB to Frank Churchill, 17 June 1864, RU 7002, Box 38.

13. SFB to Edward Shepard, 10 October 1876, RU 53, Reel 72; SFB to General William T. Sherman, 24 November 1882, RU 7002, Box 9; SFB to George A. Boardman, 28 January 1887, RU 7002, Box 11.

14. SFB to W. F. Parker, 25 April 1874, RU 7002, Box 6; SFB to Charles Hallock, 26 August 1874, Ru 7002, Box 6.

15. SFB to Molly Biddle, 14 July 1887, RU 7002, Box 38.

16. Allard, "Spencer Fullerton Baird and the U.S. Fish Commission," 160.

17. SFB to Peter Parker, 13 February 1873, RU 7002, Box 5.

18. *Annual Report . . . Smithsonian Institution . . . 1888*, 710.

19. John S. Billings, "Memorial," 17 April 1889, RU 7098, Box 2.

Chapter 11. Assistant Secretary, 1865–1878

1. SFB to J. A. Hooker, 12 March 1872, RU 7002, Box 4.

2. SFB to Sewall Cutting, 18 December 1872, RU 7002, Box 5.

3. SFB to H. L. Dawes, 15 December 1870, and to Committee on Appropriations, 3 January 1871, RU 7002, Box 4.

4. Joint Resolution H.R. 468, 41st Cong., 3d Sess., 18 January 1871.

5. SFB to John Cassin, 21 December 1850, RU 7002, Box 2.

6. *New York Times*, 19 November 1898, Post, *1876*, 79.

7. Circular letter from SFB to Centennial Exposition exhibitors, 1 February 1882, RU 7081, Box 44.
8. *Annual Report . . . Smithsonian Institution . . . 1877*, 41.
9. For a full and clear account of this issue, see Allard, "Spencer Fullerton Baird and the U.S. Fish Commission."
10. SFB to Asa Gray, 12 March 1878, RU 7002, Box 7.
11. *Annual Report . . . Smithsonian Institution . . 1878*, 10.

Chapter 12. Secretary

1. SFB to Asa Gray, 12 March 1878, RU 7002, Box 7.
2. Billings, "Biographical Memoir of Spencer Fullerton Baird," 155.
3. See Appendix for a full list of Baird's honors and awards.
4. Goode, "The Three Secretaries," 188, 189.
5. Allard, "Spencer Fullerton Baird and the U.S. Fish Commission," 250; Darrah, *Powell of the Colorado*, 112, 152.
6. SFB to George B. Goode, 10 August 1882, RU 7002, Box 22.
7. John W. Powell to SFB, August 1883, Department of Anthropology, National Museum of Natural History, BAE File 4677, p. 290.
8. SFB to John W. Powell, November 1883, RU 7081, Box 11.
9. John W. Powell to SFB, 6 November 1883, BAE File 4677.
10. SFB to William J. Rhees, 30 August 1883, RU 64, Box 1.
11. SFB to F. W. True, 2 August 1883, RU 54, Box 1.
12. SFB to George B. Goode, 1 July 1884, BAE File 4677.
13. Anthropological, Biological, and Philosophical Societies of Washington, *Proceedings*.
14. William J. Rhees to SFB, "Remarks Relative to the Organization of the Smithsonian," 27 December 1884, RU 64, Box 9.
15. SFB to William J. Rhees, 22 July 1876, RU 64, Box 1.
16. SFB to William J. Rhees, 2 August 1880, RU 7002, Box 8, and 9 September 1884, RU 7002, Box 10.
17. William J. Rhees to SFB, "Remarks Relative to the Organization of the Smithsonian," 27 December 1884, RU 64, Box 9.
18. Taylor, "Professor Baird as Administrator," 721.

Chapter 13. United States Fish Commissioner

1. Galtshoff, *Story of the Bureau of Commercial Fisheries Biological Laboratory*, 1.
2. Jordan, "Spencer Fullerton Baird and the U.S. Fish Commission," 104.

3. Galtshoff, *Story*, 27.
4. Ibid.; Allard, "Spencer Fullerton Baird and the U.S. Fish Commission," 317.
5. Rhees, ed., *The Smithsonian Institution*, 1879 edition, 2:1048.
6. SFB to Colonel E. Jewett, 24 February 1871, RU 7002, Box 4; Billings, "Biographical Memoir of Spencer Fullerton Baird," 146.
7. A. E. Verrill, "Report upon the Invertebrate Animals of the Vineyard Sound and the Adjacent Waters, with an Account of the Physical Characters of the Region," in *Report, 1871–1872*, U.S. Commission of Fish and Fisheries (Washington, D.C.: Government Printing Office, 1873).
8. Galtshoff, *Story*, 36.
9. Allard, "Spencer Fullerton Baird and the U.S. Fish Commission," 40.
10. Galtshoff, *Story*, 44–45.
11. SFB to Daniel Gilman, December 1882, RU 7002, Box 9.
12. SFB to Thomas B. Ferguson, 7 December 1886, RU 7002, Box 11.
13. Thomas B. Ferguson to SFB, 7 May 1887, RU 7002, Box 20.
14. Felix Anton Dohrn (1840–1909) was a German zoologist who in 1874 established in Naples, Italy, the first laboratory designed specifically for marine studies. Dohrn's laboratory became the prototype for all that followed. Allard, "Spencer Fullerton Baird and the U.S. Fish Commission," 106.

Chapter 14. Friends and Associates

1. Stillman, "The Philosophers' Camp," 601.
2. Marsh, *Life and Letters of George Perkins Marsh*, 324; George P. Marsh to SFB, 3 March 1852, RU 7002, Box 29.
3. George P. Marsh to SFB, 3 March 1852, RU 7002, Box 29.
4. SFB to George P. Marsh, 5 June 1851, RU 7002, Box 2.
5. SFB to George P. Marsh, 2 May and 14 November 1853, RU 7002, Box 2.
6. George P. Marsh to SFB, 17 February 1857, RU 7002, Box 29.
7. SFB to George P. Marsh, 8 April 1859, RU 7002, Box 3.
8. John Cassin to SFB, 24 December 1853, RU 7002, Box 29.
9. John Cassin to SFB, 22 April 1852, RU 7002, Box 17; SFB to John Cassin, 23 April 1852, RU 7002, Box 2; Cassin to SFB, 26 April 1852, RU 7002, Box 17.
10. SFB to William M. Baird, 25 February 1867, RU 7002, Box 3.
11. SFB to Thomas B. Wilson, June 1846, in Dall, *Spencer Fullerton Baird*, 137–38.
12. SFB to Thomas M. Brewer, 17 April 1872, RU 7002, Box 4.
13. SFB to C. P. Blackly, 6 September 1877, RU 53, Reel 82.
14. SFB to Thomas M. Brewer, 4–5 March 1878, RU 7002, Box 7, and 23 November 1878, RU 7002, Box 8.
15. Rivinus, "Spencer Fullerton Baird, the Collector of Collectors," 1061–65. Af-

ter Baird's death, his widow donated to the Smithsonian Institution his personal collection of 1,173 postage stamps. The Baird collection constituted the seed from which has grown the National Philatelic Collection, currently located in the National Postal Museum.

16. Thomas M. Brewer to SFB, 31 March 1867, RU 7002, Box 15.
17. SFB to P. L. Sclater, 21 May 1865, RU 7002, Box 3.
18. Henry Bryant to SFB, 23 December 1865, RU 7002, Box 16.
19. Henry Bryant to SFB, 25 December 1865, RU 7002, Box 16.
20. SFB to Henry Bryant, 1 January 1866, RU 7002, Box 3; Bryant to SFB, 2 January 1866, RU 7002, Box 16.
21. Dall, *Spencer Fullerton Baird,* 171.
22. SFB to John H. Clark, 3 October 1852, RU 7002, Box 2; Mary Baird to SFB, March 1854, RU 7002, Box 37.
23. SFB to John H. Clark, 10 March 1855, RU 7002, Box 2.
24. SFB, Journal, 22 April 1861, RU 7002, Box 43; SFB to Mary Baird, 5 August 1863, RU 7002, Box 37.
25. SFB, Journal, 26 June 1865, RU 7002, Box 43.
26. SFB to Mary Baird, 1 February 1873, RU 7002, Box 37.
27. John H. Clark to SFB, 14 April 1882, RU 7002, Box 17; SFB to Clark, 22 April 1882, RU 7002, Box 9.
28. Cutright and Brodhead, *Elliott Coues,* 37.
29. Ibid., 30; Elliott Coues to SFB, 1872, RU 7002, Box 18.
30. Cutright and Brodhead, *Elliott Coues,* 256.
31. SFB to George N. Lawrence, 30 July 1878, RU 7002, Box 8.
32. Cutright and Brodhead, *Elliott Coues,* 285.
33. *Dictionary of American Biography,* 4:381; SFB to George B. Goode, 29 June 1886, RU 7002, Box 11.

Chapter 15. The Manner of the Man

1. Goode, "The Three Secretaries," 194.
2. Robert Kennicott to SFB, 15 November 1857, RU 7002, Box 26; William Lauber to SFB, 27 September 1846, RU 7002, Box 29.
3. SFB to William M. Baird, 15 May 1858, RU 7002, Box 36, and to George P. Marsh, 5 June 1851, RU 7002, Box 2.
4. Hume, *Ornithologists of the United States Army Medical Corps,* 26–27.
5. Baird revealed his ship model collecting interest in a letter of October 3, 1877, to Captain W. W. Hunt of Neponset, Massachusetts. He thanked the cap-

tain for information about models available but added, "I do not dare do any-thing at present for purchasing models for my collection until after I get back to Washington and see how the funds stand." Baird noted his desire to obtain a model of "the Marblehead Grand Banker," and in a postscript he offered to buy "the (Pinkey) and the Dog-body boat" if they were available for twenty-five dollars (RU 53, Reel 82). A later letter to Hunt on the same subject is re-grettably almost illegible.

6. Smiley, "Memorial to Spencer F. Baird," 2–3.
7. Dall, *Spencer Fullerton Baird*, 149–50.
8. Letters from SFB to Mary Baird, 1849, 17 June 1851, and 7 May 1854, RU 7002, Box 37.
9. SFB to J. W. Harper, 3 January 1875, RU 7002, Box 6, and to Sewall Cutting, February 1868, RU 7002, Box 5.
10. SFB to J. B. Bowman, 7 May 1868, and to Rufus King, 18 February 1872, RU 7002, Box 5; *Annual Report . . . Smithsonian Institution . . . 1888*, 718.
11. Goode, "The Three Secretaries," 193.

Chapter 16. Ave Atque Vale

1. Joseph Henry to Alexander Bache, 3 July 1852, RU 7053, Box 3.
2. SFB to R. N. Gordon, 29 May 1872, RU 7002, Box 5, and to Mary Baird, 30 January 1873, RU 7002, Box 37.
3. Baird's health diary, 18 November 1855, RU 7002, Box 43.
4. Ibid.
5. Ibid.
6. SFB to Daniel Leech, 10 May 1887, RU 7002, Box 11.
7. Dall, *Spencer Fullerton Baird*, 406.
8. John W. Powell, "The Personal Characteristics of Professor Baird," 76.
9. Thomas L. Hartman, M.D., to E. M. Youssef, 9 January 1989.
10. Mary Baird to William J. Rhees, 23 August 1887, RU 64, Box 3.
11. *American Angler*, 12:24, RU 7002, Box 69.
12. Rhees, ed., *Smithsonian Institution: Documents Relative to Its Origin and History*, 2:1104.

Chapter 17. The Baird Heritage

1. Ridgway, "Spencer Fullerton Baird," 703–15.
2. Jordan, *Days of a Man*, 174.
3. Billings, "Biographical Memoir of Spencer Fullerton Baird," 149.

4. Richard C. Banks to E. F. Rivinus, 2 May 1988.
5. Dall, *Spencer Fullerton Baird*, 447.
6. Cockerell, "Spencer Fullerton Baird and the U.S. National Museum," 79–80.
7. Merriam, "Baird the Naturalist," 594.
8. Richard H. Pratt to SFB, 1 September 1879, RU 7002, Box 31.
9. Galtshoff, *Story of the Bureau of Commercial Fisheries Biological Laboratory*, 51.
10. More recent recognition of Baird's contribution to the marine research at Woods Hole is found in the newly established Woods Hole waterfront park, which encloses the American Fish Society's memorial stone and where Baird was commemorated in direct dedication ceremonies on August 8, 1992.

Bibliography

Agassiz, Professor and Mrs. Louis. *Journey to Brazil*. Boston: Ticknor & Fields, 1868

Aldrich, John W. *The Biological Society of Washington: A Centennial History, 1880–1980*. Bulletin of the Biological Society of Washington, no. 4. [Washington, D.C.: Biological Society of Washington], 1980

Alexander, Edward P. *Museum Masters: Their Museums and Their Influence*. Nashville: American Association for State and Local History, 1983.

Allard, Dean C. "Spencer Fullerton Baird and the U.S. Fish Commission: A Study in the History of American Science." Ann Arbor, Mich.: University Microfilms, 1969.

————. "Science, Diplomacy, and Rum: The Halifax Fisheries Commission." In *Ships, Seafaring, and Society*, edited by Timothy J. Runyan, 119–27. Detroit: Wayne State University Press for the Great Lakes Historical Society, 1987.

Allen, David E. *The Naturalist in Britain: A Social History*. Harmondsworth, Middlesex, Eng.: Penguin Books, 1978.

Annual Report of the Board of Regents of the Smithsonian Institution . . . Washington, D.C.: Government Printing Office, 1851–1905. Reports of the secretary, assistant secretary, and National Museum, and on researches and explorations.

Anonymous [probably William J. Rhees, ed.]. *An Account of the Smithsonian Institution: Its Origin, History, Objects, and Achievements*. Washington, D.C.: Smithsonian Institution, 1895. Booklet distributed at the Atlanta Exposition, 1895, and at the Louisiana Purchase Exposition, 1904.

Anthropological, Biological, and Philosophical Societies of Washington. *Proceedings at a Meeting Commemorative of the Life and Work of Spencer Fullerton Baird.* Washington, D.C.: Judd and Detweiler, Printers, 1888. Includes articles by Garrick Mallery, William B. Taylor, W. H. Dall, and John Wesley Powell.

Audubon, John James. *The Birds of North America, from Drawings Made in the United States and Their Territories.* New York: George R. Lockwood, 1839.

Baird, Spencer F. *Birds.* Vol. 9 of *Reports of Explorations and Surveys to Ascertain the Most Practical and Economical Route for a Railroad from the Mississippi River to the Pacific Ocean.* Washington, D.C.: A. D. P. Nicholson, 1858.

———. "The Distribution and Migrations of North American Birds." *American Journal of Science and Arts,* 2d series, 41 (January–May 1866): 78–90, 184–92, 337–47.

———. "Scientific Intelligence." Baird's regular contributions to *Harper's Weekly,* 1877–79.

Baird, Spencer F., "with the cooperation of" John Cassin and George N. Lawrence. *The Birds of North America.* Philadelphia: J. B. Lippincott Co., 1860.

Banks, Richard C. Letters to E. F. Rivinus, 2 and 15 May 1989.

Bartlett, Richard A. *Great Surveys of the American West.* Norman: University of Oklahoma Press, 1962.

Bates, Ralph S. *Scientific Societies in the United States.* Cambridge: MIT Press, 1965.

Berlandier, Jean Louis. *Journey to Mexico during the Years 1826 to 1834.* 2 vols. Austin: University of Texas Press and Texas State Historical Association in cooperation with the Center for Studies in Texas History, 1980. See especially "Introduction" by C. H. Muller.

Billings, John S. "Biographical Memoir of Spencer Fullerton Baird, 1823–1887." In vol. 3 of *Biographical Memoirs,* 141–60. Washington City: National Academy of Sciences, 1895.

Bolton, Henry Carrington. "The Smithsonian Institution: Its Origin, Growth, and Activities . . ." *Appleton's Popular Science Monthly,* January 1896.

Bonta, Marcia. "From the Wilds of Carlisle: Spencer Fullerton Baird and the World of Nineteenth-Century Naturalists." *Pennsylvania Naturalist* 2, no. 3 (February–March 1980).

———. "Baird of the Smithsonian." *Pennsylvania Heritage* 6, no. 3 (Summer 1980).

Bruce, Robert V. *The Launching of Modern American Science, 1846–1876.* New York: Alfred A. Knopf, 1987.

Bureau of American Ethnology Archives. File 4677, Baird-Powell Correspondence, Smithsonian Institution, National Museum of Natural History, Washington, D.C.

Carmichael, Leonard, and J. C. Long. *James Smithson and the Smithsonian Story.* New York: G. P. Putnam's Sons, 1965.

Coan, Eugene. *James Graham Cooper: Pioneer Western Naturalist.* Moscow: University Press of Idaho, a division of the Idaho Research Foundation, 1981.

Cockerell, Theodore D. A. "Sketch of Spencer F. Baird." *Popular Science Monthly* 33, no. 4 (August 1888).

———. "Spencer Fullerton Baird." *Popular Science Monthly* 68, (January 1906): 63–83.

———. "Spencer Fullerton Baird and the U.S. National Museum." *Bios* 13 (March 1942).

Coulson, Thomas. *Joseph Henry: His Life and Work.* Princeton: Princeton University Press, 1950.

Crosette, George. *Founders of the Cosmos Club of Washington, 1878.* Washington, D.C.: Cosmos Club, 1966.

Cutright, Paul Russell, and Michael J. Brodhead. *Elliott Coues: Naturalist and Frontier Historian.* Urbana: University of Illinois Press, 1981.

Dall, William Healey. "Baird the Man." *Science* 57 (16 February 1923): 194–96.

———. "Spencer Fullerton Baird." *Nation* 44 (1 December 1887).

———. *Spencer Fullerton Baird: A Biography.* Philadelphia: J. B. Lippincott Co., 1915.

Daniels, George H. *American Science in the Age of Jackson.* New York: Columbia University Press, 1968.

———. *Nineteenth-Century American Science: A Reappraisal.* Evanston: Northwestern University Press, 1972.

Darrah, William C. *Powell of the Colorado.* Princeton: Princeton University Press, 1951.

Deane, J. Ruthven. "Unpublished Letters of John James Audubon and Spencer F. Baird." *Auk* 21 (1904): 255–59; 23 (1906): 194–201, 318–34; 24 (1907): 53–70.

Deiss, William A. "Audubon: Influences on an American Naturalist." In *John J. Audubon, 1785–1851: A Georgia Tour Exhibit Catalogue.* Roswell, Ga.: Chattahoochee Nature Center, 1984.

———. "How Spencer F. Baird Dodged a Bullet: The Early Debate over the Nature of the Smithsonian Institution and the Emergence of Consensus on the National Museum." Paper presented at the joint meeting of the Society for the History of Natural History, the American Society of Ichthyologists and Herpetologists, the American Elasmobranch Society, and the League of Herpetologists to celebrate the seventieth anniversary of the American Society of Ichthyologists and Herpetologists, Charleston, S.C., 1990.

———. "The Making of a Naturalist: Spencer F. Baird, the Early Years." In *From Linnaeus to Darwin: Commentaries on the History of Biology and Geology,* pp. 141–48. Special Publication, no. 3. London: Society for the History of Natural History, 1985.

———. "Spencer F. Baird and George N. Lawrence: An Ornithological Friendship." Paper presented at a meeting of the Society for the History of Natural History, London, 1989.

———. "Spencer F. Baird and His Collectors." *Journal of the Society for the Bibliography of Natural History* 9 (1980): 635–45.

Dickinson College. *Catalogue of Dickinson College for the Academical Year MDCC-CLVI–VII.* Carlisle, Penn.: Printed at the Herald Office, 1857.

———. *The Commencement Exercises of the Two Hundred and Sixteenth Academic Year.* May 21, 1989.

Dupree, A. Hunter. *Asa Gray, 1810–1888.* Cambridge: Harvard University Press, Belknap Press, 1959.

———. *Science in the Federal Government: A History of Policies and Activities to 1940.* Cambridge: Harvard University Press, Belknap Press, 1957.

Elman, Robert. *America's Pioneering Naturalists: Their Lives and Times, Exploits and Adventures.* Tulsa, Okla.: Winchester Press, 1982.

Fielding, H. Garrison. *An Introduction to the History of Medicine.* Philadelphia: W. B. Saunders Co., 1913.

Fleming, James Rogers. "Meteorology in America, 1814–1874: Theoretical, Observational, and Institutional Horizons." Ph.D. diss., Princeton University, 1988.

Foster, Mike. "The Permian Controversy of 1858: An Affair of the Heart." *Proceedings of the American Philosophical Society* 133, no. 3 (1989).

Fowler, Don D., and Catharine S. F. Fowler. "Anthropology of the Numa: John Wesley Powell's Manuscripts on the Numa Peoples of Western North America, 1868–1880." In *Smithsonian Contributions to Anthropology.* Washington, D.C.: Smithsonian Institution Press, 1971.

Galtshoff, Paul S. *The Story of the Bureau of Commercial Fisheries Biological Laboratory, Woods Hole, Massachusetts.* Circular no. 145. Washington, D.C.: U.S. Department of the Interior, 1962.

Goetzmann, William H. *Exploration and Empire: The Explorer and the Scientist in the Winning of the American West.* New York: W. W. Norton, 1966.

Goode, George Brown. "The Founding of the Institution" and "The Three Secretaries." In *The Smithsonian Institution, 1846–1896: The History of Its First Half Century.* Washington, D.C.: Devine Press, 1897.

———. "The Published Writings of Spencer Fullerton Baird, 1843–1882." In *Bibliographies of American Naturalists.* Washington, D.C.: Government Printing Office, 1883.

Greene, Constance McLaughlin. *Washington: Village and Capital, 1800–1878.* Princeton: Princeton University Press, 1962.

Guenther, Albert C. L. G., ed. "Record of Zoological Literature: Vertebrate Sec-tions." In *The Record of Zoological Literature*. London: John Van Voorst, 1865–91.

Guide to the National Archives of the United States. Washington, D.C.: National Archives and Records Commission, 1974.

Gwinn, Nancy E. "The Smithsonian Libraries: Afoot in Three Camps." *College and Research Libraries* 50 (March 1989): 206–14.

Hafertape, Kenneth. *America's Castle: The Evolution of the Smithsonian Building and Its Institution, 1840–1878*. Washington, D.C.: Smithsonian Institution Press, 1984.

Hedgepeth, Joel W. "The U.S. Fish Commission Steamer *Albatross*." *American Neptune* 5 (January 1945):5–26.

Hellman, Geoffrey. *The Smithsonian: Octopus on the Mall*. Westport, Conn.: Greenwood Press, 1978.

Henry, Joseph. *An Account of the Smithsonian Institution, Presented to the American Association for the Advancement of Education at its Annual Meeting Held in Pittsburgh, Pa., August 10th, 1853*. Newark, N.J.: A. Stephen Holbrook, Printer, 1854.

Herber, Elmer Charles. "Spencer F. Baird, Nineteenth-Century Naturalist." *Proceedings of the Pennsylvania Academy of Science* 29 (1955): 43–47.

———. "Spencer Fullerton Baird." *Historical Review of Berks County, Pennsylvania* 21, no. 3 (April–June 1956): 86.

———. "Spencer Fullerton Baird: Pioneer American Naturalist." *John and Mary's Journal* 9 (Winter 1984): 11–21.

———. "Spencer Fullerton Baird and the Purchase of Alaska." *Proceedings of the American Philosophical Society* 98 (1954): 139–43.

Herber, Elmer Charles, ed. *Correspondence between Spencer Fullerton Baird and Louis Agassiz—Two Pioneer American Naturalists*. Washington, D.C.: Smithsonian Institution Press, 1963.

Hinsley, Curtis M. Jr. *Savages and Scientists: The Smithsonian Institution and the Development of American Anthropology, 1846–1910*. Washington, D.C.: Smithsonian Institution Press, 1981.

Holder, Charles F. "Spencer Fullerton Baird." In *Leading American Men of Science*. 269–81. New York: Henry Holt and Co., 1910.

Houghton, William E. *The Victorian Frame of Mind, 1830–1870*. New Haven: Yale University Press, 1957.

Hume, Edgar Erskine. *Ornithologists of the United States Army Medical Corps*. Vol. 1. Baltimore: Johns Hopkins University Press, 1942.

"In Memoriam: Frank Hamilton Cushing." *American Anthropologist* 2, no. 2 (1900).

Irby, J. R. McD. "On the Works and Character of James Smithson." Paper "prepared at the request of the Institution," September 1878. Copy in Smithsonian Institution Archives, RU 7098, Box 19.

Jordan, David Starr. *Days of a Man.* 2 vols. Yonkers-on-Hudson: World Book, 1922.

———. "Spencer Fullerton Baird." In *Leading American Men of Science.* New York: Henry Holt, 1910.

———. "Spencer Fullerton Baird and the U.S. Fish Commission." *Scientific Monthly* 17 (August 1923).

Kastner, Joseph. *A Species of Eternity.* New York: Alfred A. Knopf, 1977.

———. *A World of Watchers.* New York: Alfred A. Knopf, 1986.

Kellogg, Remington. "A Century of Progress in Smithsonian Biology." *Science* 104, no. 2693. (9 August 1846).

Kohlstedt, Sally G. *The Formation of the American Scientific Community: The American Association for the Advancement of Science.* Urbana: University of Illinois Press, 1976.

———. "A Step toward Scientific Self-Identity in the United States: The Failure of the National Institute, 1844." *Isis* 62 (1974): 339–62.

Langley, Samuel Pierpont. "James Smithson." In *The Smithsonian Institution, 1846–1896: The History of Its First Half Century.* Washington, D.C.: Devine Press, 1897.

Leatherwood, Stephen, et al. *The Whales, Dolphins, and Porpoises of the Eastern North Pacific and Adjacent Arctic Waters.* New York: Dover Publications, 1982.

Lindsay, Debra J. "Science in the Sub-Arctic: Traders, Trappers, and the Smithsonian Institution, 1859–1870." Ph.D. diss., University of Manitoba, 1989.

Linton, Edwin. "The Man of Science and the Public." *Science* 48 (12 July 1918): 25–34.

Lurie, Edward. *Louis Agassiz: A Life in Science.* Chicago: University of Chicago Press, 1960.

Madden, Henry Miller. "Xantus, Hungarian Naturalist in the Pioneer West." Ph.D. diss. Columbia University, Linz, Austria, 1949.

Mallery, Garrick. "Baird and Participating Societies." *Washington Philosophical Society Annual Report, 1888.*

Manning, Thomas G. *Government in Science: The USGS.* Lexington: University of Kentucky Press, 1967.

Mark, Joan. "Frank Hamilton Cushing and an American Science of Anthropology." *Perspectives in American History* (Howard University) 10 (1976): 449–86.

Marsh, Caroline Crane. *Life and Letters of George Perkins Marsh.* Vol. 1. New York: Scribners, 1888.

Meltzer, David J. "North American Archaeology and Archaeologists 1879–1934." *American Antiquity* 50, no. 2 (1985): 249–60.

Merriam, G. Hart. "Baird the Naturalist." *Scientific Monthly* 18 (June 1924): 588–95.

Minasian, Stanley M., Kenneth C. Balcomb III, Larry Foster. *The World's Whales:*

The Complete Illustrated Guide. Washington, D.C.: Smithsonian Books, 1984.

Noelke, Virginia H. McK. "The Origin and Early History of the Bureau of American Ethnology, 1879–1910." Ph.D. diss., University of Texas, 1974.

Oehser, Paul H. *Sons of Science: The Story of the Smithsonian Institution and Its Leaders.* New York: Harry Schuman, 1949.

Orosz, Joel J. "Disloyalty, Dismissal, and a Deal: The Development of the National Museum at the Smithsonian Institution, 1846–1855." *Museum Studies Journal* 2 (1986): 22–33.

———. "In Defense of the Deal: A Rebuttal to S. Dillon Ripley's and Wilcomb Washburn's `Response'." *Museum Studies Journal* 3 (1987): 7–12.

Pachter, Mark. *Telling Lives.* Washington, D.C.: New Republic Books, 1979.

Page, Jake, and Eugene S. Morton. *Lords of the Air: The Smithsonian Book of Birds.* Washington, D.C.: Smithsonian Books and Orion Books, 1989.

Poesch, Jessie. *Titian Ramsay Peale, 1799–1885, and His Journals of the Wilkes Expedition.* Philadelphia: American Philosophical Society, 1961.

Post, Robert C., ed. *1876: A Centennial Exhibit.* Washington, D.C.: National Museum of History and Technology, Smithsonian Institution, 1976.

Powell, John Wesley. "The Personal Characteristics of Professor Baird." *Bulletin of the Philosophical Society of Washington* 9 (1887): 71–77.

Rabbit, Mary C. *John Wesley Powell, Pioneer Statesman of American Science.* USGS Professional Paper no. 669A. Washington, D.C.. Government Printing Office, 1969.

Records of the Secretary's Office. Smithsonian Institution Archives, RU 28 and RU 33.

Reeves, H. M., A. S. Hawkins, R. C. Hanson, and H. K. Nelson, eds. *Flyways: Pioneering Waterfowl Management in North America.* Washington, D.C.: U.S. Department of the Interior, U.S. Fish and Wildlife Service, 1984.

Reingold, Nathan, ed. *Science in Nineteenth-Century America: A Documentary History.* New York: Hill and Wang, 1964.

Rhees, William Jones. Correspondence Files. Smithsonian Institution Archives, RU 64 and RU 7081.

———. "James Smithson and His Bequest." *Smithsonian Miscellaneous Collections.* Vol. 21. Washington, D.C.: Smithsonian Institution, 1880.

———. *Life and Writings of James Smithson.* Smithsonian Miscellaneous Collections, no. 330. Washington, D.C.: Smithsonian Institution, 1880.

———, ed. *The Smithsonian Institution: Documents Relative to Its Origin and History.* Washington, D.C.: Smithsonian Institution, 1879.

———, ed. and comp. *The Smithsonian Institution: Documents Relative to Its Origin and History, 1835–1899.* 2 vols. Washington, D.C.: Government Printing Office, 1901.

Ridgway, Robert. "Spencer Fullerton Baird." In "Biographic Memoirs," *Annual*

Report of the Board of Regents of the Smithsonian Institution . . . for the Year 1888. Washington, D.C.: Government Printing Office, 1889.

Riedman, Sarah R. *Trailblazer of American Science: The Life of Joseph Henry.* New York: Rand-McNally & Co., 1961.

Ripley, S. Dillon, and Wilcomb E. Washburn. "The Development of the National Museum at the Smithsonian Institution, 1846–1855: A Response to Joel J. Oroz's Article." *Museum Studies Journal* 2 (Spring–Summer 1987): 6–11.

Rivinus, E. F. "Spencer Fullerton Baird, the Collector of Collectors: His Collection Was the Beginning of Stamp Collecting at the Smithsonian." *American Philatelist* 103, no. 11 (November 1989): 1061–65.

———. "Spencer Fullerton Baird, Educator." *Dickinson College Magazine,* October, 1989, 15–17.

———. "Spencer Fullerton Baird, Nestor of American Ornithologists." *Atlantic Naturalist* 39 (1989): 26–33.

Rosenberger, Homer T. "Spencer Fullerton Baird (1823–1887)." *Cosmos Club Bulletin* 10, no. 2 (February 1957).

Sampson, J. A. "The True Nature of Ovarian Endometriosis (Chocolate Cysts). *Archives of Surgery* 3 (1921): 245–323.

Saxon, A. H. *Selected Letters of P. T. Barnum.* New York: Columbia University Press, 1983.

Sellers, Charles Coleman. *Mr. Peale's Museum: Charles Willson Peale and the First Popular Museum of Natural Science and Art.* New York: W. W. Norton & Co., 1980.

Sherwood, Morgan B. *Exploration of Alaska, 1865–1900.* New Haven: Yale University Press, 1965.

Shor, Elisabeth N. *The Fossil Feud between E. D. Cope and O. C. Marsh.* Hicksville, N.Y.: Exposition Press, 1974.

Shufelt, Robert W. "Bairdian Reminiscences." *Medical Life* 30, no. 6 (1923): 277–82.

Smiley, Charles W. "Memorial to Spencer F. Baird." *American Monthly Microscopical Journal* 9 (January 1888).

Smith, Henry N. "Clarence King, John Wesley Powell, and the Establishment of the USGS." *Mississippi Valley Historical Review* 34 (1947).

Springer, Victor. Letter to E. F. Rivinus, 21 March 1989.

Stanton, William R. *The Great United States Exploring Expedition of 1838–1842.* Berkeley: University of California Press, 1975.

Sterling, Keir B. *Last of the Naturalists: The Career of C. Hart Merriam.* New York: Arno Press, 1977.

Stillman, W. J. "The Philosophers' Camp." *Century Magazine* 46, no. 4 (August 1893): 601.

Taylor, William B. "Professor Baird as Administrator." In "Biographic Memoirs,"

Annual Report of the Board of Regents of the Smithsonian Institution . . . for the Year 1888. Washington, D.C.: Government Printing Office, 1889.

Terrell, John W. *The Man Who Rediscovered America: A Biography of John Wesley Powell.* New York: Weybright and Talley, 1969.

Terres, John K., ed. *The Audubon Encyclopedia of North American Birds.* New York: Alfred A. Knopf, 1982.

Thomas, Greg. "The Smithsonian and the Hudson's Bay Company." *Prairie Forum* 10, no. 2 (Autumn 1985): 283–305.

Tomalin, Ruth. *W. H. Hudson: A Biography.* London: Faber and Faber, 1982.

True, Webster Prentiss. *The Smithsonian: America's Treasure House.* New York: Sheridan House, 1962.

———. *The Smithsonian Institution.* Smithsonian Institution Scientific Series, vol. 1. New York: Smithsonian Scientific Series, 1929.

Tyler, David B. *The Wilkes Expedition: The First United States Exploring Expedition (1838–1842).* Philadelphia: American Philosophical Society, 1968.

U.S. Congress. House. *Report of the Special Committee of the Management of the Smithsonian Institution.* 33d Cong., 2d sess.

U.S. Congress. Senate. *Report of the Special Committee of the Board of Regents Relative to the Fire.* 38th Cong., 2d sess., 21 February 1865. S. Rept. 129.

Viola, Herman J. *Exploring the West.* Washington, D.C.: Smithsonian Books, 1987.

Viola, Herman J., and Carolyn Margolis. *Magnificent Voyagers: The U.S. Exploring Expedition, 1838–1842.* Washington, D.C.: Smithsonian Institution Press, 1985.

Washburn, Wilcomb. "Joseph Henry's Conception of the Purpose of the Smithsonian Institution." In *A Cabinet of Curiosities: Five Episodes in the Evolution of American Museums.* Charlottesville: University Press of Virginia, 1967.

Willey, Richard R. *The Tucson Meteorites: Their History from Frontier Arizona to the Smithsonian.* Washington, D.C.: Smithsonian Institution Press, 1987.

Williams, Frances Leigh. *Matthew Fontaine Maury, Scientist of the Sea.* New Brunswick: Rutgers University Press, 1963.

Wing, Rev. Conway P. *History of Cumberland County, Pennsylvania.* Carlisle, Penn.: Herald Printing Co., 1982.

Xantus, John. *Travels in Southern California.* Translated and edited by Theodore Schoenman and Helen Bendele Schoenman. Detroit: Wayne State University Press, 1976.

Yochelson, Ellis N. *The National Museum of Natural History: Seventy-five Years in the New National Museum.* Washington, D.C.: Smithsonian Institution Press, 1985.

Zinnser, William, ed. *Extraordinary Lives: The Art and Craft of American Biography.* Boston: Houghton, Mifflin Co., 1986.

Zwinger, Ann H. "A Hungarian in Baja." *Audubon* 87 (1985): 128–39.

————. *John Xantus: The Fort Tejon Letters, 1857–1859.* Tucson: University of Arizona Press, 1986.

————. *Xantus: The Letters of John Xantus to Spencer Fullerton Baird, from San Francisco and Cabo San Lucas, 1859–1861.* Baja California Travels Series, vol. 48. Los Angeles: Castle Press for Dawson's Bookshop, 1986.

Index